China Inside Out

*10 Irreversible Trends
Reshaping China and Its
Relationship with the World*

China Inside Out

10 Irreversible Trends Reshaping China and Its Relationship with the World

Bill Dodson

WILEY

John Wiley & Sons (Asia) Pte. Ltd.

Published in 2011 by John Wiley & Sons (Asia) Pte. Ltd.

2 Clementi Loop, #02-01, Singapore 129809

Other Wiley Editorial Offices

John Wiley & Sons, 111 River Street, Hoboken, NJ 07030, USA

John Wiley & Sons, The Atrium, Southern Gate, Chichester, West Sussex, PO19 8SQ, United Kingdom

John Wiley & Sons (Canada) Ltd., 5353 Dundas Street West, Suite 400, Toronto, Ontario, M9B 6HB, Canada

John Wiley & Sons Australia Ltd, 42 McDougall Street, Milton, Queensland 4064, Australia

Wiley-VCH, Boschstrasse 12, D-69469 Weinheim, Germany

Library of Congress Cataloging-in-Publication Data

ISBN 978-0-47082643-0 (Hardcover)
ISBN 978-0-47082645-4 (e-PDF)
ISBN 978-0-47082644-7 (e-Mobi)
ISBN 978-0-47082646-1 (e-Pub)

Typeset in 10/14pt, Meridien-Roman by Thomson Digital

Printed in Singapore by Saik Wah Press Pte Ltd

10 9 8 7 6 5 4 3 2 1

For my parents, William R. and Norma Dodson,
in gratitude for their patience and sacrifices.

Contents

Acknowledgment

China Inside Out has been a collaborative project with numerous individuals who have contributed both directly and indirectly over the past decade. More than a few of the insights expressed in the book were born through the countless conversations I've had with those who have lived, studied, and worked in China for many years, many of whom were North Americans and Europeans. These discussions often were excavations of their experiences, their observations, and their reflections about the swift and dramatic changes in China they've become part of.

In particular, I would like to express my gratitude to longtime China veterans Peter Holmes and Keith Cairncross, who through long hours of conversation, have helped me to put many of my own China experiences and musings in perspective. Other close friends and China veterans also have shared their experiences and thinking, especially Palle Linde, Michael "Mickey" Duff, Mark "Six" Kissner, Doug Wack, and Oscar Hernandez. I also feel a need to sound a note of deep appreciation for my counterparts at the Blue Marlin "Think Tank" in the Suzhou Industrial Park—professionals and their families who have a combined hundreds of years of experience from all over China, and whose warmth and humor have provided me a home away from home.

Certainly, my colleagues Bhavesh Mistry and Basile Waite at TrendsAsia in Greater Shanghai have been invaluable critics and tireless reviewers of the manuscript as well as great listeners when I needed to bounce ideas off individuals with an intelligence and sensitivity to Chinese modern society. Andrew Hupert, an adjunct professor at the Shanghai campus of New York University, will always be my first stop for stimulating conversation about the intersection between culture, government policy, and commercial interests in China. Scott Tong, who was the China bureau chief for the Marketplace program on Public Radio in the U.S. from 2007 through mid-2010, was always willing to swap the latest China news and hearsay with me over cups of coffee. I have to thank the prolific Paul French of the China consumer market-research company Access Asia for his encouragement during the project, and for his guidance *vis-à-vis* getting around the publishing world. I am also grateful to my once-colleague and forever-friend Franziska Gloeckner for the fresh eyes she provided me through her years living and working in Nanjing. Justin Lusk, also a China longtimer and the general manager of a foreign-invested operation in China, is singular in my mind for the amazing support he provided this writing project before the book found a home with John Wiley & Sons.

Of course, I have to thank the many hundreds of Chinese I've met in China over the past 10 years who have shared with me their own stories and thinking during the past decade of tumultuous change in their society. In particular, I would like to thank Robert Kong, a longtime friend in my adopted Chinese hometown of Suzhou, near Shanghai, for explaining to me over innumerable get-togethers in a balanced, dispassionate manner the dynamics of Chinese relationships in families, and between friends and coworkers. I must also thank a Shanghai family I admire and appreciate, the Chai brothers, Guoxing and Guofeng, for helping me get oriented and for being so supportive when I first began traveling to Shanghai on business and asking a million questions about everything but business.

Since 2003, local government officials across China have provided me with thousands of hours of tours, conversation, and education about their local cultures and economic development progress over the years, many of whom continue to provide me with updates. Some of the most delightful experiences I have had in China were spent at banquet tables with some of these individuals, who were always warm and engaging hosts. Some have even become friends. One of my greatest pleasures has been and will continue to be dropping by their towns and cities to see them again and to learn of the changes they have helped facilitate.

I owe a debt of gratitude to my publisher, Nick Wallwork, who is based in the Singapore office of John Wiley & Sons. It was Nick who first seemed to figure out what I was getting at with *China Inside Out* and helped me craft the project into something readable and saleable.

Editorial Executive Jules Yap took on the project and remained my primary liaison through the editorial and production processes. My copyeditor Jennifer Wells was tireless in encouraging me to write what I meant and to mean what I wrote. The professional efforts of the production team as a whole for the book, led by Fiona Wong, could not have made birthing the project any more fulfilling for me.

Finally, my gratitude to my wife, Jessica Zhou, who was pregnant with our first child throughout most of the writing phase of the book. Sometimes I think she was the charm that brought the book to life. Neither of our individual labors was easy; hers, however, was the most rewarding: our lovely son Ashley Xavier.

Foreword

Men and women in China have the right to dress as they please: plaids, stripes, purples, reds, acid-greens, fuchsias, rhinestones, tight skirts, baggy T-shirts—all at the same time, even, if they choose to experiment (which some do). They can buy at bargain basement prices or, those who can afford it, can shop at expensive boutiques. They can dress as peculiarly as they like—or as fashionably—as the glittering catwalks of Shanghai have spotlighted since the opening years of the twenty-first century.

China hasn't always been that way, though. As the bad old days of the Cultural Revolution closed in the late 1970s and the country sought its way out of the economic and social chaos that had defined the lives of generations, the Mao-suit was all the fashion. Actually, it was pretty much the *only* fashion for adults, available in the most drab shades of gray, blue, and green conceivable. The statement the social uniform made was "we are all equal," though, of course, Communist Party members were more equal than others. For the 30 years after Mao Zedong announced the liberation of the People's Republic of China, Communist Party *apparatchiks* tightly controlled *all* parts of Chinese life: where one lived, if one attended university, what discipline one would study, where one worked, where one shopped, how much one could buy (if shelves were stocked at all), even who to marry (dating was illegal). In other words, up until about 1980, China's government was totalitarian, interested mostly in exercising its power and ideology at every level of its citizens' existence.

Now, Chinese citizens have freedoms those aged 45 and over could hardly have imagined in 1980. They can start their own businesses, they can purchase as many homes as they can afford, they are increasingly owning their own cars—once the sole entitlement of Party officials—they can choose where to send their children to school, and, if they have enough money, even completely escape the onerous university examination system and send their child abroad for study. Television programming and commercials are as mind-numbing as any in the developed world now, with as many cable stations. The country now sports a wide choice of newspapers and magazines, many of which are simply "lifestyle" publications that give a growing middle class hints on how to dress, how to put on makeup, how to pick up girls, and the best ways to bring your man (or your woman) to climax. Then there is the impact of the Internet, which is perhaps the single greatest lever that has pried open the society to what is possible in the modern world. In some aspects, Chinese society has more freedom than many societies throughout the world.

Of course, as is already well-known, the Communist Party still censors whatever it considers seditious, or anything that could destabilize society; or rather, what could upset its increasingly tenuous control of Chinese society. It regularly arrests and jails political dissidents, it still applies its one-child policy with gusto, its judiciary for the most part is still embryonic and shackled to political expediencies, and its lack of consideration of intellectual property rights is still atrocious. The Chinese government has become authoritarian. In other words, it can no longer totally control the lives of its citizens to the same extent it had 30 years before. Economic progress, the development of a high-maintenance middle class, the need to present continuing, uninterrupted economic opportunity to 20 percent of humankind, have forced the Communist Party to reform itself as an oligarchy with visibly reduced powers over its citizens. The Communist Party's *modus operandi* has changed from impressing its will unilaterally on citizens to survival of its dwindling power base and managing the *genii* it has let out of the bottle of history.

The Party has been learning, though, *genii* do not return to their abodes upon command. Instead, the transformative, almost magical forces, once released, must run their course, with unimaginable consequences for Chinese society and the world.

China Inside Out is about the stresses and strains along social fault lines that have developed as the Party's entrenched interests in control and self-enrichment rub against economic growth demands, commercial priorities, middle-class requirements, generational warfare, criminal rivalries, and international standards of engagement and responsibility. Daily, it seems, social and political progress occurs as the battle lines between social and political blocks in China shift with first one faction pushing successfully into the domain of another, and then giving up "territory" on another front, each time with a great deal of energy released in unpredictable bursts of creative destruction.

Most international commentators on China—and many Chinese scholars themselves—ascribe the country's rapid transformation to one or another Party genius or dissident-hero or corporate maven—the so-called "great person" theory of history. Instead, China is shooting economic and social "rapids," the untamed flow of which is the confluence of technological, social, and economic trends. The world is "flatter" than it's ever been in human history, as Thomas Friedman wrote in his book *The World is Flat*, and China is taking advantage of the leveling to heft itself into the twenty-first century. International business, Western consumers, and the Chinese Communist Party, for the most part, have been able to capitalize in the most literal sense on this juxtaposition of trends.

The chaos of the Cultural Revolution reduced the Communist Party to one of two courses through which to pursue its future. It could accompany its eastern neighbor North Korea further in the direction of totalitarianism, insularity, and poverty, or it could allow the shoots of Western-style entrepreneurship that had already begun to sprout in farming communes in the early 1980s to take hold and to thrive, and to rebuild industry from a capitalist orientation. The choice to allow capitalism a foothold in the society unleashed powerful social forces that had major ramifications for China's Communist Party. The citizenry began to question the Party's Mandate of Heaven—the permission from the citizenry to rule that every Emperor throughout Chinese history has required to retain power. During the events of the Tiananmen Square protests in 1989, political leaders came very close to the same fate as their Soviet cousins had that same year—expulsion and obsolescence.

Now, at the outset of the twenty-first century, the Party is as sensitive as it has ever been about the balancing act it performs in its stewardship of the country, even though it has encouraged and even accelerated the pace of social transformation. What concerns the Party most is that the currents it has chosen to follow have passed beyond its absolute control. The cascade of activities and events that form the trends discussed in *China Inside Out* are irreversible now, to the extent that to drastically alter the direction and/or speed of any of the trends would be to rupture a society just injecting itself into modernization. Disruption could possibly result in protests and riots greater in scale than even those recently seen in the autonomous regions Tibet and Xinjiang. Termination of any of the trends is not an option for a government that wants to maintain some semblance of control over the country: the people will simply not submit to an untimely end to the boom times.

Each chapter in *China Inside Out* discusses an irreversible trend and its implications for neighbors near and far, and for international businesses invested in China. Chapter 1 opens with the impact the Internet is having on the shape of Chinese society, identity, policy, and moral behavior. Many Chinese are increasingly seeing unfettered Internet access as a right, not a luxury, much to the government's dismay. For the first time in Chinese history, the ruler and the ruled are on a much-leveled playing field. Chapter 2 discusses the drive nearly every Mainland Chinese has to achieve a middle-class lifestyle and the attendant anxieties and strains placed on the society, on individuals, and on institutions such as marriage and childbearing. Chapter 3 explores how the backbone of a middle-class lifestyle, mass urbanization, has created tensions between urbanites and country folk that have surfaced as a sort of policy-driven apartheid, which society actually needs to continue its economic development. Chapter 4 relates how China has needed and continues to believe polluting industries are essential to kick-start its economy and develop its interior.

Chapter 5 explores how China's insatiable appetite for land, oil, and minerals has forced it far beyond its borders to meet its industrial and consumer needs, while its growing lack of water—polluted or not—is already impacting its growth prospects. Chapter 6 is a discussion of the challenges China faces in developing its local economies and improving living conditions outside the prosperous Yangtze and Pearl River Deltas. Chapter 7 takes the reader into Chinese hospitals, its hospitality industry, customer-service care and wedding industry—likely the best-run services industry in the country—for insights into its nascent services sector, the key to full employment in China. Chapter 8 examines how China's foray into the international marketplace is showing Chinese government officials and entrepreneurs rampant offshore investment has severe shortcomings in international business dealings, and that money isn't always the most important part of a transaction in many countries worldwide. Chapter 9 delves into how China's population pressure throughout its long history has been both a boon and a liability to its economic development, and how its one-child policy is already affecting social and family structures in ways never before seen. Finally, Chapter 10 relates how modernization has exposed to the world China's national insecurity through a shrill variety of nationalism, an accelerated buildup of its military, and an inflexible foreign policy.

Ultimately, *China Inside Out* is a personal journey of discovery during one of the most important social transitions that any country has ever undertaken in human history. I wanted to dig as deeply as I could into modern Chinese society to gain insight into how a country can remake itself time and time again, and to understand what its latest incarnation means for us outsiders. The country's resurrection from the collective suicide of the Cultural Revolution is one of the most important stories to be told in this century. *China Inside Out* is my earnest attempt at relating to those who don't know China very well what I and others have observed and experienced in "the country that doesn't sleep."

Identifying the irreversible trends reshaping China was the first step in the expedition, while the travels, the people, the research, and the countless conversations made up the second. Tracing the arcs and intersections of the trends eventually brought me to three important conclusions about China's development and the challenges confronting her. First, the advancement of China's economic and social agenda is far more dependent on the stress released from friction between divisions in society than to the heavy hand of authoritarian self-styled genius. As British historian Edward Hallett Carr wrote in his book, *What is History?*, "History is, to a considerable extent, a matter of numbers." Players both famous and pedestrian fill out the roles created by the swirling eddy currents of the flow of history. However, it's how individuals respond to the predicaments thrust upon them or the roles that they have taken up in the midst of great upheaval that anchor historical narratives and make for a good read.

Second, China's domestic priorities and challenges as well as its national identity will preclude China from "ruling" the world, though the adolescence of its ascent as a world superpower will be trying at times to the international family of nations and to international businesses invested in the country.

Finally, China's Communist Party has done a colossal and impressive job of transforming itself from an intrusive totalitarian governor (with the exception of Tibet and Xinjiang) that micro-manages its citizens' lives to a form of government more similar to most of its Asian neighbors; that is, one-party rule with democratic characteristics.

If there is anything I hope readers take away from this odyssey, it's that China is now at the leading edge of history. How the society negotiates the inevitable shocks of trends that come into confluence, and how, most importantly, it manages the eventual wind-down of those powerful social and economic forces in the next 10 to 15 years, will have major repercussions for its citizenry, its neighbors, international businesses invested in the country, and for Western civilization.

China's success is just that important to us all.

Bill Dodson
Suzhou, China
October, 2010

CHAPTER **1**

The Rise of
Generation W(eb)

HUMAN FLESH SEARCHES

On the evening of May 10, 2009, Deng Yujiao, an attractive 21-year-old waitress, greeted the three guests entering a private parlor at a bathhouse in Badong Xiongfeng Hotel just as she normally would any other evening. Badong is a township in Hubei Province, nestled in tree-lined mountains, an ancient callous on an elbow of the Yangtze River, deep in the interior of China. The bathhouse was not luxurious by the standards of similar Shanghai or Beijing venues, with their great marble facades and Romanesque statues surrounding the Jacuzzis, scrubbing tables, and lounges attended by smartly dressed service staff. Rather, the Xiongfeng Hotel bathhouse was much more modest in scale and offerings; it was enough, though, for the three government officials who had come for massages to feel like kings. Deng followed her customers into the private parlor to take their orders for drinks and snacks. The three men pressed Deng to offer them "special services" a code phrase in China for prostitution. Deng declined, saying that was not her job. Deng Guida (no relation to the waitress), the chief of the county investment promotion bureau, threw a wad of cash at her head. She ignored the provocation and tried to leave the room. The officials barred her exit. She tried to push past them, but they continued playing cat-and-mouse with her, blocking her escape.

Two of the administrators pushed her onto a sofa in the parlor. She broke away, only to be roughly pressed back onto the couch. She snatched at a fruit knife at a nearby table, and slashed out. One of her tormentors fell back, cut. She thrust outward again. Deng Guida, slow to realize the turnabout of events, suddenly clutched at his throat. He stumbled to the ground. Blood spurted from the wound the waitress had dealt him. Slipping into shock, she phoned the police about the incident, and told them one of the guests was bleeding.

Deng Guida died in the ambulance on the way to the hospital. Local police arrested Deng Yujiao for murder.

Chinese Internet users around the country flew into a rage over the arrest. Immediately, online Bulletin Board Systems (BBS) and forums on Chinese websites such as Sina.com, Tianya.com, and Netease.com as well as countless bloggers flooded cyberspace with thousands of threads of arguments and condemnations of government officials. One post from People.com stated a common sentiment: "How come these officials have so much money? During the dispute, the victim hit the girl on the head with a wad of money. How could a public servant on a salary have so much to spare without any thought or scruple? Was it public funds or embezzled money perhaps? How could they visit entertainment venues so frequently and are obsessed with 'special services' so much? [sic]"[1]

The online furor of hundreds of thousands of Internet users spread all the way to Beijing. Local police, in a preemptive move to forestall any edicts from high-level Central Government officials, reduced the charges against Deng Yujiao to "excessive use of force." Still, the reduction in charges was not enough to satisfy Chinese netizens. Nearly every commentator responded that it was clear Deng Yujiao was defending herself against the officials, and that she should be freed. Eventually, the police dropped the charges and released her at the end of May 2009, to much fanfare. She even received an offer from a Chinese movie director for a role in a film he was making.

China's government officials at national and local levels are both thrilled and petrified at the potential the Internet holds for the welfare of the country and for their continued control of the economy and society. They have enthusiastically embraced the possibilities for greater monitoring and filtering of information, as well as the new avenues for government propaganda that shapes Chinese views on domestic and international issues. Indeed, China has more Internet users than the entire population of the United States, according to the China Internet Network Information Center. By January 2010, China had 384 million Internet users, an increase of nearly 50 million users from the end of June 2009, which itself was a 13 percent jump since the end of 2008. China supported a penetration rate of 29 percent of its population who could use the Internet.

In 2010, China's State Council Information Office set a goal of raising the penetration rate to 40 percent before the year 2015. Factors such as rapid economic growth, increasing wealth and disposable income, and greater access to the Internet in large cities, small towns, and households have made China the largest user base in the world. Central government and citizens alike see no chance of the country going back to pre-Internet days. Internet use has passed from being a privilege of a few to a right of the many millions who have already invested their livelihoods and even identities in the technology medium.

Though only a third of potential users in China currently log onto the Internet—compared with more than 70 percent in the United States, according to a study by the Pew Internet and American Life Project—nearly half a billion Chinese will be Internet users by 2012.[2] Chinese users create nearly 3,000 websites daily, with 162 million bloggers in 2009 tracking and commenting on an assortment of social issues and government policies.[3] The wealth the new technology is creating for private e-commerce companies, advertisers, and state-owned media is without bounds. Already, a US$20 billion industry has been built around Internet cafes, which serves up 40 percent of the US$2.5 billion in online gaming revenue annually.[4] Total revenue for all Internet companies in China in 2007 was US$5.9 billion. Though only a quarter of the revenue generated by American firms in the U.S. in the same year, industry income is set to increase double digits annually.

But the Internet as it is evolving in China means more than just a money-making opportunity. It is also more than just another way for the Communist Party to control its citizens. No other medium so transparently reflects the tectonic fault lines between dramatically disparate parts of Chinese society: government *apparatchiks*, mob rule, legitimate business interests, gamers, bloggers, social networkers, political activists, and underworld snakeheads. Factions collide and collude online to reveal a nation grasping to promote collective interests, to shape and project a modern national identity, and to push back boundaries for creativity and expression.

The relatively low cost and high-level sophistication of the technology means that Big Brother's own wards can and are keeping an eye on Big Brother nearly as effectively as Big Brother himself. The quite visible gaps between the lifestyles of many government officials, the *nouveau riche*, the new middle class, and the country folk has made anyone a target who seems to have become wealthy through ill-gotten means.

One of the most daring and brazen wiki-style detective efforts on the Chinese Internet involved the search for the identity of a government official from Shandong Province, in China's north, who tried to push a little girl into the men's washroom of the Plum Garden Seafood Restaurant in the Nanshan District of Shenzhen on October 28, 2008. Shenzhen is in China's deep south, near Hong Kong, a large frontier city that has grown with the rise of manufacturing in China from a seaside village to one of the four largest cities in the country in a mere 20 years. A grainy closed-circuit video clip shows a fat, puffy-faced man in his mid- to late 50s asking an 11-year-old girl where the bathroom is. The girl shows him the way. Footage then shows the man cuffing the girl at the neck near the entrance of the men's room, followed seconds later by the girl rounding the wall and hotfooting it back to the restaurant lobby, sobbing. Her parents see her crying; she explains how a big man had tried to force her into the men's washroom. The man himself strides up to the parents, elbows akimbo as though he's about to draw pistols. The parents begin shouting at the man. The man shouts his admission that he tried to get the little girl into the bathroom: "I did it. So what? How much money do you want? Give me a price! I will pay it!" He pushes at the father: "Do you know who I am? I was sent here by the Beijing Ministry of Transportation. My level is the same as your mayor. So what if I pinched a little child's neck? Who the f*** are you people to me?! You dare f*** with me? Just watch how I am going to deal with you!"

The family knows it's licked. It has no legal recourse against the official, no hope of bringing the man to justice. Chinese Internet social networks, however, swiftly filled the vacuum of inaction.

Within a short time of the video footage being posted, Chinese Internet users mobilized a Human Flesh Search Engine to determine the government official's name, address, position, and current whereabouts. Human Flesh Search Engines—a Chinese term—involves hundreds and sometimes thousands of Internet users banding together to scour cyber- and physical-space for information about individuals they agree should be publicly excoriated for their actions. The Human Flesh Search Engine in the case of the Plum Garden Seafood Restaurant brought the issue to national attention and to the desks of the official's supervisors in Shandong Province. His name was Lin Jiaxiang, the Search announced, the party secretary of the Shenzhen marine affairs bureau.

Angry posts appeared in online forums and bulletin boards echoing the sentiment of one user: "Dammit! Shenzhen Nanshan District Police!!! The entire country's masses will be watching how you handle this!!! If you do not give a statement, the masses will give you guys a statement!!!" [sic]

Lin Jiaxing was fired soon after the incident, but cleared of child molestation charges.[5]

Human Flesh Searches are particular to today's modernizing Chinese society. The natural question arises, then, as to why Chinese feel so inclined to hunt individuals down in digital lynch mobs and make their targets miserable. Common responses from Chinese themselves on the bulletin board of popular web portal Netease.com about why Chinese find Human Flesh Searches an appealing means of expression included:[6]

"As long as it [Human Flesh Search] is used reasonably and correctly, this is also our right as citizens."

"Human Flesh Searches is an embodiment of the common people's right of expression and right of supervision. One reason this kind of embodiment has a big impact upon some people in society is because the common people do not have better channels embodying these two rights." [sic]

"The people have the right to know the truth."

However, despite China having a constitution, Chinese citizens in Mainland China are far from sure or secure in what their individual rights actually are. Chinese find it much safer personally to work through social networks.

And from the popular Chinese online forum QQ.com:

"It is time to consider how to use Human Flesh Search as a means of *public* supervision."

Comments on the blog chinaSMACK, in response to officials in the small city of Xuzhou, in northern Jiangsu Province, making Human Flesh Searches illegal, voiced a more thoughtful note:[7]

"Hard to support Human Flesh Searches of corrupt government officials and other evildoers (as a replacement for a free press and government accountability to the people) without some relatively innocent people having their privacy violated over relatively innocent and inconsequential matters." [sic]

As one user succinctly reasoned:

"1. People constantly got pissed off [sic] in real life so they need somewhere to vent off frustrations, or repair their self-esteem.

2. Herd mentality and intolerance on the uneducated mass.

3. Being Mr. Anonymous feels great."

China has very little judicial recourse for disputes of even the most minor sort. Whereas the U.S. court system, for instance, has a small claims court, a probate court, a civil court, and the like, China has a primordial court system that individuals neither trust nor believe in. Compounding the lack of faith in the Chinese court system is the lack of enforcement of judgments. China does not have the mechanisms in place to ensure the decisions on minor injustices are carried out. The system for more serious crimes such as murder, theft, drug trafficking, and corruption is draconian, in which guilt is considered a fact and the rest is discussion and prescription. Serious crimes result in prison sentences and sometimes in death.

The lack of a mature and impartial judicial system that can decide on even the most trivial matters is an accepted fact of life in China, despite great strides in the country economically. When an incident or major disagreement occurs, participants are intent on seeing justice done immediately and before the parties separate to possibly duck enforcement. As a result, Chinese streets are often home to squabbles and outright fights between individuals, which tend to draw large, anonymous crowds that sometimes become involved. At the tipping point of a critical mass of individuals and highly charged contention, Chinese crowds explode in singular activity that is raucous at best, savagely violent at worst. Human Flesh Search Engines are expressions of the same sort of *ad hoc posse*(s) found in the real world in China.

Authoritarian rule coupled with restricted channels for adjudication have squeezed expression of daily discontent and wrongdoings that many in China witness into online channels. Web users band together into great, anonymous—and, simultaneously, amorphous—mobs that feel they have a power unparalleled elsewhere in their lives. The power enables them to be judge, jury, and executioner, all in one, all at the same time, without having to justify their actions to anyone, including the government. Chinese still brawl on the streets and vent their discontent with their lives and with their government through mass protests, but that has now spilled over into cyberspace, where the anonymity of avatars—customized personas—has made coming together even easier.

The "Young Digital Mavens" study, conducted by U.S. Internet company IAC and the U.S. advertising agency network JWT, in November 2007, found ". . . more than half the Chinese sample (51 percent) said they have adopted a completely different persona in some of their online interactions, compared with only 17 percent of Americans." The study also reported that ". . . more than three-quarters (77 percent) of the Chinese sample agreed computer/console games are much more fun when played against others online, compared with a third of Americans. While fans of virtual communities are in the minority in both countries, "second-lifers" (those who agreed that "I feel more real online than offline") account for just four percent of the U.S. sample compared with 24 percent of Chinese respondents."

"THIS POST DOES NOT EXIST"

Despite how slow dial-in access was to the Internet in the late 1990s, the Chinese government still took to blocking access to content on the World Wide Web. The earliest websites blocked in China referred to any domestic or international references to the Tiananmen Square massacre, which had occurred almost a decade before in 1989. Any derogatory references to Mao Zedong in particular, or to Communist Party activities or history that discredited the regime were blocked as well. In 1999, China's Internet population hit a critical mass of seven million users,[8] up from just tens of thousands in 1996.[9] The Chinese government wasted no time in blocking Western news media outlets such as *The New York Times*, *The Washington Post*, CNN and the BBC. The government did not open the BBC to Chinese readership until 2008, though the Chinese version of the BBC was still blocked at the end of 2009.

By 1999, it was difficult to find any information on the Internet about the outlawed Falun Gong, the spiritual movement that had flexed its might in numbers against the criticism meted out by Communist Party leaders. Authorities had quickly and violently disbanded the group, and all practice of its exercises and philosophy were made illegal. The government blocked access to any websites and BBS that referred to the group, as well as to Taiwan and democracy movements. By 2002, the government had reached a major milestone in implementation of its Golden Shield project, which it had launched in 1998. The initiative was meant to create an information and civil-service infrastructure that would systematically filter any content that authorities considered socially or politically unacceptable. "The Great Firewall of China"—a reference to the expansive and ineffective efforts of ancient Chinese emperors to keep the marauding hordes from the north from sweeping southward into the homeland—is the part of the Internet that automatically blocks content that the central government considers unacceptable. Now, the Great Firewall monitors and filters items that were off-limits in the 1990s as well as pornography, references to the Dalai Lama and Tibetan liberation, and most criticisms of the central and local governments.

Users who request sites that the government deems off-limits will see any variety of display errors on an otherwise blank web page. The most common error is one that simply indicates the website could not be found. Another kind of "error" resets the online session, so that users have to exit from their web application (for instance, Internet Explorer, Firefox, or Google Chrome), then re-launch the application.

Another obstacle puts requests into an endless loop that also forces users to restart their Internet session. The upgrade to the Great Firewall involved a reset of pages that had been mirrored to censors' servers, reviewed, and deemed unacceptable. Censorship programming would then break the link to the page; additional attempts to access the page within certain time limits would actually extend the time limit for access to the page. So, if you wanted to view an article on the Dalai Lama from within China, you would likely receive an error that indicated the link was reset. Try refreshing the link within two minutes, and you will receive the same error, except that the timeout will last five minutes; try again within five minutes, and the blackout time may be extended to 30 minutes.[10]

The Beijing Summer Olympics of 2008 saw government censors amping up control of the Internet with its clampdown on websites and blogs that sounded any note of political dissidence. Access to references in China to the Tibetan Riot earlier in the year and to the deaths of thousands of children in the Sichuan earthquake just a few months before, were conclusively blocked. Notices about severe environmental degradation and, especially, local governments' collusion in green crimes, were also blocked. The construction accompanying the Olympics and the promise of wealth the event would bring to real estate developers and *apparatchiks* in the capital saw the wholesale destruction of thousands of homes affecting millions of people in and outside the city. Government censors blocked online references to the demolition of entire neighborhoods, as well as to the scores of mass protests and jailing of dissidents who objected to the roughshod manner in which local governments were going about their urban-renewal projects.

China's print, TV, and online propagandists directed by the central government took advantage of Chinese protests focused on the Olympic torch's relay in Western countries during the summer of 2008 to divert attention from domestic issues ranging from government collusion with business owners operating highly polluting factories to unscrupulous property developers swindling land from farmers. National government encouraged local journalists to complain in the media the world was against China's "rise." The media also turned up the pitch of nationalism to the extent that Chinese consumers boycotted French companies Carrefour and Auchan, the hypermarket chains, and such products as

French perfumes and fashion brands. Westerners were warned by their countries to stay away from potentially violent protests at French venues, where mobs grew into the thousands. Chinese websites, portals, bulletin boards, and blogs also took up the nationalistic beat, focusing attention on grievances with countries that did not "show respect" to China during the preparations for the Beijing Olympics. The environment was reminiscent of the 2005 anti-Japanese protests that China's leadership promoted online and through traditional media. The Chinese government wanted to show through an informal and emotional referendum its displeasure with Japan's printing a history textbook that ignored atrocities committed by Japanese soldiers in China during World War II, and to protest Japan's lobbying to gain a permanent seat on the United Nations Security Council.

The Net Nannies—as Westerners who live in China call Chinese government censors—were their most heavy-handed, though, with the Uighur riots of 2009, the largest uprising against Communist Party rule since Tiananmen Square. These censors had proved themselves quick studies. Earlier that year, in June 2009, the Iranian government staged its elections for a new leadership. The *vox populi* had chosen Mir Hussein Moussavi, while the sclerotic theocracy that actually run the show put their stamp of approval on Mahmoud Ahmadinejad. Ahmadinejad would remain president, the imams commanded. The people revolted *en masse*.

However, it wasn't the suspect election results that was unique in political spheres, or even the protests that turned into massacres of unarmed civilians; instead, it was *how* the news circulated around the world that became the talking point. Protesters used their mobile phones with built-in cameras to snap shots and footage of the government's heavy-handed response. They also used their phones to access the real-time information network Twitter to "tweet" in sometimes cryptic phrases of fewer than 140 characters to mobile phones and websites around the world a blow-by-blow account of the government's response to public displays of discontent. Iran's supreme leader Ali Khamenei had thought it had built a sufficiently robust dam against information getting into and out of the country; instead, the information dam quickly developed cracks through which pictures, snapshots, and personal accounts were flooding to the outside world, out of the government's reach.

Just a few weeks later at the start of July 2009, Urumqi, the capital city of the Xinjiang Uighur Autonomous region, erupted in protests by the indigenous Uighur population. Uighurs, ethnically Turkic, are Muslims. The unrest originated in an earlier demonstration by Uighurs demanding redress for the murder of Uighurs in Guangdong Province. Chinese workers had spread rumors that a group of Uighurs working in a Guangdong factory had raped two Chinese women—claims that eventually proved to be untrue. Nonetheless, hundreds of Chinese workers went on a rampage in the factory and hunted down and killed a handful of Uighurs in a real-world Human Flesh Search.[11] Local authorities at first did little to solve the case. Though state-run channels had said that the mob of Chinese had only killed two Uighurs, graphic photos spread on the Internet showed at least a half-dozen bodies of dead Uighurs. Their Han Chinese pursuers stood over them, shouting in victory. Though the Chinese government blocked the photos and even deleted footage each time activists published the material on new web addresses, protesters simply reposted the material elsewhere, including on overseas servers, beyond the grasp of Chinese censors.

Incensed by footage of the lynching that had been posted on the Internet, thousands of Uighurs in Urumqi assembled for a mass protest, the numbers of which the Chinese government had not seen since the Tiananmen Square protests of 1989. Demands for a proper government investigation into the crimes in Guangdong very quickly morphed into Uighur calls for greater protections of Uighur cultural and social interests in their own province, Xinjiang.

The Communist Party, since retaking the province in 1949, had been surreptitiously expunging the Turkic heritage of the people in the region and "sinofying" the society and economy. Former Chinese army soldiers who had left the army in the region were encouraged to stay to help in the construction, oil, and mineral industries. The provincial government provided tax incentives and subsidies for Chinese from other parts of China to move to Xinjiang to homestead and create their own businesses. Not only the *best* jobs in state-owned enterprises went to the Han Chinese, but *most* of the jobs went to them, with discrimination rampant in workplaces that employed both Chinese and Uighurs.[12]

Government censors moved quickly to staunch the flood of video, BBS posts, blog accounts, emails, and even tweets about the lynching of the Uighurs in Guangdong. The national government immediately ended services to all mobile phones in Urumuqi to keep users of digital cameras and video recorders from beaming out to the world images of the increasingly violent protests and the unremitting manner in which jack-booted paramilitary troops beat and shot protesters. Censors also blocked the Twitter service, so observers and participants would not be able to send real-time comments about the conflict to the outside world. Censors even extended the block to the Chinese Twitter knock-off, Fanfou. National level censors also blocked the popular social networking site, Facebook, which supports its own e-mail service as well as posts on "walls" for invitees to read and answer. Even the Urumqi city and Xinjiang regional governments took their websites down to ensure a complete blackout of the province.[13] A territory about the size of Alaska was completely cut off from the world.

The popular YouTube online video service continued to be blocked during the Urumqi uprising. It had been initially shut down a year before during the 2008 Tibetan riots because activists posted video footage of the government's brutal tactics in quelling the rebellion. During the Tibetan riots, protesters had taken advantage of the spotlight that the Beijing Olympics had brought to China. The Tibetans communicated the violence of the government crackdown by taking digital photos and video of the police action and posting the drama on YouTube, virtually as it was happening. Though months later, the central government lifted the communications blackout on the region, Twitter, Fanfou, Facebook, and YouTube all remained blocked indefinitely.

Contrary to the gag placed on Internet services that supported amateur media during the explosive events in Urumqi, major newspapers with online articles about the protests and ensuing violence remained accessible in China. *The New York Times*, *Financial Times*, *The Economist*, and news agencies such as Reuters and the BBC remained open for viewing. Likely, the central government considered the absolute number of readers in China who could read and appreciate what English-language media outlets were writing too small to be considered dangerous to the message the government wanted to spin. However, the Great Firewall did not release its blocks from longtime censored blog host blogspot.com, nor from bloglines.com, a news and blog aggregator that likely provided a channel for antigovernment blogs from outside China to make their way to a readership inside China.

The government also deployed a second line of defense against disseminating information that ran counter to its policies on Xinjiang— or information that simply embarrassed central government—called Search Engine Manipulation (SEM). SEM involves the government filtering a list of search results based on the most probable key words that "techno-chiks" (that is, technology-inclined *apparatchiks*) believe interested readers are most likely to query. Popular Chinese sites such as Baidu, Sina.com, Google.com, and Google.cn posted government-approved search results of the uprising in Urumqi, with a high density of articles from Chinese news organizations Xinhua and *People's Daily*, both mouthpieces for Beijing. Surprisingly, major international news outlets, including Reuters, the BBC, and *The New York Times*, were allowed to display up-to-date results that could be accessed for online searches such as "Urumqi" and "Urumqi protests".

However, it's the Net Nanny that is probably most effective at ensuring Chinese cybernauts cleave to the government's point of view on the Xinjiang riots and other sensitive issues. The Net Nanny simply eliminates content it doesn't like by wiping entries from servers. As the often-humorous blog site Chinayouren.com recently described: "The Nanny's power comes from the menace of closing down a page, taking away the business license, or directly imposing 'stern punishment' on offenders. Stern punishment can involve stiff fines, jail time, loss of a job, or, if a business, loss of the business license."

Hence, the Internet in China hosts very little in the way of debate about the nature of the protests in Tibet and Urumqi. Mostly, surviving blog posts by Chinese nationals have nicely fallen in line with party policy. One hyper-politically correct blogger posted the following on Sina.com.cn: "Resolutely smash the splitist forces and terrorists!"[14]

Another blogger, known as "Chang Qing," said: "Destroy the conspiracy, strike hard against these saboteurs, and strike even more fiercely than before."[15]

"The blood debt will be repaid. Han compatriots unite and rise up," wrote "Jason" on search engine www.baidu.com.[16]

The odd domestic voice does squeak through the bristles of the Net Nanny's broom. For instance, Reuters cited one blog entry just after the

Urumqi crackdown that said: "If your family members who have no rights or power are discriminated against and made fun of, not only will your family collapse, you will already have sown the seeds of hatred."[17]

However, media observers noted the Net Nanny maintains its scrutiny of domestic websites. For instance, pchome.net, a Shanghai-based site that supports a BBS, had numerous comments during the Urumqi unrest that all vanished within hours of being posted, each replaced with the line: "This posting does not exist."[18]

THE REVOLUTION WILL NOT BE ONLINE

Chinese dissidents were hardly idle as the government censors thickened China's walls against online criticism and soapbox proclamations. Liu Xiaobo's Charter 08, an online Declaration of Independence the former Beijing Normal University professor posted at the end of 2008, was the boldest affront to central authority mandate in years.

I first met Lu Xiaobo during the 2007 Chinese Spring Festival in Beijing. Liu Xiaobo is a well-known dissident who has been struggling against the Chinese government since the Tiananmen Square uprising nearly 20 years ago. He has been in and out of prison as a political prisoner for years. An old friend of his, a former Beijing lawyer, had invited me to dinner along with several of her friends from the Tiananmen days. Liu Xiaobo and his wife had come as well. It had been months since they were without the public security shadows who typically tailed them. I was struck by how small both he and his wife were, and how much alike they both appeared. They both wore dark, baggy clothes and sported shaved heads. They seemed ready at any moment for Liu to return to prison; his wife was simply ready for the marathon sessions involving government entreaties and inter-national communications to get her husband released.

Most of the discussion that evening at the restaurant revolved around the mistakes students and agitators made during the standoff at Tiananmen Square, which finally led to the army routing the protesters and killing hundreds—perhaps even thousands—of people.

The Chinese friend with whom I had come to the dinner encouraged me to continue the discussion at Liu's home. The prospect of a foreigner interested in what they had to say seemed to delight the dissident couple.

They were in high spirits from a combination of the animated dinner conversation and the sense of freedom from house arrest, however short-lived. They lived in a modest apartment block within walking distance from the restaurant. As we walked down the driveway into the residential compound, Liu pointed at an empty sentry's box and commented on how even the public security guard assigned to keep an eye on their home had retired for the holiday.

Two things struck me when I entered their home for what would be the first and last time: how the walls of books made such a beautiful montage of color that brightened their sanctuary; and the prominent position of a personal computer in their living room. Liu Xiaobo explained that he spent most of his time in front of the computer, writing e-mails and political tracts for international consumption. The four of us spent the rest of the evening drinking wine and debating the merits of Western-style democracy.

A year and a half later, in December 2008, Liu Xiaobo would co-author the most politically explosive tract ever to be posted on the Internet. Called Charter 08, the article was essentially a Chinese declaration of independence from the authoritarian rule of the Communist Party. The opening of the Charter states: "A group of 303 Chinese writers, intellectuals, lawyers, journalists, retired Party officials, workers, peasants, and businessmen have issued an open letter—'Charter 08'—calling for legal reforms, democracy, and protection of human rights in China." Even more infuriating to Chinese authorities was that scores of scholars and intellectuals from around the world digitally signed the declaration. The government security apparatus moved quickly, blocking domestic access to the site on which the pronouncement had originated, and arresting Liu Xiaobo. In December 2009, judges sentenced Liu to 11 years in prison for his attempts to destabilize the society, the toughest sentence ever passed down to a dissident, including those arrested just after the Tiananmen Massacre in 1989. In 2010, Liu was awarded the Nobel Peace Prize for his unwavering stance.

Government censors took additional steps to sweep the Internet clean of any content they felt inappropriate for consumption by the Chinese masses under the guise of sanitizing the web of pornography. The authorities started their cyber-purge by closing down the controversial online forum, bullog.com, a prominent website published and read by progressive Chinese thinkers who had written extensive commentaries and analyses of the implications of Charter 08. The charter had amped the momentum of the central government's mission to sanitize the Internet of opposition to its hegemony. *The China Digital Times*, a popular blog based at the University of California critical of Chinese government policy, called the police action "the most vicious crackdown in years."[19]

Censors electronically blocked hundreds of blogs and arrested some writers to make an example of them. By mid-February 2009, the government had closed nearly 2,000 websites and 250 blogs that supported online-discussion forums, instant-messaging groups, and text-messaging boards. The government justified its actions as an antipornography drive; however, it was clear that any platforms that discussed politically sensitive issues were prime targets for elimination. An entrepreneur named Wang Zhaojun sued his blog-host service, Sina.com, in late winter of that year for closing his blog on the eve of Chinese New Year. Once himself a local government official, Wang demanded the portal explain its actions given his right to free speech as written in the Chinese constitution. His case was not helped in the least as he had written a diatribe against the country's one-party system, along with references to the Falun Gong sect, the Tiananmen Square massacre, and Charter 08—all red capes to the government bulls-in-waiting, who by late 2010 had still not published a judgment in the case.[20]

THE GRASS-MUD HORSE STRIKES BACK

While adopting a nationalistic line toward the Tibetan and Xinjiang protests and the furor over the Olympic torch relay, average Chinese netizens also increasingly voiced consternation with government intrusion into what they saw as personal space, as users came to identify more and more with their online avatars. Shortly after Liu published Charter 08, Chinese netizens began resisting the government's restrictions on the Internet in ways Western users may consider sophomoric, creating cartoon characters, animations, songs, and even fictional countries in which to play out their fantasies of rebellion.

By March 2009, a fictitious alpaca had become a social phenomenon in China. The three Chinese characters of its name (*cao ni ma* 草泥马)

translated in English as "Grass-Mud Horse"—three seemingly innocuous and rather innocent-sounding words that can slip through any censorship-software program. However, another set of Chinese characters for the exact same words *cao ni ma* 操你妈—pronounced with different tones—translates as "F*** Your Mother." The play on words was like flipping a middle finger at government censors who believed they were making solid progress on eradicating what they called "spiritual pollution" from the Internet.[21] The intention behind the entire Grass-Mud Horse movement was to show the government censors that no matter how clever they thought they could make their blocking and deletion software, they could not block all of what the Chinese Internet community thought and discussed—at least, not without bringing all the traffic on the Chinese information superhighway to a screeching halt in an attempt to block every innocuous word put to ironic intent.

The Grass-Mud Horse had cartoons, comics, online videos, and even songs dedicated to its existence. I recall walking through a shopping district of Suzhou, near Shanghai, that spring and seeing Grass-Mud Horse stuffed animals in shop windows available for sale. The heroic alpaca lived in a desert that had another rude name, *ma le ge bi* 马了个屄, and was confronted by the onslaught of voracious "river crabs." "River crab" in Chinese sounds a lot like the word for "harmony," one of the central planks of the national government's policy on creating a "harmonious society." In Chinese cyberspace, though, "harmony" has become a code word for censorship. When a Chinese blogger said his blog had been "harmonized," he was really saying his site had been blocked or outright deleted.

Indeed, the Grass-Mud Horse was so successful in eluding capture through government-placed Internet filters that YouTube—before it was blocked in China—chalked up 1.4 million viewers of a children's song about the heroic bovine. An online cartoon about the alpaca registered a quarter million more views, and a parody of a documentary that would make *National Geographic* proud followed the Grass-Mud Horse around in its natural habitat, chalking up 180,000 views. Professors and think tanks published real treatises about the social significance of the virtual animal.

It took several weeks after the Grass-Mud Horse had slipped its leash before the government eventually understood it had lost control of the Internet, despite its online temperance movement. Near the end of March 2009, authorities posted on websites and BBSs the notice, "Any content related with the Grass-Mud Horse should not be promoted and hyped." The Communist Party then fell back on a surefire cure for domestic ills—blame the West. "The overseas media has exaggerated the incident as a confrontation between netizens and the government."

At the beginning of June 2009, the Chinese government announced that from July 1, 2009, all personal computer vendors—including those in the West selling to the China market—would have to pre-install a software program called Green Dam-Youth Escort on machines destined for the Chinese market. Ostensibly, the government was promoting the software as a means of protecting society's youth from smut and politically incorrect content on the Internet. For the Chinese government, pretty much anything challenging the Communist Party's control over the society, its self-image, and the image of the society at large are off-limits. So, while the Green Dam software did block the racy photos of Hong Kong pop stars, it also blocked websites that referred to the spiritual group Falun Gong, the Tibetan liberation, and the Dalai Lama. Also off-limits were any unflattering references to Mao, the Cultural Revolution, the Great Leap Forward, and any other self-inflicted catastrophes.

Though the Grass-Mud Horse had been banned and blocked, Chinese Internet users had another cartoon hero—or rather, heroine—up their imaginative sleeve to protest the installation mandate: the Green Dam Girl. The Green Dam Girl looks very much like the wide-eyed school girls popular in Japanese comic books and animated TV shows and movies. She sports a miniskirt in the forest-green color of a PRC uniform, which highlights her long, sexy legs; she wears a badge with a crab (symbol of the censorship services the government extends to web content it deems unwarranted); and she carries a cute, furry, stuffed bunny rabbit, mascot of the author of the software, Jinhui Computer System Engineering Company. She also hauls around a bucket of paint or soy sauce to cover up unacceptable content she finds on the Chinese web.

Like the Grass-Mud Horse, the Green Dam Girl has cartoons, stories, songs, and poetry dedicated to her tireless efforts to "harmonize" the

Chinese Internet. She even had a few pornographic sketches done of her and circulated throughout websites and blogs in much the same way as the Grass-Mud Horse—through the most inoffensive of written Chinese characters that eluded the most sophisticated filtering software.

Though the fictitious online characters certainly irritated censorship authorities, the government was still intent on forcing its spyware onto every computer in China. It seemed the harder the government pushed the issue publicly, the more reactionary Chinese Internet users became. Finally, some Chinese Internet users posted their own warning to the Chinese government on websites and bulletin boards nationwide on the last week of June 2009 in response to the government directive to put censorship software on every computer used in China. "Hello, Internet censorship institutions of the Chinese government," one post said. "We are the anonymous netizens. We hereby decide that from July 1, 2009, we will start a full-scale global attack on all censorship systems you control."[22]

The people's ire was not to end just with threats of crashing government servers. Less-sophisticated Chinese Internet surfers launched a telephone-call assault on Jinhui Computer, maker of the censorship software, lodging more than 1,000 phone calls harassing staff in one month alone. Human Flesh Search Engines dug up personal information on Jinhui employees, including details about the general managers' private life. One caller threatened to kill the manager's wife and child.[23] The digital world had tipped into madness, forcing the central government to backpedal on its decree. July 1 came and went and still, as of this writing, computers bought and sold in China for private and corporate use have not had censorship software installed directly on their hard drives.

WHEN NETWORKING BECOMES THE RAGE

Malcolm Gladwell's book, *The Tipping Point*, popularized the relationship between the spread of viral infections in a society and in human social networks. Whether typhoid fever or word of mouth about the latest indie rock band, communicability follows the same nonlinear development pattern: a few small, seemingly unrelated "outbreaks" crop up, between which connections eventually self-organize to spread like wildfire throughout the network at a rate that grows exponentially. The tipping point exists at the edge of chaos, in which communicability runs amok, uncontrollable.

Companies use relatively low-cost "viral marketing" methods to reach potential consumers of their products to convert them into sales agents who will further spread the word about the wonders of the products throughout the wired world. Indeed, Western companies invested in China have used the Internet to create Chinese "buzz" about their products. Consultancies in Beijing and Shanghai meanwhile gauge the buzz and report back to clients about the effectiveness of viral tactics.

The Chinese government also plays the Internet the same way, though with less contagion than Human Flesh Searches. Central authority pays Chinese citizens 50 cents for each blog and forum post that spreads the gospel of the Communist Party through cyberspace. It was these "50-centers," as they're called in Chinese, who posted proclamations such as, "Resolutely smash the splitist forces and terrorists!" Such blatant propaganda, however, falls on deaf ears amongst the post-Cultural Revolution generation, which has no experience with that terrible period in Chinese modern history and little interest in knowing about it, either. Instead, Generation W(eb) is far more interested in entertainment content, in the salacious and the raucous. Recall that more Chinese per capita, compared with Americans, consider their lives as real (or more real) on the Internet than in the physical world.

Chinese government efforts to curb Chinese netizen access to the wider world by fortifying the Great Firewall, and through corporate self-censorship of blog and forum posts, actually have an effect *opposite* that which the government is hoping to achieve. The Internet has become an increasingly engaging and titillating realm in which to slip into alternative personalities, express oneself, discuss, and even act on opinions under the nose of Big Brother. It also has become a closed resonance chamber in which tidal waves of communications and dissent reinforce each other to eventually burst into the real world as mass action. The ubiquity of recording technologies and the long tail of information posted on the Internet invites social networks to quickly form and develop in an incubator that seems tailor-made for a culture that for thousands of years has loved to gather in groups to trade information, swap gossip, and form opinions and judgments in *ad hoc* juries. Viral protests are inevitable in an electronic medium that is increasingly becoming denser with users and more insular through government censorship.

Though clusters of dissent may form through the sacrifices of men such as Nobel laureate Liu Xiaobo, the great firestorms of civil disobedience on the scale of tens of thousands of Chinese citizens will increasingly come from the policies and actions of government representatives and business leaders who netizens believe, simply, are cheating them. It is nearly impossible, though, to determine what action, what word and what glance will leap social synapses to tip local critical state conditions in China into mass action. A critical state is the territory that lies between stability and utter chaos. In the same way, one never knows in China just what particular incident might lace together independent gangs of cyber-malcontents, just as one is never sure how the next pandemic might start or how the next forest fire will ignite or what will trigger the next earthquake. Further, as Mark Buchanan writes in his book, *Ubiquity: Why Catastrophes Happen*, forest fires, earthquakes, avalanches, wars, and mass movements don't know how big they will be when they start. The Tiananmen Square protests are a prime example. What began as a handful of Chinese students mourning the lost virtues of a deceased *apparatchik* mushroomed into one of the dramatic sit-ins in recent history.

Tipping points abound in a China modernizing at a rate never before seen in its history, using tools and technologies that only bind its users closer to one another in a critical state increasingly in disequilibrium. Such is the power and the necessity and the resonance of the electronic social networks now lashing Chinese society together that when one girl in the Chinese countryside is falsely accused of a crime, an entire local government comes under threat of being turned out by ordinary citizens thousands of miles away. As long as the central government chooses not to encourage an independent judiciary able to "clear the underbrush" of relatively minor social discontent, the Internet will remain a tinderbox of discourse and rebellion, eventually creating a cascade of discontent over which central government may be forced to black out information exchange throughout the country, just as it had in the autonomous regions of Tibet and Xinjiang.

Ironically, the central government knows it requires these mass communications channels to reach into and hold onto a modernity the West has defined. China needs the sort of incisive minds and creative personalities that will truly make the country a superpower. The newly urbanized and gentrified in China, research institutions ensconced in glittering high-rises, research and development centers pushing the frontiers of technology, exporters in the countryside that rely on e-mail and web portals through which to conduct business, and foreign-invested firms have much to lose if the central authority believes it needs to throw some great information circuit breaker to squelch popular dissent. Western companies that rely on constant network communications between their headquarters and their China facilities, manufacturing operations using the Just-in-time inventory strategy, and retail outfits that daily consolidate transactions from disparate outlets, need to ensure their backup systems are robust and communications lines can be quickly rerouted in the event of a nationwide information blackout. Large multinationals, in particular, risk losing millions of dollars in the blink of an eye. And China risks subsequently losing foreign direct investment projects valued at hundreds of billions of dollars, as well as losing credibility in the global marketplace as a steward of international business.

What, though, do Chinese citizens have to fret about online during the boom times of the early twenty-first century? What grievances tip angry online blog posts into mass protests on the streets of Chinese villages and cities? What are some of the greater fractures in Mainland Chinese society that may well one day shake Wall Street and Main Street?

Sometimes in China, answering such weighty questions is as easy as stepping out the door of one's home.

END NOTES

1. "Waitress Stabs Chinese Official Trying to Rape Her," chinaSMACK, May 18, 2009 http://www.chinasmack.com/2009/more/waitress-stabs-government-official-during-rape-attempt.html.
2. "Chinese Consumers in 2020: A look into the Future," *Euromonitor Report*, March 11, 2009.

3. "China Web Users Keep Track of Government Missteps," Reuters, March 31, 2009.
4. "China's Internet Cafes Study 2008," Research and Markets.
5. "Netizen Satire Defends Nanjing Commissioner Zhou," chinaSMACK, December 26, 2008, http://www.chinasmack.com/stories/netizen-satire-defends-nanjing-commissioner-zhou/.
6. "Xuzhou Government Outlaws Human Flesh Search," chinaSMACK, January 21, 2009, http://www.chinasmack.com/stories/xuzhou-government-outlaws-human-flesh-search/.
7. Ibid.
8. Seth Faison, "China's Grip on the Net," *The New York Times*, February 11, 1996.
9. Mark Landler, "In China, Visions of Internet riches in a PC-short land," *The New York Times*, December 20, 1999
10. James Fallows, "The Connection has been Reset," *The Atlantic Monthly*, March 2008.
11. Yu Le and Ben Blanchard, "China Detains 15 over Ethnic Brawl Linked to Riot," Reuters, July 7, 2009.
12. Edward Wong, "Clashes in China Shed Light on Ethnic Divide," *The New York Times*, July 7, 2009.
13. Michael Wines, "In Latest Upheaval, China Applies New Strategies to Control Flow of Information," *The New York Times*, July 6, 2009.
14. Ben Blanchard, "China Tightens Web Screws after Xinjiang Riot," Reuters, July 6, 2009.
15. Ben Blanchard, "Chinese Go Online to Vent Ire at Xinjiang Unrest," Reuters, July 7, 2009.
16. Ibid.
17. Ibid.
18. Ben Blanchard, "China Tightens Web Screws after Xinjiang Riot," Reuters, July 6, 2009.
19. Michael Wines, "A Dirty Pun Tweaks China's Online Censors," *The New York Times*, March 11, 2009.
20. Kathrin Hille, "Beijing Court to Rule on Political Blog Case," *Financial Times*, February 2, 2009.
21. Michael Wines, "A Dirty Pun Tweaks China's Online Censors," *The New York Times*, March 11, 2009.
22. Kathrin Hille, Joseph Menn, and Richard Waters, "Control, Halt, Delete," *Financial Times*, June 26, 2009.
23. "Threats Made to Maker of China Filtering," Associated Press, June 24, 2009.

CHAPTER **2**

The Anxious Class

PROPERTY RIGHTS AND WRONGS

A crowd suddenly roared outside the patio doors of my high-rise apartment. Something very dramatic must have been happening for me to be able to hear the clamor clear up to the seventeenth floor, I thought. Typically, my adopted Chinese hometown of Suzhou was a rather placid city, just 65 kilometers outside Shanghai. The Lakeview Garden apartment complex in which I made my home was the very model of a modern middle class: all propriety, privacy, and just enough show of wealth to let others know where on the socioeconomic ladder one perched. Whatever the matter was, I considered, it sounded violent. A fight? A drunken brawl? Another protest perhaps? The Suzhou spring evening was warm without the usual heavy humidity. The perfect evening for an outdoor performance. I hurried out to the balcony to catch the show.

I couldn't have been more surprised or amused. A small, yellow, scorpion-like backhoe was pulling down the half-meter thick wall that had blockaded owners of the apartments in the complex from half their property. A Singaporean real estate development corporation had built the wall to bar the tenants from further spoiling its delayed construction project for two more residential towers on the land. I scurried down to the ground floor to take in the action, still in my T-shirt and sandals.

Lakeview residents had pushed down the first wall two months before, upset the property developer had reneged on the initial sales plan to build a courtyard with an elaborate garden and playground. The local government had provided construction permits to the developer, who began building the towers without getting consent from apartment owners. The barricade was constructed of mere cement and used-bricks, which they easily felled with a few well-placed shoves. The developers then built a new, thicker, taller wall to thwart the citizen revolt, and whitewashed the construction to advertise its permanence. A skeleton crew began working from 5:30 a.m. until past 10 p.m. every day to lay in place the first tower's foundation. I woke each morning and prepared for bed each evening to the sounds of construction equipment driving 10-meter cement pilings into the ground, backhoes scraping away at the mushy soil, and dump drunks carrying away the evidence of the proposed site for a neighborhood playground.

Now, two months on, local residents were at war again with the developer. As I exited the luxury apartment building, I saw a handful of police in the parking lot having a shoving match with some of the residents. Communist Party marching music blared from one of the lower level apartments in protest of the project, providing a revolutionary backdrop to the drama. The management company's security people milled about the crowd seemingly without direction. Some bystanders looked up over my head at the building I had just exited. I turned around and looked up myself to see blood-red banners that stretched from the top floor of the high-rise down two-thirds the length of the building. One of the banners read in big yellow Chinese characters: "We would rather die than give up our homes!" More police arrived, presumably to protect the construction site from further damage.

At ground level, I could see a young Chinese man, tall and skinny, in his early 20s, dressed in blue jeans and a flimsy white, short-sleeved shirt, piloting the errant backhoe. He accurately and without hesitation continued on his mechanized rampage of the battlement without concern of groups of men shouting at him. He had already wrecked perhaps 30 meters of the whitewashed barrier.

Eventually, some police and local Chinese construction-company project managers made their way to the backhoe to haul the assailant out of the cockpit. The managers were fat, middle-aged men sporting bad comb-overs. The construction crew pulled the young man from the booth of the digger and dragged him away from the scene of devastation. Building residents yanked back at the boy, and argued angrily with the white-helmeted police defending the project managers.

The residents broke the boy free from the officers. He began to run. After only a few steps, though, project managers caught the boy again and tore at his clothes. They took the boy inside the perimeter of the construction site, perhaps to crucify him, I wasn't sure. The boy had to rely on the might of the residents who had come to his rescue to disengage him from the beating he was receiving by the fists and feet of the construction managers. Residents grabbed at any limb the boy was able to flail. Other residents had the officers pinned down with arguments and shoving.

Suddenly, the boy wrenched free of the project managers. He flew fast as the wind out of the construction area, over the wreckage of the wall he had single-handedly brought down, and out a back way from the parking area. He clearly had a plan of escape in place, and knew how to find his way out the compound with its winding pathways. I don't think his feet ever touched the ground. I was happy for the kid, and found myself smiling at the impotent police, building security staff, and project managers, their comb-overs disheveled from the tug-of-war in the warm spring breeze.

The next morning at 6 a.m., company backhoes and dump trucks returned to the site scraping at the grounds like chickens scratching for food scraps. The spine of the wall lay crumbled in heaps. A lone police cruiser with a bored public servant sat inside the vehicle to protect the ruins and discourage further public assembly. It was during that clear, early morning I realized I had seen played out one of the greatest fears that China's nascent middle class harbors: a capricious, complete, and irrevocable loss of their newly acquired wealth and position, seemingly overnight. Their anxiety is increasing as growing numbers of the newly affluent take additional slices of a wealth-pie whose plate has a finite circumference.

Tsinghua University in Beijing reported in early 2010 that 90 percent of the country's white-collar workers were highly stressed. People interviewed in the study listed the escalating cost of owning a home in China as the primary cause of stress, followed by education costs and the competition for jobs.[1] The new middle class also has the added burden of a relatively expensive and overstretched health-care system with which to contend. The Four Stresses—if the Communist Party were to label top middle-class anxieties—remain as powerful blasting caps in the society's efforts at creative destruction of its past to shape its future. How well the central government handles the needs, wants, and anxieties of a growing, better educated, and increasingly homogeneous social group will determine its ability to sustain the legitimacy of the Communist Party and maintain its relative stability with other Asian economies.

China's urban population stands near 600 million, with anywhere from 100 million to 175 million people in its burgeoning middle class, depending on which analyst you ask.[2] At an average growth rate of about 10 percent a year, the middle class is set to expand to about 700 million people by the year 2020—the largest in the world. While the disposable income of the average Chinese family was about US$1,327 in 2005, an IBM study in 2007 found the annual middle-class family income to be in the range of between US$3,000 and US$6,000, sufficient to buy goods and services from the developing mass market. The upper middle class in China in 2007 was about 15 million people strong, who were on average making more than US$32,000 a year.[3]

The middle class of any modern society is already familiar with some of the challenges confronting China's middle class. The Chinese middle class, though, is very young. It didn't get its start until 1998, when China liberalized property ownership in the cities. Property ownership became the "chassis" and the "engine" of growth for the middle class, providing a way for the once-poor to invest their earnings and reap some sort of return. (After all, everyone in China was poor until as late as 1985, when farming communes began to sell their surplus onto the cities for profit.) Further, property ownership propagated entire industries and sectors, from construction through to the manufacture of concrete, the forging of steel, and furniture making. The new properties also required a service sector involving real estate development, brokerage, interior design, and decoration. There were also the ancillary services that rose directly from the wealth that property ownership bestowed: restaurants, office management, tourism, and more. The Communist Party needs to nurture the already existing middle class as well as the opportunities to get there to solidify the bit of legitimacy it still has to rule over nearly 1.5 billion people.

Certainly, China's middle class will only grow larger. The McKinsey Global Institute projected in 2008 that China's middle class would increase from 43 percent of the population to 76 percent by 2025; that's more than one billion people that will comprise the third-largest consumer market in the world at that time. Its development of the middle class is a direct determinant of the central government's ability to maintain control over the society and the economy. Should entry to the middle class be systematically barred to anyone with the wherewithal and income level to make it to the threshold, and channels to maintain those standards blocked, the Communist Party will find its mandate to rule in peril.

However, middle-class China's realities are more fragile than one would find in North America or in Europe. The middle class is a power base in the West; Western middle-class values and channels for expression of discontent have been established for nearly 70 years. Models for civil society have existed for centuries in the Western hemisphere, as well. Without civil institutions and an independent judiciary that protects what the Chinese middle class values, the country's new *bourgeoisie* will remain anxious about suddenly losing the gains it has made in the past decade. It is afraid of losing its money, its property, its jobs, its businesses, its health, its future opportunities for its children, and its lifestyle after retirement. Personal misfortune aside, the single power great enough to take it all away—almost as great as Heaven's own, some Chinese would argue—is the central government itself and its organs at the local levels. Sometimes, the local apparatus can be downright Orwellian when it comes to the rights of its own citizens. The Chinese governments—far from monolithic culturally, but singular in their obsession with control and self-aggrandizement—can at any time issue policies, directives, or decisions that wipe out the fortunes of families overnight. For instance, in the spring of 2010, angry homeowners in the Yangtze River Delta town of Changshu petitioned the central government about plans by local government and developers to demolish 800 villas to make way for new villas.[4] This is a source of anxiety that the middle class in rich countries such as the United States, Japan, Germany, or even Italy do not have to contend with. Even if the government in one of the wealthy countries was to exercise undue power over middle-class citizens, complainants have recourse to justice through independent judiciaries that permit escalation of issues that remain unresolved to a complainant's satisfaction.

So, though it is nearly gospel to every economist that China's middle class will only grow larger in the coming decades, the middle class's sense of security will develop in an inverse-proportion relationship; that is, the larger and richer the Chinese middle class becomes, the less safe and more anxious it will feel.

Homeowners in China in particular have a lot to lose. Average Chinese home prices in 2009 were eight to 14 times average annual household income. Governments of Organization for Economic Co-operation and Development (OECD) member countries—the "rich" economies—consider a ratio of more than four times household income an overheated market. Other Asian countries have ratios of five to seven times income. While nearly 80 percent of China's middle class own their own homes, only a quarter of them have a mortgage.[5] The average mortgage in China in 2009 was only 46 percent of the property's value. U.S. homeowners were leveraged as much as 75 percent of the value of their property.[6] China's home buyers whose residence permits were from the town in which they were buying property had to put down a minimum deposit of 20 percent, while out-of-towners were on the hook for 30 percent. Those buying a second home—usually for investment—had to ante up a 40 percent deposit in 2010 to dampen speculation. In other words, homeowners in China entering the second decade of the twenty-first century had a lot of cold, hard cash to lose should a local government arbitrarily decide on a course of action that would severely devalue middle-class property holdings, or even eliminate them altogether.

The year 2008 saw massive and violent protests by middle-income homeowners in Shenzhen and Hangzhou. Central government strictures implemented months before to cool the overheating property market had begun deflating property values for the first time since the property market had been liberalized in the late 1990s. Chinese homeowners had expected the value of their properties to continue to rise; they had never before experienced market downturns. The inexperienced property owners trashed the Hangzhou offices of Vanke, the largest real estate developer in China, in 2008. The company had slashed the prices of flats just months after buyers had put as high as a

30 percent deposit on the original asking price. Beijing and Shenzhen also saw scenes of homeowners protesting and complaining bitterly to real estate development and management companies about the sudden devaluation of their property.

The Great Recession of 2008–2009 was providential to property owners as the central government lifted controls on the real estate market and injected new capital into housing-development projects. Citizens and real estate developers had money to spend, thrusting property values to new stratospheric heights in early 2010. By mid-2010, the central government saw the property bubble expand to dangerous extremes, with rent-to-purchase-price ratios returning to highs in the range of 1-to-400 in some cities. The international standard indicating dangerous speculative activity is 1-to-200. Chinese middle-class wealth is precariously perched on a house of cards supported only by the next round of self-reinforcing purchases—and the good graces of central government policy and local government patronage.

UNIVERSITY AND BEYOND

I stepped out onto the outdoor patio of a cafe in Suzhou to find a group of five young girls uncomfortably squeezed onto two wooden benches, the table between them crowded with Chinese workbooks, cups of coffee, and glasses of tea. They chirped and chittered at each other, disgorging passages of memorized text, and frantically flipping through worn pages of exercise books.

I asked them if they were studying for their college-entrance examination. They all called out, "Yes!" in unison, and tittered at the odd Westerner who took an interest in what they were doing. "When is the exam?" I asked.

"This afternoon!" they responded in perfect cadence. The question seemed to remind them they had better get back to work. They buried their heads back in the workbooks and mumbled Chinese mnemonics to themselves, now self-conscious.

The *gaokao* 高考, or high examination, is a Chinese citizen's hottest ticket to a better life. Each year, more than 10 million high school students take the three-day university examination, which can mean extending the wealth and status of a middle-class family or, for those from the poor countryside, a passage into the urban middle class. In 2000, the central government doubled the number of higher-education institutions to 1,900. Nearly 19 million students were enrolled in three- and four-year universities across the country in 2009.[7]

The examination system requires that students who want to get into the best schools in China study up to 16 hours a day for at least the year leading up to the examination. Each June, nearly 10 million students sit for the three-day battery of tests that will determine their fate. To get into one of the best schools, such as Beijing University or Tsinghua University, or even a second-tier school like Nanjing University or Zhejiang University means assurance that your child will be able to find a good job after graduation that will give your family face and additional wealth; face, through the splendid reputation of the child's school and, by extension, the company he or she works for, and the quality of the mate attracted for marriage. Much of the wealth a child generates after he or she graduates and begins working gets mixed into the entire family's pot.[8]

Though the energy of the group of young ladies at the neighborhood cafe was frenetic, they hardly seemed nervous to me. Perhaps it was the phenomenon of a traumatic experience shared that put them at ease, or perhaps they had already gone through the worst of the exam. The fate of young Chinese rests on this single set of exam, their desires compressed from below by family expectations and from on top by prejudicial government policies.

Still, the *gaokao* 高考 is one of the few avenues talented young people in the countryside may have to escape poverty. If a student scores high enough, she may be able to go to a first or second-tier school in a larger city, such as Beijing or Shanghai. Even the smaller cities of Suzhou or even Hangzhou will still be worlds apart from a farming village for job opportunities and channels for self-improvement. Students who graduate from local universities and subsequently find employers in their new city may then apply for a change in *hukou* 户口, or residence permit. The change means that one may be eligible for the social services of the city, while your child will be able to receive a legitimate education in the city.

However, the standards that students in the countryside have to meet are greater than those in the cities. Indeed, *People's Daily* reported in 2007 that a child in rural China had a third the chance of entering university as a child raised in the city, since most of the resources required for passing the entrance exam are concentrated in urban centers.[9] In 2005, only 30 percent of the students enrolled in university in China came from the countryside; as recently as 20 years before nearly 70 percent of university students were from the countryside. Part of the problem is escalating university fees. In the 1980s, university was all but free, but by 2005, the annual average tuition of 6,000 yuan (about US$890) was far too expensive for families with rural incomes. In 2005, the average rural family made about 2,000 yuan (about $295). Moreover, rural families that have sacrificed all so their children can enter university also have to beat a rationing system that is stacked against them. Most university seats go to local residents; the majority students at the prestigious Beijing University, for instance, are from Beijing. Even students at the less prestigious Soochow University are for the most part from Suzhou, where the university has been located since it was established by American missionaries a century earlier.

Jennifer, a student at Soochow University, told me in June 2008 during one of the examination periods just how desperate students had become to get into and stay in university. Jennifer was a typical local girl with a pretty smile and conservative tastes. A fellow student had just asked Jennifer to sit in for her during a battery of tests on a Sunday afternoon. Jennifer at the last minute demurred, choosing to simply not attend the sitting, and not giving the classmate a call. Apparently, Jennifer's student ID photo somewhat resembled her classmate's face. She talked about cheating on the exam for her classmate just as she would the weather; matter-of-factly, without shame. The reason she decided not to sit in for her friend, she said, was that she did not want to get caught, which might disqualify her from graduating from university. Ironically, the radio broadcast on the downtown Suzhou bus we were on was just announcing a report about hundreds of students who had been caught that weekend cheating on their university exam.

Still, she said, some students had resorted to putting listening devices into their ears from which they could receive the answers to the exam they were taking. In some instances, parents bribed teachers to remain at the ready to transmit the answers to their stressed children. Students also resorted to the age-old approach of scribbling answers on tiny scrolls they plaited in their hair and would palm when proctors were not looking. One father allegedly equipped his child with a mini-scanner and had nine teachers at the ready to provide answers to the test.[10]

Rich parents will bribe their children as well: They offer expensive cars, money, and extravagant parties. Preparation for university exam also can include more unusual strategies, such as having students inhale full tanks of oxygen to increase the efficiency and clarity of their thinking (or so believe the parents). Some parents have even put their daughters on birth control pills so the girls will not be inconvenienced by menstrual cramps during the exam period.

Other parents don't even bother with having their children take the university exam. Many from the middle to upper middle class can afford to send their children to private middle school, where the students learn and practice English language skills. "A lot of the students' parents are local government officials," one Western history teacher told me. He taught at the oldest middle school in Suzhou, which 1,000 years before had been where Confucian scholars would study for the imperial examination. "Most of the students will be going to university in Canada." Canadian student visa requirements are not as draconian as those in the United States, and Canadian universities are more affordable for international students than are American schools.

Another approach parents use to get their children into university is to simply buy the school records of other students who would have gone on to university in China. Local teachers and government officials sometimes collude with parents to steal the documents of children who had managed stellar grades and test results. In 2005, several teachers in Jilin Province were caught selling the school documents of two students for US$2,500 and US$3,600. Police believed the ring had more school records they planned to sell had they not been caught.[11] In early 2009, police in Hunan Province arrested a small town government official for buying the school and examination records of his daughter's classmate. He exercised his *guanxi* 关系—special relationships involving swapping favors—to get a new ID for his daughter at the local public security bureau, forged education records, and intercepted an acceptance letter for admission to a local university. When the arrest became public, the university the official's daughter had attended revoked her college degree.[12]

Very early on in their marriages, young middle-class couples begin feeling the stress of providing their children with an education that will lift their toddlers' prospects for a good life on the Mainland. Even couples born into the middle class who obtain university degrees and good jobs lead high-pressure lives because—after the expense of buying a new home—they begin saving for their child's education, which can begin as early as age three in China. They know from personal experience just how competitive Chinese society is with its hundreds of millions of students vying for a relatively few university seats; and then onward into the adult world where nearly every job has hundreds of applicants who are willing and able to fill precious vacancies.

Saska was fast approaching 30 years old when she and her husband of several years chose to have their child before they both grew much older. Already, Saska had a successful career with a major Singaporean commercial real estate company, her first job out of university. Unique at the time, in the late 1990s, Saska had gone to university in Finland, where she said she spent the loneliest four years of her life, and then another two years studying for a master's degree in the United Kingdom before returning to China to work. Originally from Hunan Province, she chose to work in Shanghai, even though her husband's work kept him in Hunan.

"My parents think I've been distracted long enough by the birth," Saska told me in the lounge of a five-star international hotel in Shanghai. She showed me a photo on her mobile phone of her seven-month-old daughter. "You know, the time it took to carry the baby, and then the six months I spent at home with the baby," she said.

"The most stressful thing right now is thinking about how to support the baby's education. It's going to be so expensive to get the baby the best education at the best schools." She seemed to shudder at the thought. "My parents want me to change jobs from real estate to financial services. There's more money in finance, they keep telling me. They think commercial real estate has no future and I'm not making enough money." Parents spend a great deal of money on extracurricular education programs for their children—math, science, Chinese language—all so their children can pass the university exam.

Most Chinese do not like the examination system, but few have any thoughts on how to revise the system, which is based in hundreds of years of Confucian tradition. James Fallows, author of the book *Postcards from Tomorrow Square*, hosted a discussion thread on his blog about the efficacy of the Chinese examination system.[13] Chinese believe that Western systems of university admittance—letters of recommendation, community involvement, extracurricular activities, essays, grades, and test scores—can be too easily rigged and even faked in China. Though certain cities have lower standards of entry for their own residents than for those from other cities—especially those students from the countryside—Chinese see the exam as flawed yet objective-as-they're-ever-going-to-be measures of intellectual ability and stamina, difficult to corrupt.

One young Chinese woman in Fallows's thread who had just graduated from university and was heading off to Harvard for graduate school made the point that it is not the examination system that is so much at fault as that schools are locally funded. Her argument really isn't much different from the arguments in the United States about how local schools are funded by the property taxes of the communities in which the schools are located: the ghetto gets zip while the suburbs (or wherever one finds the affluent in America) get a great deal more.

The young woman's point was that no matter the examination system in use, if the schools are well-funded and teachers are sufficiently trained, then the Chinese would be passing the exam in the tens of millions each year, instead of just the millions. As it is, the central government is having difficulty generating enough jobs for the graduates of the new millennium, of whom there are now twice as many graduating a year as there were a decade ago. Imagine if the government was then responsible for the creation and maintenance of high-end jobs for half its population, which would be the highest proportion of well-educated Chinese in the country's history, instead of just the small, elite fraction it is now.

Certainly, the current elite (whether political and/or the *nouveau riche*) would find themselves under threat by a new, brighter group that would be far larger than their existing clique and emboldened to rock the boat in the manner of a Tiananmen Square show of solidarity. The lack of opportunities and lack of forgiveness over how the elite have "rigged the system" to benefit itself would become too much for millions expecting entry into China's middle class to remain silent.

Too much equality, after all, does not fit well with China's version of Communism.

China has nearly 2,000 colleges and universities, nearly double the number available 10 years ago. Realizing the dearth of the country's well-educated, the central government gave the go-ahead to increase the number of university seats in 1999. The number of college-bound students in China increased from 1.08 million in 1998 to more than 17 million in 2003.[14] The six-fold jump since 1999 in the number of students enrolled in tertiary education institutions has meant an overcrowded job market, in which competition is fierce at best, cutthroat at its most dramatic. Despite the breakneck pace of growth of China's economy, the society has not created enough jobs to sop up the additional university graduates. Nearly eight million students each year graduate from higher-education institutions in China, immediately making their way to a job market that has not matured enough to absorb all of them. At the end of 2009, nearly 50 percent of all college graduates that year had not yet found jobs. Nearly three million students who did not have the family connections, or an appropriate degree, or lacked work experience, or who were simply at the wrong place at the wrong time were unemployed after they and their families had made Herculean efforts to get them into and through university. Another one and a half million university graduates who had finished their degree programs the year before also still had not found jobs.[15]. Many students have traded their dreams for high-paying jobs to work in China's growing service sector—in hotels, in the travel industry, and in such food-and-beverage companies as Starbucks, Burger King, and McDonald's—a path with which graduates in the West are more than familiar. Some students like Liu Wei simply give up and commit suicide, ashamed they cannot repay their families for the sacrifices that parents and siblings have endured to see them through to graduation. Wei, a 21-year-old university graduate hailed from a small farming village 320 kilometers south of Beijing, in Hebei Province. She did not have the connections or the money to pay bosses to hire her. She felt she had failed her family, and had no other option than to free them from the shame that she had brought upon them.[16]

Many of China's yuppies are metaphorically killing themselves at work because of people like young Liu Wei. They know there are dozens—perhaps even hundreds—of people willing to do whatever it takes to be in their position. Today's foot soldiers of the middle class— junior managers, engineers, technicians, secretaries, accountants, project managers, software developers, and more—all have a deep-rooted sense of insecurity about their jobs because they feel there are armies of bright young people coming up the ranks to take their places.

However, the stresses and strains of finding a middle-income job in China and keeping it in China's metropolises has come to the attention of Chinese researchers. The Chinese Academy of Sciences Institute of Psychology reported in 2010 that in a sampling of 50,000 urban workers, 60 percent were "sub-healthy." The report stated, "While one in 10 Americans will encounter situations where they need help from mental health professionals, most Chinese turn to their families and friends when they need help," according to the *China Daily*.[17] Chinese culture believes mental health issues are shameful, a loss of face to the disabled individual and to his family. The isolation that those in need of care suffers magnifies their sense of dissociation from family, friends, and society.

Unfortunately, China's health-care system is ill-equipped to help the many thousands in need of counseling and therapy; nor are medical institutions ready professionally and financially to cope with the increasingly sophisticated maladies of a middle class under attack.

PRECARIOUS HEALTH CARE

The Chinese middle class is worried about losing its recent financial gains through ill health or catastrophic accidents that see them sinking their savings into health care. Indeed, despite the prosperity of the over-all economy in China, the Chinese have spent less of their income and saved more. As recently as the late 1990s, most Chinese were employed in state-owned enterprises (SOEs) that covered their health-care costs. With the privatization of the majority of SOEs over the following 10 years, 80 percent of Chinese workers lost the health-care safety net they had always relied on. As a result, family savings increased. In 1990, private consumption made up nearly half of the country's wealth;

in 2008, private consumption had fallen to just over a third of China's gross domestic product (GDP).[18]

In 2006, a single average hospital admission at a state hospital cost 12,650 yuan (US$1,870), which is about 90 percent of the average Chinese family's wealth. Nearly half of the country's population of 1.3 billion had no insurance coverage at all. China ranks among the lowest of industrialized countries in public financing of health care, with an individual responsible for paying more than half his or her salary for hospital care, and the government picking up less than 20 percent of the tab; company-based social insurance benefits contribute the remainder of the bill. Ninety percent of China's 18,000 hospitals are state run, with prescription drugs bringing in about half their income, the expense of which is picked up by the hapless patient. Health-care costs have exploded. Despite GDP per capita increasing nearly 30 folds from 1980–2005, total health expenditures per capita increased 40 folds. Out-of-pocket spending on health care, though, exploded more than a 100 folds![19]

Just as in the United States, health-care costs can ruin a family. A family in Suzhou I came to know fell from middle-class grace because of a catastrophic illness in the family. The Zou family had three daughters. The eldest daughter, Zou Huihua, had met her husband, Wang Xiaolin, when she was attending university in 2002. Wang was working on his master's degree while Zou was finishing her last year in university. It was just after Zou had graduated from university and just months before she and Wang had married that doctors diagnosed Wang with a blood disorder. In school, he was a bright, energetic student with an argumentative streak. He had the makings of a great intellectual. When he fell ill, he became weak, lethargic, and pale. He could only eat certain foods without vomiting, and required near-daily blood transfusions. Blood transfusions are expensive in China, costing about 2,000 yuan (US$300) for each transfusion, which is equal to an average worker's monthly salary.

In 2006, expensive blood transfusions forced migrant and local workers in a poor district in the Beijing municipality to extremes. Families afflicted with blood diseases in the area pooled their money together to buy their own blood transfusion machine from a local hospital. The group of 17 patients—all of whom required blood transfusions on a regular basis—found their purchase to be the most cost-effective means of staying alive. Local police confiscated the machine from a filthy and dilapidated shed slumped in an enclosed, unkempt yard. Authorities sent the patients back to their hometowns. Though the national government had promised to subsidize the former residents' blood transfusions, the patients already knew the subsidies would not be enough to pay for the transfusions in the small country towns to which they were returning. The patients also knew that when the subsidies dried up, they would be back where they had started, without sufficient funds to cover the expensive treatments.

The fact in China is that no matter how deathly ill a person is, the hospital will not treat him until he or his family or friends pay cash up front. Stories abound of patients left unattended in wheelchairs, bleeding to death from some accident, because no one would pay cash for the treatments. Employees in hazardous manufacturing conditions may or may not have a boss who is "kind" enough to ante up the cash for doctors to attend to a severed arm or a smashed hand. In the instance of a near-fatal collision between a speeding truck and the Volkswagen that a Danish friend in Suzhou was driving, my friend was fortunate that the truck company's owner came to the accident site when the truck driver called him. The owner accompanied my friend to the nearest public hospital and paid several thousand yuan so my friend could be accepted into the emergency ward.

Zou and her new husband had no such benefactor. Wang's family could not help with the cost of the transfusions—they were even poorer than Zou's family, which, though not rich by city standards, was far better off than Wang's family in the countryside of Anhui Province. Zou's mother, the strong matriarch of the family, took the condition of her son-in-law to heart and paid for the medicines and transfusions Wang required to stay alive. She approached family members for loans to help pay for the treatments. Few would help her; most said she was stupid for spending so much money on someone who was going to die anyway.

When the family had spent its savings and exhausted the few loans from relatives they were able to get, Zou was beside herself with sorrow. She cried for days, inconsolable, and cursed her parents for not doing more to save her husband, who had grown weaker by the day.

So, Zou's mother finally put their home up for sale. The family was very attached to their 1,500 square-foot, three-bedroom apartment, which had a pretty garden in a backyard walled off from a neighboring factory. Property prices in the mid-2000s had increased dramatically since the government had privatized property in 1998, so the sale was quite profitable. However, the medicine and blood transfusions to keep Wang alive were no less expensive. The family rented a much smaller flat in which the five of them—including the youngest daughter—did their best to keep young Wang fed, clothed, sheltered, and alive.

Wang died in the spring of 2005, aged 26. Four years later, Zou still lived with her parents and with the middle sister. The youngest sister had married and moved out of the family's rented flat. Unable to afford the high property prices ushered in by China's economic boom, Zou and her family lived in a small, run-down, two-bedroom apartment with a drafty, closet-sized bathroom and a poorly lit nook for cooking. A dilapidated leather sofa that came with the place faced a small TV beside a shoulder-height refrigerator that cannot be used because it is blocked by a scuffed wooden card table that the family pulls to the center of the floor when it's time to eat.

The central government is fully aware of stories like the Zou's and has been drafting reforms to remedy the lack of protection against catastrophic illnesses. Health-care administration and insurance reform, however, have taken a back seat to government investment in the heavy industries that have pumped up the country's GDP growth. In 1994, the central government launched its first attempt at state-sponsored insurance coverage beyond the SOEs. The Urban Employee Basic Medical Insurance was an employment-based program that covered city residents. Employers and employees contribute to a large pool of premiums that support the formally employed, those laid off from SOEs, and migrant workers. Though the plan nationally covered more than half the population of 340 million for whom it was intended, it did not cover children in the cities, nor those in urban centers who had lost their jobs in private companies or those who had retired. In China, a worker can retire as early as the age of 55. In 2008, the Urban Resident Basic Medical Insurance (URMI) project began trial in 79 cities. The plan provides government subsidies of 80 yuan (US$12) per person per year—raised to 120 yuan (US$18) in 2010—with premiums paid by individuals. The program essentially covers city dwellers for catastrophic incidents that require inpatient care. The urban poor were the most helped by the program during the pilot. Premier Wen Jiaobao was impressed enough with the results to direct the pilot project be extended to half the cities in China in 2008, and cover all cities by 2011. The URMI will one day dovetail with the new Rural Cooperative Medical Insurance (RCMI) project to create a health-care safety net for all residents. The RCMI is similarly structured to the URMI, though with a much lower per-person subsidy from the government.[20] The global economic downturn in late 2008 and early 2009 gave the national government further motivation to build what it called a "safe, effective, convenient, and affordable" health-care system by 2020. Its plan was to spend US$123 billion to extend coverage that it already had in place. By 2011, the government intends to have 90 percent of China's citizens covered by some form of health insurance.[21] Still, even into 2020, patients may still have to pay all the costs of health-care coverage up front, in cash, and hope for speedy reimbursement.

Coverage for a catastrophic illness or accident will solve only a portion of China's health-care troubles. Bureaucracies and fiefdoms will need to be dissolved and leaner processes put in places to enable hospitals to operate more as service providers instead of as state-owned enterprises meeting production quotas for the number of patients administered during any given five-year plan. Administrations need to implement reward structures to incentivize doctors and nurses, and to weed out the incapable. Staff will need to have their pay sharply increased to reduce doctors' dependence on commissions from pharmaceutical companies whose drugs they push. Entirely new hospitals will need to be built with up-to-date equipment and staff training to support new technologies. Though there are private hospitals in China, they are much too expensive for any but the *nouveau riche* or corporate expats to afford. Most private hospitals are situated in the tier-1 cities: Beijing, Shanghai, and Guangzhou. As one 32-year-old Chinese office worker described the differences in hospital-delivery costs: "It was US$5,800 for the whole procedure and aftercare [at a private hospital]. For a general baby delivery in a public hospital in Beijing, it's U$400 to US$700. Plus, I can't get reimbursement for insurance [at a private hospital]."[22]

That said, with the private hospitals I have personally patronized in Shanghai, it seems well worth the premium to have to pay only once—when treatment is complete—and to have, on-balance, considerate if not polite staff, and to know the nurses and doctors are not mere cogs in bureaucratic machines who do not treat patients as such either. Chinese consumers, historically cost-conscious, themselves will require consumer education on the value and efficacy of their medical institutions achieving and maintaining such standards.

Increasing the fitness of the health-care system will prove to be a challenge as daunting to government leadership as building the manufacturing export sector that is the foundation of the wealth that China's middle class is afraid to spend for fear of going to the hospital.

HOLDING IT ALL TOGETHER

The rise of China's middle class has proved a bonanza for foreign-invested and domestic companies doing business in China. Whether they are Australian mining companies providing the raw ores smelted to become part of China's new urban development programs, automobile makers excited by annual double-digit sales increase as the newly affluent replace their bicycles with the latest model cars, electrical appliance makers, furniture manufacturers, or the tourist and hotel industries that cater to a growing clientele that travels more frequently in China for business and pleasure, the economic advantages of China's rising middle class are difficult to deny.

Western and domestic employers will continue to benefit from the surfeit of university graduates coming into the job market at entry level who are impatient to grasp the middle-class lifestyle. However, these fresh graduates will also face depressed salary levels due to the large numbers continuing to graduate with few prospects of landing a job out of school. Domestic Chinese and foreign-invested companies, though, will see more experienced local staff place additional upward pressure on salary demands as they realize their value to enterprises. The rising cost of living alongside increased family expectations to grasp a piece of the good life will also weigh heavily on career decisions.

As more individuals aspire to join China's middle class and compete for a limited amount of property, university seats, jobs, and resources such as food, energy, and water, the newly affluent will come under greater stress. Reform of the health-care system is essential to manage the growing number of stress-related ailments and diseases that attend middle-class lifestyles, magnified by the dense population numbers and rapid pace of economic development of the society at large. Burps of random violence and mass protests similar to what I had experienced at my Suzhou apartment building in 2007 will become more commonplace as long as education levels, connectivity with the wider world, and expectations for a better life come into opposition with local and central government imperatives for revenue, control, and self-preservation.

During the spring of 2010, China saw an alarming increase in dramatically violent incidents directly related to the schism between individual expectations for a Hollywood-feel-good sort of life and the reality of muddling through existence in the most populated and arguably the most competitive country in the world. Over a span of three months, half a dozen individuals in different regions in China wielding knives murdered scores of children attending kindergartens and elementary schools. Meanwhile, a spate of nearly a dozen worker suicides during the same season at a single facility in Shenzhen, owned by Foxconn, the world's largest contract manufacturer of electronic gadgets, underscored the stresses individual workers were experiencing in an environment that treated them more as robots than as thinking, feeling human beings. Further, mass strikes—some of which became violent and required a heavy police presence to mollify crowds—stopped factories throughout China so workers could elevate their salaries or improve hazardous working conditions. All these incidents have been encouraged by the hope or disappointment of reaching and remaining in the promised land of Middle Income bliss. Even more meaningful, the events have brought the appropriateness of China's tarnished economic model as the "Workshop of the World" into the glare of Chinese public debate. The deaths have also been forcing some Western consumers to reflect on the origins of many of their inexpensive gadgets, toys, and clothing, the trappings of a middle-class lifestyle toward which hundreds of millions of Chinese still aspire, and millions more struggle to retain.

END NOTES

1. Peng Yining and Duan Yan, "Constant in a Fast-Changing Society: Stress," *China Daily*, May 21, 2010.
2. Justin Chan, "The Rise of Retail," *Insight*, May 2008.
3. "A Shopper's Paradise," *China Economic Review*, February 2007.
4. Michael Wines and Jonathon Ansfield, "Trampled in a Land Rush, Chinese Resist," *The New York Times*, May 26, 2010.
5. Hao Zhou, "Owning a Home the Most Important," Chinadaily.com, June 28, 2007; http://www.chinadaily.com.cn/bizchina/2007-06/28/content_905025.htm, accessed October 12, 2009.
6. "Bull in a China Shop," *The Economist*, October 8, 2009.
7. Sharon LaFraniere, "China's College Entry Test Is an Obsession," *The New York Times*, June 12, 2009.
8. Ibid.
9. "College Entrance Exams Make or Break in China," *People's Daily*, June 6, 2007.
10. Sharon LaFraniere, "China's College Entry Test Is an Obsession," *The New York Times*, June 12, 2009.
11. Sharon LaFraniere, "Files Vanished, Young Chinese Lose the Future," *The New York Times*, July 26, 2009.
12. "Former Chinese Official Detained in Theft of ID in Daughter's College Entry," Xinhua, May 11, 2009.
13. James Fallows, "In Defense of the 高考: Chinese, Foreigners Rally to its Support!" May 14, 2009, http://jamesfallows.theatlantic.com/archives/2009/05/in_defense_of_the_gaokao.php.
14. "Chinese Students a Major Market Force," *Asia Times*, June 23, 2009.
15. Jamil Anderlini, "Rule of the Iron Rooster," *Financial Times*, August 24, 2009.
16. David Eimer, "Wave of Suicide Sweeps China's Graduate Class," *The Daily Telegraph*, July 25, 2009.
17. Peng Yining and Duan Yan, "Constant in a Fast-Changing Society: Stress," *China Daily*, May 21, 2010.
18. "The Spend is Nigh," *The Economist*, July 30, 2009.
19. Gordon G. Liu, "Taking Care: China's Health Reform and Policy Dynamics," BusinessForum China, November-December 2008.
20. Ibid.
21. "Sickness of Savers," *The Economist*, May 12, 2009.
22. "Caring for a Profit," *China Economic Review*, May 2009.

CHAPTER **3**

A Tale of Two Countries

MIGRANT WORKERS: SEPARATE AND UNEQUAL

One temperate evening in the spring of 2007, I was sauntering through Xintiandi, a renovated cobblestone neighborhood in Shanghai that is popular with both tourists and locals who stroll through the trendy strip to see and to be seen. Just as I was about to cross the narrow lane that separates the plaza in two parts, I saw a middle-aged Chinese man in shabby blue working clothes craning his neck to look into the plaza across the lane from me. He was smaller than the average urbanite—as so many people from the countryside are—and his gnarled hands were outsized. A private security guard—a pale, young man dressed in a forest-green uniform two sizes too big for him—walked up to the workman and blocked his view. The guard gestured crossly, leaned down into the workman's face, and shouted at the peasant. The workman became agitated and responded in kind. The security guard stepped menacingly nearer the workman, who stepped back, offered one last word in defense of his self-respect, then walked the direction from whence he had come.

As the lane opened for pedestrian crossing, I considered that the workman was clearly from the countryside—one of the "floating population 流动人口" that local governments need to build their roads and buildings and clean their streets and apartments—and that he may even have participated in the renovation of the very same neighborhood that had become a cash cow for its private owners and government patrons. Yet, there he was, denied access to a public venue by a kid who was more likely than not himself from the countryside. Though there were no signs outside the walking street that prohibited the entry of migrant workers it was clear Shanghai practiced a bifurcated social system against fellow Chinese citizens. Ironic, as likely 80 percent of all Chinese now in the Chinese cities are first- or second-generation country "bumpkins" themselves. Indeed, city dwellers consider it an insult to call them *nongmin* 农民, or peasants.

Most of the protests that have sprung up in China since Deng Xiaoping announced in the 1980s that it was glorious to get rich reflect the stresses and strains of a country that is irreversibly urbanizing at a rate not seen in nearly a century, when *emigrés* to America, just off the boat at Ellis Island, would have their names homogenized at the exit gate and shunted to ethnic ghettos that bulged with old world kin.

In China, though, the leadership has given itself a mandate to actively move a population greater than the United States into cities before the year 2030—nearly 400 million souls. About 600 million people already live in Chinese cities. In the same way American neighborhoods in New York boroughs rumbled with the latest immigrant ethnic groups, Chinese in cities of all sizes are trying to adapt to the waves of peasant migrant workers who wish to make a better life in urban centers. Throughout the country, great stresses and strains between country folk and city slickers manifest themselves daily, and sometimes erupt in violent and unexpected ways.

Yet China needs its migrant workers from the countryside to build the dozens of new cities the country needs to modernize its economy. In the same way America needed immigrants from Europe to build its cities and workers from China to construct its railroads; in much the same way as Germany required Turkish labor to rebuild its war-ravaged towns; and the rich Arab countries need Indian and Filipino workers to modernize their sandy real estate, China needs its peasants. Without the numbers and "hunger" of their country cousins, the cities can neither have the hands and backs they need to build and expand its urban centers, nor will they have the bodies to reside in the acres and acres of flats that now lay empty, waiting for a strange alchemy that will turn them from fool's gold into something practical, yet likely unobtainable by the millions who built them.

The flip side of the bifurcation of Chinese society is that in the nascent stages of China's modernization, the have-nots who reside outside the cities or who have gravitated to urban centers for work will increasingly resent their urban counterparts. If the have-nots feel disenfranchised without viable opportunities for realizing their own dreams—an apartment, a car, health-care coverage, and ample opportunities for their offspring—then they may vent their discontent through mass, perhaps even violent, protests. Central and local governments throughout China consider mass protests direct threats to their leadership, and at times, subdue organized protests with extreme prejudice.

Meanwhile, tensions mount as city dwellers at the lower rungs of urban society resent the competition and social complications their country cousins inject into an environment with limited opportunities and resources. A taxi driver in the small city of Suzhou put it to me succinctly: "The rich have so much money, and the poor don't have a chance." I judged by his craggy face and knotted hands that he was in his mid-fifties, a local whose pressed blue uniform showed his pride in his job. I asked him if he thought today's living conditions were better than, say, 30 years before, and that the rapid development had been worth it. "Thirty years ago, everyone was the same; everyone had about the same thing. Now, either the government officials or *waidi ren* 外地人 [literally, the 'outside people,' a reference to Chinese from other parts of China who invade a prosperous city] have sent real estate prices far beyond what we locals can afford." Country folk admire urbanites; and city dwellers hate their country cousins.

The World Bank expects the population of China's cities to swell to one billion by the year 2030. Just 20 percent of all Chinese lived in cities in 1980; the Chinese government has a national policy in place to have 70 percent of its citizens living in cities by 2030. That is the combined population of Germany, France, Britain, Italy, South Korea, Spain, Poland, and Canada. The McKinsey Global Institute cites the number of cities that currently have at least 10 million people will rise from two

(Beijing and Shanghai) to eight by the year 2025, and 15 super-cities, each with a population 15 million or more, will have sprung up. (New York City has slightly more than 8.4 million residents.) The number with five million to 10 million residents will rise to 15 cities from 12; cities with between 1.5 million and five million people will grow to a staggering 115 from 69; while small cities of 500,000 to 1.5 million will rise in number even more dramatically to 280 from 173. Tellingly, towns of less than half a million residents will decline to 521 from 602. The large cities along the east coast will get larger as migrants become permanent residents, while the smaller cities in the interior will also develop their infrastructure to become urban magnets for country-folk in the surrounding regions.

The story of migrant workers in China since the mid-1990s has been and will continue to be for the first quarter of the new century one of ebb and flow: migrants travel to the cities from the countryside and back again depending on the health of the economy. When the size and so-phistication of the urban landscape in China's historically poorer interior rivals the promises of the richer east coast, labor migration *en masse* to the cities will become a distant memory. Though China will still have sizable inequities between rich and poor for the foreseeable future, urbanization and the easing of residency requirements will gradually blur—though not eradicate—the tensions, expectations, and differences between the two worlds as most Chinese eventually become city folk.

FACTORY LIFE: NOT THE TICKET IT USED TO BE

The Gu family is a typical case of how residents in China's countryside in the mid-1990s made their way to the cities, ushering in the mass migration movement that would transform the face of the nation. Mother and Father Gu each had seven siblings, all of whom had one or, in a few cases, two children. Some of the family moved from the farms of Chuzhou, a very small town outside Nanjing, to Hefei, the capital of Anhui Province. Others moved to Suzhou, closer to Shang-hai. By the standards of the time, Suzhou was a thriving, prosperous town, well-known for its ornate gardens and silk industry. In 1994, Gu's eldest brother, who was a director at one of the largest fertilizer factories in China, offered the Gus the opportunity to work in the

Suzhou Number 2 Fertilizer Company. It was state-owned—one of the largest SOEs of its kind in China until its closure in 2003—and employed thousands of workers. Not only would they receive a steady income, but the company would also take care of all their health-care costs. The Gus couldn't take their children along with them to the city, so they—like so many other migrants—left their children with relatives in Chuzhou. After a year of hard work, however, they were able to move to a larger company-owned apartment so their children could join them in Suzhou.

Eventually, the family would put down roots in the small city. The national policy of privatization of real estate property enabled them to buy their own home in 1998. Family relationships with local government officials allowed their children to receive education in the city, though their residence permit—called a *hukou* ⊡—remained of the countryside. Some of the children of the families would go on to pass the dreaded university examination, go to university in the city, and settle down to take jobs in the same location. The Gus lived the dream of the hundreds of millions of migrants who were streaming into China's cities seeking a better future.

Most migrant workers with little education have not been as fortunate as the Gus, though. After the year 2000, it became very difficult for migrants to own property in a city that was not their hometown. The Gus had come during the post-Tiananmen Square economic boom in the 1990s, which saw the central government experimenting with liberalizing the majority of its state-owned enterprises and encouraging private businesses to prosper. By the early 2000s, private enterprise became another piston in China's economic engine, with most of the action occurring in the Pearl River Delta, near Hong Kong, and in the Yangtze River Delta, with Shanghai at the epicenter of manufacturing activity in the region. The employment model shifted from SOEs agglomerating workers through family and friend networks to privately owned factories hiring young people from the countryside who intended to work in the cities until they made enough money to return to their hometowns, get married, and start their own cottage business. "Up to a third of our assembly people from the countryside do not return to the factory after Spring Festival," Robert Gong had told me in 2005. Robert was the Chinese human resources director of a consumer-electronics manufacturer based in the Suzhou Industrial Park near Shanghai. "They wait until they get their red envelope 红包 and then they leave. They may have worked with us a year or two, then they return home to find a husband, and perhaps start their own small business." Red envelopes 红包 at Spring Festival—or Chinese New Year—represent the packet of cash that most Chinese employees receive as a "thirteenth month" of salary. Robert's company got around the loss of so many assembly people by hiring fewer migrants from faraway locations in China. Instead, it preferred to hire from the local area.

Still, while the Chinese economy was growing at a blistering 12 to 13 percent a year from 2005 through 2008, factories along the eastern seaboard were unable to find enough labor to staff their factories. Not only were orders from abroad putting greater pressure on production capacities, but life in the small towns whence migrant workers hailed was also improving. A government survey held in 2007 found that of 2,749 villages in 17 provinces, 74 percent of the villages had no one remaining fit enough to work in the factories along the coast. Essentially, the labor pool had dried up, exacerbated by the increased numbers of young people who had gone off to some other cities for university studies.[1]

Then came the global slump in factory orders at the beginning of 2008. Factory owners and managers who treated employees as liabilities rather than as assets took the most expedient route possible to dealing with the dearth of business. They took the money and ran. Literally. Throughout Guangdong Province, where Hong Kong and Taiwanese owners and managers of factories dominate, and as far north as Shandong Province, where South Korean factories churn out goods, managers were stuffing suitcases full of cash and escaping under the cloak of night to return to their home countries. By car and by ferry in the south, the Hong Kong businessmen would sneak back to Hong Kong, while Taiwanese and South Korean industrialists were sneaking flights back to their homes.

Millions of migrant workers returned to their factories from two weeks of spring holiday in their hometowns to find the gates to companies chained shut and the lights turned off on the production lines. The workers, though, hadn't been paid final wages to terminate their contracts. Huge crowds of disgruntled and angry workers formed at the gates of shuttered operations up and down China's seaboard in the spring of 2008. The police did not try to disperse the groups, not only understanding the plights and complaints of the workers, but often sympathizing with them as well.

City officials from where the defunct factories were based met with the workers, trying to mollify their anger. The central government in Beijing had begun pushing the localities to adhere to a policy of forbearance regarding the displaced workers. The local police were not to use force to disband the protests. The leadership in Beijing believed that using violence to break up the protests would only inflame the situation, the news of which would likely spread to other precincts, creating larger conflagrations of discontent. Some of the stranded migrant workers were able to find new work at other factories, while most eventually returned to their hometowns in the countryside.

By mid-2009, when the Chinese economy began to pick up again, many migrant workers simply refused to return to the cities along China's east coast to work in the factories. The decision to remain near their hometowns was made easier by the central government's response to the global economic downturn. In 2009 and the beginning of 2010, the Chinese government ordered its state-owned banks to flood the economy with loans to commercial interests, local governments, and private individuals. In a 13-month period, banks lent more than US$1.5 trillion, mostly to SOEs. The infusion of capital into the sagging economy had three effects: to accelerate infrastructure development within cities, to spur urban-renewal projects in the larger cities along the east coast, and to provide financing for the development of the poorer cities in China's interior as well as the transportation infrastructure connecting the cities to one another and to the urban hubs on the east coast.

By the end of Chinese New Year 2010, hundreds of thousands of factories along China's eastern seaboard were actually without factory workers, despite the resurrection of the export markets for China-made goods. Economic success in the countryside, migrant workers discovered, was the sweetest revenge against the exploitation many of them had suffered in the sweatshops of Guangdong, Zhejiang, Jiangsu, and Shandong provinces. As migrant workers became more aware of their labor rights, and as Chinese and foreign-invested industry vied for skilled workers, factories and service-sector employers were being forced to come to terms with what staff require: better working conditions, training programs to improve their skills, and career paths. Increasingly, as Alexandra Harney writes in *The China Price*, tomorrow's workers will be settling in the cities to which they have migrated. They will be looking at the factories as stepping stones to a better life in the city, instead of as a return ticket to the countryside as their parents had. They will be looking toward working to live, instead of living to work. Tomorrow's workers will want to change their *hukou* 户口 (or place of residence) from the countryside to the cities that will have become their children's homes. Families, like the Gus nearly 20 years before, will once again have their shot at the good life—and stability.

However, one of the greatest obstacles to the long-cherished dream of Chinese peasants to make better lives for themselves is the Chinese national policy of *hukou* 户口.

HUKOU 户口: A LIFELONG SENTENCE

After the Communist Party took control of the country in 1949, it implemented a system of town-level residency called *hukou* 户口. *Hukou* 户口 were strict residency permits that froze one's abode to a single location. Traveling to other towns and cities was forbidden without special written permission from local governments. Often, it was only through special relationships and perhaps even bribery that permission could be obtained. The *hukou* 户口 system is why, from an official standpoint, there is no migration and there are no migrant workers in China: local *hukous* 户口 are all still in place, with few applications for transfer to other locations.

Hukou 户口 became the way through which the central government could keep one of the greatest variables—and therefore risk of failure—of central planning fixed; that is, the movements of the Chinese population. Under central planning, towns, cities, and provinces in China had economic and strategic roles to play in rebuilding the country in the socialist mold. For instance, the countryside's role—and therefore that of the peasants—was to grow food to send to the cities. Cities like Daqing, in the extreme northeast corner of China, were geared toward oil extraction; Dalian, further south, to moving natural resources down the east coast and into other parts of China. Shanghai was geared toward low-end manufacturing. The mountains of central China became the hiding places of China's own military-industrial complex, to protect the sector from possible nuclear attack. The Chinese leadership had made the Chinese landscape into a (Chinese) chessboard, and its citizens into useful pieces dedicated to developing and promoting the good of the country.

The effects of the *hukou* 户口 were devastating to the lives of Chinese, especially during the Cultural Revolution. City dwellers in Beijing, Shanghai, and even Nanjing had educational and work opportunities that they taken for granted stripped away during the mass political movement. Mao Zedong professed the best education for many young people in the cities was to send them to the countryside to learn from the peasants. Films such as *Xiu Xiu: The Sent-Down Girl* (directed by Joan Chen in 1998) depict the desperation and isolation many young Chinese with their own dreams experienced when they lost control over their lives because they had a *hukou* 户口 from a big city. Many young urban dwellers had to become peasants tilling the land even after the end of the Cultural Revolution because the system simply forgot about them, or they married a local and had children of their own in the countryside. I am still amazed at the number of young Chinese I meet today who were born to Chinese parents who had been "sent down" to Xinjiang, in the isolated northwest corner of China, or to Inner Mongolia. It was only because the next-generation Chinese had scored high enough on their university entrance examination that they were able to return to the fold of a modernizing urban China.

When I first visited Beijing—just before the fiftieth anniversary of the establishment of the People's Republic of China on October 1, 1949—I commented to an American acquaintance, Ben, who had lived in Beijing for several years, on just how clean and orderly the streets were. "There are no hawkers!" I observed, pleased at not being harassed by anyone who had anything to sell.

Ben replied crisply: "That's because the Beijing government sent them all back to their homes in the countryside." He was referring to the migrant workers that had become the underground economy of the city. Beijing did not want any camera crew—especially those from Western countries—filming how the disenfranchised were actually being treated by a system that Beijing itself encouraged. Fast forward nine years into the future, to the months in the runup to the Beijing 2008 Olympics and very little had changed in the central government's view of migrant workers. Indeed, the crackdown on *hukou* 户口 was so severe in Beijing that many of the *nouveau riche* complained of difficulties in keeping their apartments tidy without their cleaners from the countryside, and construction sites having difficulties meeting completion deadlines (if they were not directly related to the Olympics) because their workers had been expelled beyond city lines. The message was clear during the international celebrations: your presence is not desired during Beijing's big party.

Migrant workers who have *hukou* 户口 from the countryside suffer a stunning lack of rights in the cities in which they work. Migrant workers do not have the right of abode without temporary permission, which can last several months to one year. If they do not have the temporary license, they are treated as squatters, and are under constant threat of immediate expulsion if the local government pleases. Whether they have temporary license to work in the city, they have no rights to social welfare benefits or services in their adopted city and their children have no right to a public education or medical treatment in hospitals. Authorities say without the *hukou* 户口 system, cities would be ringed by the same kind of shantytowns one sees in India and Africa, with no way to moderate urbanization rates. In Turkey, refugees from the countryside who move to the outer edges of cities create *gecekondu*, which means, literally, "landed overnight," a reference to the ramshackle shelters that miraculously appear at dawn's light with a family already making a home within. Chinese migrant workers live in extremely cheap tenements in the cities; or, if they are construction workers, in dormitories built by property developers near construction sites and in the half-finished apartments and offices the workers themselves are building.

Indeed, the *hukou* 户口 policy combined with the necessity of migrants to build and service the cities is creating a lost generation of children who have no access to proper education in the neighborhoods in which their migrant parents live. If children of migrant workers are fortunate enough to receive an organized education, it is officially illegal, and is in danger of being shut down. The classrooms are often in ramshackle quarters hidden away in back alleys so that it is difficult for police to locate.

Many migrant workers simply find it easier to leave their children with their own parents in their hometowns. Entire villages in the interior of China are bereft of working-age residents who have taken employment in faraway cities. Back in the villages, elderly retirees take care of their grandchildren as full-time jobs, with the expectation that once a year at Spring Festival, the parents will return to their hometowns to spend some time with their families.

In March 2010, popular discontent with the *hukou* 户口 system bubbled over with the publication of an editorial on the front page of 13 newspapers across China demanding the abolition of the *hukou* 户口 policy. "We believe in people born to be free and people possessing the right to migrate freely," the editorial proclaimed.[2] It was the first time in Party history that strong criticism about a pillar of society had been strategically levied by publications patronizing the Party itself. The declaration coincided with the opening of the third session of the Eleventh National People's Congress and the Chinese People's Political Consultative Conference in Beijing, which would position the announcement for maximum visibility by the Party leadership. Zhang Hong, the editor-in-chief of *Economic Observer*, an influential financial newspaper in China, wrote the commentary. He was fired days after the editorial hit newsstands. The Communist Party believes in the years to come there is still a need for the institution as a moderator for urbanization and channel for distribution of wealth and power in the country.

By the beginning of 2010, however, some cities were not waiting for an official go-ahead from the central authority to dissolve the *hukou* 户口 system. Northeast China's Jilin Province announced it would gradually abolish the rural *hukou* 户口 and establish a unified household registration system that no longer categorized the people into rural and non-rural residents. It remains to be seen if the central government will shut down the initiative.

A DAY IN THE COUNTRY

The first visceral encounter many people in the countryside have with encroaching urbanization is the acquisition of their land, sometimes negotiated, sometimes not. Until 2004, many local governments could negotiate land-transfer agreements to potential leaseholders without first conferring with the tenants of the land. As the thinking goes, the Communist Party represents the People, so the government is the rightful custodian of the land. In other words, China has no real private land ownership laws. Instead, tenants can lease the land for terms of 50 to 75 years. Land by default outside the cities is zoned as land for agricultural use. The local government—and sometimes, the municipal and even provincial governments, depending on the amount and the potential profit from a land sale—must approve transfer of the land from agricultural use to commercial use.

From 2001 until the new land-transfer policy in 2004, local governments transferred land from agricultural use to commercial use, with or without the consent of tenants. After 2004, the central government froze all transfers of land slated for agricultural use to commercial use. Land transfers were supposed to require approval from provincial or national level authorities, and auctions to make land sales equitable for residents. Local governments and property developers, however, found ways around the restriction, so that by 2007 there was actually an acceleration of illegal seizures of land and property that still continues. Profits from land transfers and the subsequent transaction taxes have become a major revenue stream for local government administrations.

Inadequate compensation for land acquisition is one of the main drivers behind the increasing number of protests mounted by tenants who raise crops for a living. The government is supposed to negotiate a fair offer to tenants in return for their land. However, local officials will sometimes pocket the difference between what they should offer tenants and what they actually give tenants. In Kunshan in the mid-2000s, I was exiting the main administration building of the city's flagship economic-development zone—the Kunshan Economic and Technological Development Zone—when the promotion officer with whom I was walking and I noticed a group of women speaking loudly in the voluminous foyer of the high-rise office building. They were all dressed similarly, in black, baggy cotton pants and dark smocks with dark cloth wrapping around their heads. They were of a previous generation—country folk who had known Kunshan when it was a backwater.

"What are they upset about, do you think?" I asked my escort, an elegant woman with an immaculate hairdo. "They're probably not happy with the offer they're getting for their land," she said matter-of-factly. Her nonchalant reply led me to feel that the protest was a common enough occurrence to no longer rile the local officials.

Many times, though, locals do not know their land has been slated for transfer by fiat until the demolition squad has shown up on their doorstep. Just outside the Jiangsu province city of Changzhou, as well as in the roughhewn hills of the Chongqing municipality, in the middle of China, government representatives have excitedly shown me land still occupied by tenants as ready for commercial investment. "All this can be yours," I've been told by more than one government administrator, who swept a dramatic arm across a vista of houses that would inevitably be displaced, if not by the manufacturing investment projects that I was representing, then by another commercial interest. Meanwhile, not more than a stone's throw away, residents who were either stubborn or who did not believe they would ever be displaced from their land watched on with—I imagined—a mixture of curiosity at the foreigner poking around their land and anxiety that they might be forced from their homes by police brandishing batons. I was glad to be working for clients who had enough conscience not to be the ones to destroy these people's homes, no matter what terms were offered. Still, demolition was unavoidable, whether by a commercial project that would be built from scratch, or by the land simply being leased. The fate of the nearby houses and their occupants was sealed.

Nearly half of the hundreds of thousands of protests that China has experienced during the first decade of the twenty-first century involved the displeasure of peasants with the settlements that local governments offered them for the land on which the farmers lived. Corruption compounded inequity as local government officials—individually and in groups—have taken kickbacks, shares, or even property from real estate developers. The phenomenon is one of the main reasons for the development of the China's real estate valuation bubble in 2009 and 2010. From 2002 through 2008, China penalized nearly 9,000 local government officials and jailed more than 1,000 over illegal land-title transfers.[3] For instance, the head of a government land-management division in the Suzhou municipality (which administrates six cities in the Yangtze River Delta) had been found guilty of enriching himself with kickbacks from a residential real estate developer, as well as property given to him for free that he could later sell at a profit. Further investigation revealed the entire department had been on the take. Many in the division had been given villas as thanks for their cooperation in approving the land transfer and facilitating construction approvals. Those believed to be guilty were ordered to pay the monies back "to the People," or face sacking or worse consequences. However, the probability of the subordinates losing their jobs over the affair was in fact minimal, as the work of the entire administrative division would come to a grinding halt and the mass firing would surely raise eyebrows. So villa owners throughout the compound instead raised rents to repay the kickbacks they had taken from the developer, in some cases by as much as 30 percent.

Without the right to own the land they till—and therefore be eligible to get loans or even to sell the land—residents in the countryside remain at a huge economic disadvantage to their urban cousins. In the late 1990s, the national government privatized residential property, converting what had been state-owned assets into private property. Overnight, millions of homeowners were born. As property prices in the cities rose, so too did the wealth of many of the residents. The Communist Party, however, has been loathe to enact a policy of land ownership rights in the countryside primarily for two reasons. First, land sales and resulting transaction taxes are one of the few ways left to local governments to generate revenue streams to support local services, develop infrastructure projects, and line pockets. Second, the national government is afraid farmers will sell off their land to finance a mass exodus to the cities, the infrastructure of which cannot support a sudden, large influx of outsiders.[4]

By law, local governments that displace tenants in the countryside are responsible for housing them. This means officials have to build new apartment buildings for former land occupants, taking care of moving expenses and subsidizing the cost of ownership of the new units. The local government moves displaced tenants to live far away from expensive prime real estate locations to reduce the ancillary costs; the uprooted residents will likely live far away from other family members, friends, and former neighbors. The new districts typically have little or no public transport. A sense of isolation and alienation easily creeps in to fill their days, especially among middle-age and older residents who haven't the stamina or skills to work in a modernizing China. They are destined to spend the rest of their lives as part of China's underclass.

LOOKING AHEAD: THE UNITED STATES OF CHINA?

China will continue to need an underclass even after its cities are built. There will still be a need for the have-nots who furnish the society with a cheap source of labor, doing the menial jobs that "city slickers" refuse to man. The vital role the underclass plays in Chinese society is best described in an article on migrant workers in *The Economist* (April 2000):

> "Increasingly, too, rural migrants are doing the urban class's dirty work in the big cities. In Beijing, the construction work-ers are from Shandong Province. The nannies are from Anhui or Hunan. The rubbish collectors are from Henan. And the prostitutes, well, they are from everywhere."

This will not change.

The *hukou* 戶口 system deepens a social divide in which, as Jim Yardley, a correspondent for *The New York Times*, writes: "China's migrants are like the illegal immigrants in the United States. The farmer from Ecuador who pays a trafficker to smuggle him to a job in an American chicken plant is not much different from a peasant from the rural Henan Province who follows a construction boss to Shanghai. Both are exploited and work with few legal protections. Both share crowded apartments or with other migrants. But both send back much of what they earn to relatives left behind."[5]

This social phenomenon will continue, just as it has in the U.S., in the U.K., and in the European Union at large. Modern societies need their underground workers, who are seen but not recognized, scorned for doing the very necessary operations that keep any developing and modernized society running.

In a way, China's development of its cities and the urban absorp-tion of immigrants is very much like that of America's own struggles a hundred years ago. Then, thousands of immigrants each day streamed into American cities, unfamiliar with the New World's ways, lingo, and technologies. The majority of immigrants from those grimy times were from Europe, and came over in great waves: English Protestants gave way to Italian Catholics who gave way to Irish Catholics (and Protestants) who gave way to German Jewish refugees and so on. Competition for resources, for utilities, for transportation, for housing infrastructure, as well as for public health and education services, was fierce. However different, though, the languages and foods of the immigrant waves that swept into the American cities and then flowed into the American midwest and then west coast were all Europeans. Africans, as slaves, were never counted as immigrants; however, their contribution to the development of American society and wealth is well established. America as we know it today, with its vibrancy and uniqueness in history, could never have existed without the sacrifices of successive underclasses of workers who had only one direction to go in the New World they were helping to build: up.

The big difference between Western and Chinese labor models of urbanization is China's own underclass is Chinese. The singularly defining feature of China's modernization are the Chinese migrants who have filled the same position as the Turks in Germany, the Algerians in France, and the Mexicans in the U.S. The second generation of immigrants to America, however, has a greater chance of being fully accepted into U.S. society than immigrants to Europe and Asia; some countries make it clear immigrants will never be "one of them." Second- and third-generation children born to immigrants to Germany and to Japan have next to no chance of being politically or socially accepted into society through citizenship. Indeed, the immigrant populations that support shadow economies around the world are typically of different cultures, ethnicities, and languages. The cultural differences behoove modern societies to keep the back door to economic opportunity open to foreigners, as long as natural-born citizens refuse to do the work because it is either beneath them and/or the pay is too poor. The more distant the culture of an immigrant from the society in which he works, the easier it is politically for modern societies to usher the immigrants back home when they are no longer required.

China, however, through the system of segregation that the *hukou* 户口 creates, can maintain the artificial boundaries that will support its own underground economies for decades to come. However, there will come a time when those with countryside *hukou* 户口 realize they are not really getting ahead when they "cross the border" into the new cities with their high-rises and expensive restaurants and fancy cars. Instead, through government policy, they will find themselves fixed in their socioeconomic strata like some ancient trilobite that became caught in the mud and calcification of historical precedence. It is the artificial bifurcation of a singular society and the maintenance of artificial inequities that will create the greatest stresses in urbanizing China.

That is not to say that no migrant workers will be able to infuse into the middle class; that would be a near statistical impossibility. Migrants with university education and specific skill sets have been welcomed with open arms into larger east coast cities in which foreign-invested businesses predominate. It is this migrant group against whom my articulate taxi driver at the beginning of the chapter railed. An increasing number of residents with newly minted big-city *hukou* 户口 have themselves hired migrant workers less fortunate than themselves to perform menial tasks—some of whom may even come from the resident's old town.

Though there is a firm understanding by Beijing's leadership about the inequalities and limitations of the *hukou* 户口 system, it will be some time before it dies away completely. The *hukou* 户口 system defines who in China belongs in the cities and who belongs in the countryside. It decides who gets the lion's share of resources, access to markets, educational opportunities, and proximity to power. It is an apartheid policy created during the time of Mao Zedong's reign that is applied to the benefit of city dwellers and the detriment of those in the countryside. The *hukou* 户口 system provides a ready pool of laborers who have little choice than to provide services too dirty or too low-paying or too humbling by city-slicker standards to perform.

The Chinese leadership believes the *hukou* 户口 system, as the physical and symbolic divide between who-can-have and who-can-have-a-lot-less, serves a vital purpose: social stability. The *hukou* 户口 is the embodiment of the reality in China that not everyone can "have". However, the prospect of labor mobility presents the illusion of Chinese citizens one day being able to "have it all". This perception is paramount to the leadership maintaining some semblance of stable development and a mandate to lead.

The *hukou* 户口 system permits the authorities to moderate the stream of migrants that pours into China's more prosperous cities, lest the migration become an uncontrollable torrent. The *hukou* 户口 buys the leadership time to build the infrastructure necessary to support the planned doubling and trebling of the sizes of its cities. The residence permit allows the leadership to husk the cities of migrants when national pride would not be served well by the world's exposure to China's own social inequities, or when economic downturns mean urban centers cannot afford to finance the infrastructure required to support their own shadow economies.

China's black and gray economies combine to make its cities viable and vibrant by supplying power, water, streets and highways, waste management, basic public health and medical services, food and beverage offerings, and even financial services to urban dwellers. While these urban services are always essential to a stable society, they become even more precious during an economic downturn; tensions will inevitably arise when it comes to apportionment of scarce resources. Of course, migrants with their "village-of-origin" *hukou* 户口 will be on the losing end should push come to shove and urban resources are rationed. China may yet still see the resurrection of repatriation policies that forcibly remove migrants from the cities to keep urban centers from tearing themselves apart in the face of scarcity. The central government will continue to leave its options open in its maintenance of a system that is clearly discriminatory.

But while Chinese policy can always "keep a backdoor open" to its own ethnically identical Han "immigrant workers," it cannot keep that door open with the expectation that country folk will return to their poorer hometowns when there are no more skyscrapers to build, no more residential high-rises to construct, no more roads to lay down, or bridges to extend. Instead, Chinese policy must evolve to bring the standard of living in the poorer interior to a reasonable par with the east coast and institutionalize the free flow of residency, so citizens can go where the work is without fear of harassment or official prejudice.

As long as the Chinese leadership can show that it is contributing more to the economic development and opportunity of Chinese society than it is accruing through its own corruption and vanity, most Chinese will believe that through luck, a strong social network, and hard work, they can themselves become a part of the growing middle class—and perhaps even become rich. The society will tolerate forced inequalities between urbanites and country folk exacerbated by the *hukou* 户口 system as long as they all feel they and their families are making material gains. Zhang Kun, a casual laborer, remarked: "Of course, I would be lying if I didn't say I was jealous of the big cars being driven around by those rich guys. It actually makes me want to work harder, so that I can have a car like that one day." Zhang lives in the small Shanxi province town of Ankang. On the other side of town lives Tom Tang, whose family struck it rich in the underdeveloped region. "It seems unfair that our family became rich when so many others in Ankang are so poor," said Tang. "But my father came from a poor background and worked his way up. He didn't even finish primary school."[6]

With stories like those making the rounds in China's cities and the countryside, hundreds of millions of Chinese will continue to bear intense privation and humiliation to one day buy their shares in the good life.

END NOTES

1. Keith Bradsher, "Defying Global slump, China Has Labor Shortage," *The New York Times*, February 26, 2010.
2. Sharon LaFraniere and Jonathon Ansfield, "Editor Is Fired after Criticizing Registration System," *The New York Times*, March 9, 2010.
3. "Promises, Promises," *The Economist*, October 16, 2008.
4. "Fat of the Land," *The Economist*, March 23, 2006.
5. Jim Yardley, "The New Uprooted; In a Tidal Wave, China's Masses Pour From Farm to City," *The New York Times*, September 12, 2004.
6. Ben Blanchard, "Growing Rich-Poor Divide Tests China's Boom," Reuters, March 1, 2008.

CHAPTER **4**

Not in My Backyard!

AN AIR ABOUT THE PLACE

In 2004, an American executive of a *Fortune 500* company asked me to advise him on negotiations with a potential Chinese joint-venture partner that owned a factory just outside Shanghai. This and another operation in the hills of Anhui Province made the Chinese owner the largest supplier of a particular automotive component in China at the time. He greeted us at the entrance of the factory—a short, rotund man in his mid-50s, hair streaked gray. His name was Wang. He bludgeoned us with unctuous smiles and enthusiastic handshakes, then gave us a tour of the voluminous shop floor. I noticed about two dozen young girls in their late teens at wooden benches near one of the walls. Mechanically, they leaned down to the floor to dip paint brushes into gallon cans of gooey adhesive and then lathered the components they were holding with bare hands. They wore no breathing apparatus to protect them from the fumes. As we walked, I began feeling light-headed and nauseous. Within minutes, my breathing shortened and my eyes began watering. The weather was hot and the air heavy; I began to feel suffocated, almost panicky. By the time we made our way to the conference room, 20 yards from the exit of the manufacturing hangar, my head was pounding—only after a mere five minutes of exposure to toxins that the young women in the factory worked with day in and day out.

Later, after discussions with the Chinese counterparty, the executive asked me what I thought of the talks. I told him that any company that so disregarded the health and welfare of its own people in such a cavalier manner was not a fit partner. After a few more meetings with Wang on a potential joint venture, the executive eventually came to the same conclusion: the Chinese boss and his management team put profits first. The executive dropped the idea of forming a close relationship with the company.

Things, of course, get much more complicated when dealing with a society that thinks the same way. The world must engage China and its pollution challenges, since many of its environmental problems are not only making life difficult for its own citizens but are spilling across borders into the ecosystems of other countries as well.

Much of Chinese society and its leadership believe the country needs its polluting factories to modernize its economy. Sustainability is not in the Chinese psyche. Local governments and polluting businesses have become increasingly sophisticated in the ways in which they convince residents of the necessity and efficacy of the toxins their factories produce. For instance, in 2009 the Jilin government had as motivation one of the largest investments in Shandong Province as reason enough to convince the workers in a nearby yarn factory that the illnesses they had suddenly begun suffering was the result of mass hysteria. The Jilin Connell Chemical Plant was a Hong Kong-invested, US$125 million factory put into operation in the spring of 2009. Typically, projects of this size must gain approval from local and provincial level authorities before going into production. Environmental standards and approvals are meant to be rigorous. Weeks after opening, however, more than a thousand residents protested at the gates of the factory, complaining about toxic emissions that were making citizens ill. The complaint saw the company promise to repair leaks in its operations, and the government post an online warning to other violators to take Connell as an example. Hours later, the website proclamation disappeared.[1] Connell continued on with operations without making the necessary fixes.[2]

Employees of the textile factory a few hundred yards downwind of the Hong Kong operations quickly began to differ with official reports of the safety of the chemical facility. The chemical processor produced a raw material used in dyes and drugs called aniline. One worker at a textile factory near the newly opened Connell operations, Tian Lihua, began feeling nauseous soon after the chemical factory had opened, and complained her limbs had gone numb. Dizziness overcame her. She fell unconscious while still on the job. She awoke in a hospital bed around which government officials and doctors crowded. Hundreds of other employees had also been hospitalized. They assured her and the 1,200 other employees who had suffered the same symptoms that their reactions was all in their heads: the convulsions, the vomiting, and the temporary paralysis. Public health experts from Beijing agreed with the doctors, business executives, and local government officials that staff reactions were the result of mass hysteria; medical tests showed no poisoning had occurred. The experts admonished patients to "get hold of their emotions".[3] Employees who did not accept the Party line would have their medical treatments stopped and lose their jobs. The establishment had fallen in line to defend the investment. Tian couldn't afford to lose her job, so she accepted the government's terms.

The Connell affair is only one of hundreds of cases of environmental degradation in China affecting the lives of millions. There have been many others that were far more life-threatening. In early 2006, in the eastern province of Shandong, a 60-kilometer-long diesel-oil slick flowed down the Yellow River, China's second-longest waterway. The spill compelled the province to stop pumping water from the waterway, and forced the six million residents of nearby Jinan to rely on water from reservoirs. In December 2005 in southern China's Guangdong Province, a local government cut the tap-water supply to tens of thousands of people for more than a week after a state-owned smelter discharged tons of the industrial chemical cadmium into the Beijiang River. (Cadmium can cause neurological disorders and cancer.) In the same month, the people of the far northern city of Harbin were buying bottled water after their source of potable water, the Songhua River, had been polluted with a hundred tons of chemicals containing benzene that had flowed into the river after successive explosions at a petroleum refinery.

Hunan during the same winter experienced a mismanaged silt cleanup project that allowed cadmium to flood out of a smelting works and into the Xiangjiang River. The river supplied water to residents in the provincial capital Changsha, which has about six million people, and the nearby Xiangtan city, which has 700,000 inhabitants.

In 2009, in the month of August alone, Chinese media reported thousands of dead river carp suddenly appeared in a river near Shanghai, their death attributed to a lack of oxygen; 4,000 residents of the Inner Mongolian town of Chifeng became sick from an ammonia leak from a nearby pharmaceuticals factory; 1,354 children were diagnosed with excessive lead levels in their blood in Wenping, a township in southern Hunan Province; and a smelting plant was finally closed after hundreds of children in northwestern Shaanxi Province became ill from lead poisoning from a local smelter. The local government did nothing to remedy the situation until after the national media reported that hundreds of local residents had stormed and taken over the offending factory.

In all of these cases, there is an element of collusion between local authorities and business interests invested in the polluting operations. Sometimes, even local residents join in on the deception.

Local authorities—even those from the State Environmental Protection Administration—either do not want to be bothered by complaints of illnesses, or are being bribed by operators to remain inactive. Token fines cost factories mere thousands—if not less—of dollars. Typically, the local government works to keep issues local, where its power base resides, and beyond which administrators would find their careers cut short if the story broke nationally. Many local residents, clearly knowledgeable about the extent of the damage the polluting factories has on the environment and their health, collude with business owners and with local officials to hide the issue from the national media. Usually, they are more concerned with protecting their livelihood than in maintaining their health. Carbon dioxide emissions in 17 provinces in 2009 actually increased, despite more specific regulations and national emissions targets.[4] The absurdity of the situation is reminiscent of the help peasants gave local officials in the 1950s with each high-profile visit Mao Zedong or Zhou Enlai or other national figureheads would make to collective farms to review the success of their Great Leap Forward policies. The Great Leap Forward was meant to jump-start Chinese agricultural and industrial productivity. Despite themselves being near starvation levels, residents would work with local *apparatchiks* to craft elaborate Potemkin crops over which dignitaries would gush enthusiastic platitudes about how wondrously the People's State was doing. Harvests were in fact collected for display from other villages that were not on the official itinerary, and sometimes reused along the journey the officials would take.

For instance, Wu Lihong, a resident of the municipality of Yixing, at the western most rim of Lake Tai, proved on national television in 2006 how the bosses of polluting factories, local government officials, employees, and even local residents worked together to disguise the fact that textile factories in the area were painting rivers black with dyes. Lake Tai is the third-largest freshwater lake in China, just a two-hour drive west of Shanghai, a placid, shallow home to freshwater life not found anywhere else in the world. Factories along feeder streams into the lake and surrounding the lake itself had been spewing waste into the waters for nearly 50 years. Wu stole the reporters into the area a day ahead of filming a documentary about local government claims on how clean the environment was. Unbeknownst to local officials, camera crew recorded the filth ejected from the plants along the waterways. On the day of the official tours and interviews, proud local government representatives and company bosses gathered the journalists to show off how the streams were running clean and clear, sanitized the night before. The Chinese national television network CCTV subsequently aired a program about the true condition of the township's environment, entitling the show, "Youtie: The Town Whose Streams Run Black Then White."

The local government arrested Wu a year later during the summer of 2007 on trumped-up charges, just as provincial government officials forced Yixing to close its water sluices to the lake, to prevent an outbreak of noxious green algae from traveling into the city's water supply. The algae thrived on the nitrogen and phosphorus pollutants that factories dumped into the lake and feeder streams. Wuxi, a city of about two million at the northernmost curve of Lake Tai, also shut down its pump stations. Millions of people on the northwest hump of the lake were without potable water for two weeks. Companies, as well, had to stop work due to the lack of usable water in processing their parts and products. Suzhou came close to having its taps turned off, too. The central government in Beijing ordered the thousands of factories along Lake Tai be closed down, and its aquaculture industry halted.

Local officials reluctantly complied with the order. In today's modernizing China, the reward system for local officials is over-whelmingly warped toward delivering on economic growth and passing tax revenue on up to Beijing (which then doles out the proceeds according to degrees of state-sanctioned nepotism and the latest central government directive). Cronyism, however, is not just the provenance of national level officials, but of those at the lowest levels of authority as well. Local officials collude with each other to force up economic development numbers in their locale, and they collude with business owners who need speedy business approvals and lax environmental inspections.

In response to the Lake Tai disaster, Wu Xijun, the party secretary of one of the townships in the Yixing municipality that had given safe haven to polluting companies, said: "Our GDP fell from the number-three position in Yixing to number six because of the closure of these factories, but fewer people also complain about the environment."[5] Likely, he would not be getting a promotion that year either.

The Lake Tai pollution incident and the punishment local authorities meted out to the man who had devoted his life to voicing warnings about the looming disaster highlights the social reward system that drives the country's manic economic drive. James Kynge writes in his book *China Shakes the World*: "Behind virtually every environmental disaster lurks a failure of politics or policy." Throughout the Communist Party's history in China, government officials have only to regard the deeds and words of their local supervisors and superiors. Government officials and business interests at the local level massage statistical results that they then pass on to provincial levels of government, where figures are again rolled up and passed on to Beijing for review, cogitation, and more massages. The past 60 years of Communist Party rule has consistently shown officials pad their performance numbers to flatter themselves and to give face to their supervisors, who then exhibit to their subordinates their munificence.

Inflation of figures follow records all the way to the central government, who knows the padding is going on, but still needs to publish numbers for domestic and international consumption. Domestically, the numbers are used to spur on the single-minded pursuit of economic development, and to encourage local officials to continue reporting dramatic results.

One of the most dramatic examples of how the system perpetuates itself can again be found in the sad history of the Great Leap Forward, which started in 1958. Mao Zedong had pronounced that the people devote themselves wholeheartedly to the forging of steel in their backyards. "The People" meant everybody: men, women, children, peasants, and urbanites. Meanwhile, crops did not receive the attention they required. However, in order not to lose face—or their leadership positions—local *apparatchiks* reported record results for both steel production and food output. Both were lies: the steel was of low-grade quality, not even good enough to build a car, let alone a battleship; and the farms lay fallow as residents had been caught up in steel production. The outcome was the largest man-made famine in history, resulting in about 30 million people starving to death over a two year period in the early 1960s.

Now, another one of humanity's greatest man-made disasters is unfolding in China with the number of deaths related to air pollution. In 2007, the World Bank and China's State Environmental Protection Administration (EPA) concluded outdoor pollution in China was responsible for between 350,000 to 400,000 deaths. Indoor pollution from coal and wood stoves and the chemicals emitted by poor-quality construction materials resulted in another 300,000 deaths. Water pollution added another 60,000 annually to the tally.[6]

The majority of Chinese on the Mainland seem willing to accept a high level of pollution as the cost of getting wealthy, almost as though it was a patriotic duty to not complain. Consistently, Chinese will say to any Westerner that challenges their environmental issues as being wholly impractical: "Well, you Americans had a lot of pollution before you became rich." Or to the British: "Your Industrial Revolution caused high levels of pollution in your cities that killed your children." In other words, the developed world has passed down as industrialization mythology that it is all right for millions in a modernizing society to die from health problems related to pollution belched from its economic engines. China believes it needs its polluting factories to modernize its society.

I recall having lunch in Shanghai in 2008 during a business conference at which I was speaking on infrastructure-development trends in China. Three others, Chinese professionals in their mid- to late 30s, joined me in conversation at the table. All were well dressed in uniform dark business suits and conservative ties with white shirts. One of the businessmen had received his advanced degree in Germany and had lived and worked there for 10 years. Another of my lunch companions had received his advanced degree in Atlanta, and also had lived abroad for more than 10 years. Talk turned to the dangerous levels of pollution generated by industry in China. I was startled when the two managers who had lived and worked abroad agreed wholeheartedly that China's level of illnesses and fatalities due to pollution from unregulated industries was necessary and well-worth the cost for China to become a wealthy nation.

I responded matter-of-factly: "Unless it's your son or daughter who is the victim." One would have thought I had just burped out loud without covering my mouth for the frosty response my comment elicited. The table became quiet, their plates their focus for the few minutes remaining in the meal. I had caused them to lose face. Unpardonable.

"BUT THEY DID IT FIRST!"

Did my lunch partners have a point? Is massive pollution part and parcel of the industrialization of a society? Should the industrialized countries just shut up about China's pollution history, given their own sorry history on the subject?

China's argument for permitting unregulated polluting industry is that its population is too poor and too large to afford the pollution controls and enforcement of regulations that are now in force in the West, especially in Europe. Hence, its cars still do not have the catalytic converters that the U.S. automobile industry was required to install on cars in the 1970s; all gasoline is leaded in China, with little attention given to diesel; and of 661 Chinese cities surveyed, 278 still did not have sewage-treatment plants at the end of 2005.[7]

It is certainly the case that with the advent of industrialization around 1800, carbon dioxide levels in the earth's atmosphere began to climb precipitously and haven't stopped, according to ice-core samples taken from Antarctica. The United States was for the past century the number one emitter of carbon dioxide until 2008, when China statistically took that title.

Tales of the degree of pollution in Britain during the Industrial Revolution of the 1800s are legion. Untreated waste water in the cities led to high fatality rates from cholera and typhoid. The production of sodium carbonate—for use in bleaching textiles, glass, soap, and paper manufacture—and Portland cement were all highly polluting as well. Then, of course, coal was the main energy source powering the factories—unfiltered, unadulterated smog filled the skies over most British manufacturing centers for decades. Air pollution was finally taken as a serious health hazard after the Great London Smog of 1952, which resulted in more than 4,000 pollution-related deaths in the city.

The Americans picked up the industrialization model with a vengeance, creating the Pittsburgs and Bethlehems and Scrantons of lore, great urban forges of steel in which residents seldom had clear skies for the smog belching from furnaces that operated night and day.

Still, the United States created some of the greatest environmental disasters in the world through its approach to modernization. The post-World War II economic boom saw episodes of smog so thick citizens of Donora Pennsylvania (1948), New York (1953) and Los Angeles (1954) could barely see their hands in front of their faces and found themselves dizzy for lack of oxygen. Hundreds died as a direct result of the episodes.[8] Still, it wasn't until 1963 that the U.S. Congress passed its Clean Air Act, and until 1970 that companies were required to reduce emissions according to federal guidelines. Other disasters that the U.S. industry has been responsible for include a dead zone the size of New Jersey at the mouth of the Mississippi River, widened in mid-2010 by the largest oil spill in modern history; 1.1 billion liters of coal slurry mixed with arsenic and mercury contained in a reservoir maintained by a power-generation company that burst a dike and literally flooded eastern Kentucky and West Virginia in 2000; the Three-Mile Island meltdown of a nuclear reactor in 1979; the Love Canal dump site exposed in the mid-1970s as having harmed the health of local residents for more than 20 years; and, most recently, in 2008, a coal-waste spill from a local power authority that released 1.9 billion liters of coal sludge onto at least 120 hectares in Tennessee that destroyed 15 homes and left many others uninhabitable for the lead, mercury, and arsenic that suffused the ground.[9]

Even seemingly pristine Japan is not without its environmental disasters caused by heavy industrialization. The Ashio copper mine for decades at the turn of the twentieth century poisoned wildlife and residents in the surrounding countryside with pollutants washed into a nearby river.[10] The Besshi and Hitachi copper mines also despoiled the surrounding lands and sickened farmers while in operation during Japan's modernization period from the late 1800s through the early 1900s.[11] Most antipollution citizens' movements were suppressed during the reign of Japanese militarists in the decades before and during World War II, with the exception of the Osarusawa Mining and Ishikari River Kokusaku Pulp industrial actions, where waste discharge and environmental pollution problems were so intense, mass protests resulted in changes in policy in the operations. In 1955, the "Morinaga arsenic milk" problem brought a crescendo of deaths and illnesses during the transition between Japan's postwar reconstruction and the coming period of high economic growth. In 1956, "Minamata disease" was discovered not to be a disease, but instead to be the result of mercury poisoning from industrial waste discharge that caused severe convulsions in thousands of victims, intermittent loss of consciousness, repeated lapses into crazed mental states, and even permanent coma. Mothers poisoned by the effluence gave birth to children with higher rates of deformities than in unaffected regions of Japan. For hundreds, death was the only relief from high fevers.

China now has scores of Minamata throughout its interior.

CANCER VILLAGES

For thousands of years, Chinese society has been based on concentric circles of relationship with the family at the center of all survival responses. After the importance of family ties comes longtime family friends and neighbors, then township, with fealty to central government authority filling out the universe of Chinese relations. With increasing distance from central authority comes an increasing sense of autonomy that leaves a vacuum in any sort of public—or civil—space. The gray shades of law and the arbitrary interpretations and enforcement as per local officialdom's interests at that moment in time have reinforced the sense throughout China's history that as long as one had wealth and relationships with the powerful, one could pretty much do whatever one damn well pleased. Hence, flagrant dismissal of environmental laws at the local level, with the full cooperation and support in many instances of local officials and residents who want to be part of the wealthier, better-connected circles.

Still, there are some green shoots of development of a civil society. Unfortunately, the motivators that drive communities to come together and foment an action that benefits more than just a few requires a dire change in circumstances in China. One of the most dramatic knock-on effects in China's unstinting drive toward creating greater wealth for its citizens is the creation of so-called cancer villages. Cancer villages are typically small towns in out-of-the way regions of China in which the town's citizens are often undereducated, poor farmers that know little of the effects of the noxious vapors and poisonous emissions pouring out of nearby factories.

Lead poisoning is the leading cause of cancer villages in China. Excessive levels of lead in the blood stream can cause seizures, coma, and, eventually, death. In 2006, it was estimated that 34 percent of children in China had levels of lead in their blood that exceeded World Health Organization standards. Chinese manufacturers favor lead because it is highly malleable, weighty, and heat resistant. It's also a cheap additive for plastics and vinyl to make them more heat resistant, and to otherwise flimsy metal products to make them stronger. Lead dust is also sometimes used in herbal products sold by weight, to make the remedy heavier.

Factories that have been forced out of city limits to the countryside take advantage of close relations with unsophisticated local officials and with lax enforcement of environmental standards. It took several years for the farmers of Xinsi, a village in Gansu Province in western China, to realize it was the local lead smelter that was poisoning them and their land. The Huixian Hongyu Nonferrous Smelting Company had been spewing lead-laced air pollutants from its furnaces that were nearly 800 times permissible levels. The state-owned factory made lead ingots for use in television tubes and cables for export. By 2006, all 2,000 of the village's residents were thought to suffer from lead poisoning, including 250 children.

Factories enjoy setting up in the countryside because of the ignorance of local residents in matters of chemistry, health, and the environment. Xiu Minzheng, whose two children had been diagnosed with high levels of lead in their blood, confessed: "We're just simple peasants. We didn't have any awareness of what lead could do. But the government officials should have known. We just don't have the means to deal with this sort of thing."[12]

Xinsi's farmers found out about the high levels of lead in their blood through testing at medical facilities in the capital of Shaanxi Province, Xi'an. Xinhua, the national news agency and an official mouthpiece of the Communist Party, picked up the story, leading investigators from Beijing to visit the village. Pan Yue, deputy director of the State Environmental Protection Administration, accused local government officials of dereliction of their duty to safeguard the welfare of the residents in their jurisdiction and demanded severe punishments.[13] The government closed down the factory, and tore down parts of the lethal operation. Still, no mention was made of reparations to the villagers in a country in which environmental disasters are a common occurrence and no laws are in place to establish liability for health-related disasters.

Another village saw more than 600 children diagnosed with lead poisoning. Villagers marched to the Dongling Town Lead and Zinc Smelting Company on a hot August day in 2009, tore down fencing that surrounded the plant, overwhelmed the factory's security guards, and smashed trucks and other vehicles. The last protester did not leave the grounds until 6 p.m. that evening, after 200 local government officials had spent the day reasoning and listening to angry residents. When the residents asked officials why they hadn't been relocated as they had been promised three years before, when the smelter was still in the planning stages, administrators claimed a lack of funds as the culprit.[14]

The national attention the protest brought to the area spurred local officials to accelerate their plans for relocating nearly 1,500 families from the grounds affected by the smelting operation. By the end of that summer, more than 850 children had been diagnosed with alarming levels of lead in their blood. Families who lived within 1,000 meters from the facility would be moved more than three kilometers away, before the end of the following year. The Dongling Group, one of the biggest private companies in Shaanxi Province and owner of the smelter, would pay half the relocation costs. The operation, which directly accounted for 17 percent of the county's GDP in 2008, would remain in place. Beyond paying medical bills for those who had been admitted to hospital, and supplying nuts and milk to those nursed at home, villagers say little has been discussed about compensating them for their poisoned land and their lost livelihoods.[15]

In general, residents affected by mass poisonings in China wait until a quorum of the righteously angry forms, by which time scores, if not hundreds, of victims will have suffered. Locals know lodging complaints as an individual with administrators, the local constabulary, or the local judiciary will have no results, or could even be more dangerous to their health than the poisons they are ingesting from the local chemicals factory. As there is no separation of the powers in China, taking legal action is often fraught with great expense with little local scrutiny of the source of the health problems. The problem is further exacerbated in the countryside of China due to the dearth of lawyers in China as a whole; and of those who have any environmental law training or experience. Chinese lawyers, as professionals, are relatively easy to intimidate in China. They have something to lose, namely, their hard-won license to practice law, which Communist Party officials have little compunction in revoking when the harsh spotlight of recognition from superiors falls on their jurisdiction, and of course, the threat of a prison sentence.

For those who feel they as individuals have little to lose in their fight against local government malfeasance, the fight can get even nastier, affecting their families. There is very little room in China for a charismatic Erin Brockovich character with the grit, stamina, and intelligence to bring a class action suit against a local, if not national, government. (Erin Brockovich is the real-life legal assistant who tackled a major U.S. chemical refinery and launched a successful class-action suit against the company.) Simply, although there may be an appeals process, the national government will only stand so much embarrassment when major cases of health-related environmental crimes are brought to the fore. The weight of "face" in Chinese society has a strong bearing on how the government deals with such embarrassments; for the Communist Party sees such cases as criticism of its rule and of the hodgepodge system of laws and the liberal interpretations its courts make. The majority of judges in the Chinese judiciary gain their posts more as a reward for keeping the Party faith than due to any legal acuity or educational background. As such, lawsuits on the order of the melamine milk scandal of 2008—in which thousands of children were sickened by melamine-tainted milk powder—or the parents of hundreds of schoolchildren killed in the Sichuan earthquake of the same year, are squelched before they become major national symbols for further class-action lawsuits. Government authorities see mass complaint more as an aberration of society that requires suppression than as a seismic shock to the social system in which expressions of popular discontent seek release precisely to rebalance the system.

As long as China's judiciary remains quiescent, its Environment Protection Administration remains toothless, cronyism replaces the rule of law at local levels, and any plans and policies China has to promote the development of a "green" commercial sector will lack credibility, as illustrated by a mine owner in Yunnan Province who in 1997 spray-painted hectares of rock green in a quarry gouged out of a local mountain to meet local environmental protection requirements. Leaders prefer to keep environmental imperatives secondary to economic growth, to the detriment of its own citizens and the ire of its neighbors.

NOW IN YOUR BACKYARD

One of the reasons for the international concern over China's emissions is that its industrial filth is slopping over into other countries' backyards. So, even though many of the post-Industrial-Revolution countries have gone through (most of) their dirtiest development phase, they are finding that in addition to the cost and effort involved in keeping their own domains clean and their citizens healthy, they also are having to deal with foreign-born pollutants.

Chinese society's choice to place rapid economic development above environmental concerns has come onto the radars of other countries— literally. A 2008 NASA study began tracking a continent-sized brown cloud that originates from China's northeastern seaboard and covers most of the North Pacific, circulating along the Canadian coast and extending southward into Seattle. The cloud is a toxic mix of ash, acids, and airborne particles from car and factory emissions, according to the report, and from coal-burning stoves and forest fires.[16]

Much of the acid rain that falls on Seoul and Tokyo comes from sulfur dioxide and nitrogen oxides vomited by power plants by coal in China. Chinese factories throw up more of the noxious chemicals than do European facilities, despite a per capita GDP far below Europe's, indicating Chinese furnaces are incredibly inefficient. City governments in Japan have delivered official air-pollution warnings to their citizens as emissions readings from China periodically increase. The *Journal of Geophysical Research* found in 2007 that Los Angeles car pollution has mixed with particulate pollution from China to compound breathing and visibility issues in the Valley.[17]

Emissions are only growing as China brings the equivalent of Britain's entire electricity production capacity online every year— almost once a week, China fires up a new power generator. In 2007, China captured the top spot from the United States as the greatest emitter of carbon dioxide; despite American plans to continue adding coal-burning plants to its own energy inventory, China seems positioned to retain first place for decades to come. Indeed, China uses more coal to power its society than the United States, the European Union, and Japan combined. With nearly 70 percent of Chinese power generated by coal, estimates are that if the Chinese economy grows a mere seven percent annually (not the average 10 percent growth that it has experienced) it will have doubled its coal consumption within a decade.[18]

In late 2005, China's accelerated effort to catch up with Western industrialized countries resulted in one of the most dangerous chemical spills in the country had ever seen. The source of the spill was none other than Jilin, where the same Hong Kong-invested Connell Chemical Company cited at the beginning of the chapter would set up operations years later. One hundred tons of benzene spewed into the Songhua River after tanks in a chemical plant exploded. The toxic waste forced the northern Chinese city of Harbin to close its taps to water from the river, and forced the Chinese government to notify the Russian government that the benzene would cross the border between the two countries and enter the drinking reservoirs of the city of Khabarovsk. Still today, the Sungari—what the Russians call the Songhua—delivers tons of toxins downstream to the Amur River. Nearby Russian residents complain of rashes, diarrhea, and infections that don't heal. When locals cut into the ice that crusts over the waterway to catch fish, they complain of a stench from the opening, and locals believe it comes from plant and animal life killed off from the poisons.[19]

CLEAN UP YOUR ACT

The sad fact of the matter is there is little the international community can do to prod the Chinese leadership into action to curb the flow of industrial pollution as it slops into global wind and ocean currents. The Chinese leadership is beholden to no one and nothing but its own estimations and fears of mass social instability within its borders. As long as the central authority is able to provide the sort of economic opportunities to the masses that match the vision the Party offered up in the mid-1980s—with the caveat that "collateral damage" will be kept to a minimum—the average Chinese will continue supporting an economic model that has proven over the past 200 years to be incredibly harmful to the environment of every society that has embarked on the experiment. The rub comes in the social definition of "collateral damage" and "acceptable losses"—terms more often used in executing wars than in modernizing societies. The Chinese are on a mission to become wealthy. Modernization is simply the vehicle, the quickest way they have seen to generate the income levels that will enable them to recapture some sense of being a truly exceptional society.

The Chinese threshold of risk is greater than that of the richer Western countries, particularly the U.S., where everything from crib manufacture, road-crew safety to the sanitary conditions of carts that sell hot dogs is regulated and enforced. The Chinese in Mainland China, though, do not have the same sensibility. The mind-boggling numbers of its population throughout history relative to other countries; the dramatic cascade of events leading to the fall of its dynasties; and the wars and revolutions in the making of new autocracies in which the old rules no longer apply, the scale of human misery that its earthquakes, typhoons, and seasonal river floods have caused for millennia have created a kind of devil-may-care attitude to life that makes even a Western bungee-jumper blush with anxiety. Construction workers balance stories high on thumb-sized bamboo scaffolding, car drivers duck in and out of traffic without signaling, and families of three or four (including children and infants!) pile onto the backs of electric scooters without helmets to navigate highways in the rain. Chinese society has a different gauge for the relationship between risk and reward than Western society. On an individual and collective level, Chinese are willing to risk more than Westerners to attain what the West has defined as the good life. The Chinese leadership has included that greater capacity for risk in its estimation of the G-forces the society can withstand in its supersonic flight to modernity. The assessment includes the degree to which factories can pollute communities before local residents will violently protest the imposition. Meanwhile, the citizenry has also at some level assessed the degree of economic liberalization it requires before industrialization becomes a liability in the quest to live well. Excessive health issues, extreme degradation of the local environment, and a lack of government receptivity to demands to correct industrial excesses is a formula for residents to violently spotlight grievances.

Chinese leadership can support the odd protest of several hundred locals at a time. However, it finds a network effect connecting these isolated incidents in a long, unbreakable chain insupportable. Social discord can and easily does resonate in Chinese society, with the discontent that citizens feel about so many other issues in the society— income disparities, corruption in government and business, lack of protection of property rights, and more—agglomerating and combusting in a single event at a pace that quickly melts down any sense of reason or civility. The mass mind of the crowd in China is a terrifying thing to behold. The weight of China's dynastic cycles has impressed upon the soul of any Chinese would-be leader that absolute power can only be applied so long as the critical mass of public discontent is kept fragmented, with the occasional outlet for pressures provided in a measured way.

For instance, the Guangzhou local government permitted hundreds of residents in the autumn of 2009 to protest its plans to place a garbage incinerator in their neighborhood.[20] Protestors had heard that residents of another such incinerator built in Likeng village, near Guangzhou, suffered heavily from the carcinogenic toxins the furnace spewed out.

Guangzhou officials quickly retreated in its effort to locate the incinerator in such a political hotspot, much as the Xiamen government had in 2007, when it was ramming through construction of a factory that would produce massive quantities of paraxylene, a known carcinogen. Thousands of citizens protested at the Xiamen rally, many of whom were members of the newly minted middle class. Local government acquiescence to protestor demands in these instances released stress and to mollified community frustration without actually suppressing local concerns.

The Chinese leadership is fully aware of the damage its bid to remake Chinese society is causing the geography of the land and the health of its people. However, in its own bid for survival, the goal is to show its citizens that on balance, the country is moving from a humiliating and poverty-stricken nineteenth century into a proud and prosperous twenty-first century—and as quickly as possible. Political "credits," such as higher income levels, greater opportunities for economic gain, and the means by which to promote the interests of one's family, are expected to reap a dividend even after taking into account embarrassing social "debits," such as cancer villages, fouled rivers and lakes, and unbreathable air. China, with its long mercantile history, is more than familiar with the costs involved in any transaction.

Still, the richer cities along China's east coast in which the bulk of citizens have reached middle-class status have realized that overwhelming amounts of pollution are bad for their health, and for attracting industries that yield high-value products and services. Second-tier cities such as Hangzhou, Suzhou, Xiamen, and Dalian have all but kicked out such mercenary industries as textile manufacture, low-end plastics, and chemical refineries. The cities have reached a tipping point of per capita income levels—about US$4,000—allowing them to invest tax dollars in attracting more capital-intensive industries, which require their staff to have higher levels of education than found in more polluting industries. Research and development, software development, tourism, services outsourcing, pharmaceuticals, and others are pushing out the shoe makers, the cloth dyers, and the toy manufacturers in a kind of economic Darwinism that both the local governments and the residents desire.

On balance, Chinese society believes the environmental costs are worth the prize: modernity, greater wealth, and the respect (if not awe) of the international community. The question remains, however, whether China will be able to pay back Mother Nature in full for the loan it's taken out to live an unsustainable future.

END NOTES

1. Tania Branigan, "Chinese Regulators Admit Chemical Leak after Workers Fall Sick," *The Guardian*, May 29, 2009.
2. Andrew Jacobs, "Chinese Workers Say Illness Is Real, Not Hysteria," *The New York Times*, July 29, 2009.
3. Ibid.
4. Andreas Lorenz and Wieland Wagner, "China's Poison for the Planet," Spiegel Online, January 2, 2007.
5. Candy Zeng, "China Paying Dearly for Cleaner Rivers," Asia Times Online, November 14, 2007.
6. Joseph Kahn and Jim Yardley, "As China Roars, Pollution Reaches Deadly Extremes," *The New York Times*, August 26, 2007.
7. Andreas Lorenz and Wieland Wagner, "China's Poison for the Planet," Spiegel Online, January 2, 2007, http://www.spiegel.de/international/spiegel/0,1518,461828,00.html, accessed October 13, 2009.
8. "Environmental History Timeline," Radford University website, http://www.radford.edu/~wkovarik/envhist/, accessed January 10, 2010.
9. "America's Top 10 Worst Man-Made Environmental Disasters," Earthfirst .com, April 22, 2009, http://earthfirst.com/americas-top-10-worst-man-made-environmental-disasters/.
10. Wahei Tatematsu, "Pushing an Elephant Up the Stairs," *Time*, May 29, 2000.
11. Pradyumna Prasad Karan, *Japan in the 21st Century: Environment, Economy, and Society*, (Lexington: The University Press of Kentucky, 2005), 359.
12. Shai Oster and Jane Spencer, "A Poison Spreads Amid China's Boom," *The Wall Street Journal*, September 30, 2006.
13. "Local Authorities Slammed for Pollution Coverup," *China Daily*, September 16, 2006.
14. Hu Yongqi and Lu Hongyan, "Villagers Break into Lead Factory in NW China," *China Daily*, August 18, 2009.
15. "NW China Lead Victims to be Relocated," *China Daily*, November 26, 2009.

16. NASA news release, March 2008; http://geology.com/nasa/monitoring-pollution-by-satellite.shtml.

17. Joseph Kahn and Jim Yardley, "As China Roars, Pollution Reaches Deadly Extremes," *The New York Times*, August 26, 2007.

18. Andreas Lorenz and Wieland Wagner, "China's Poison for the Planet," Spiegel Online, January 2, 2007, http://www.spiegel.de/international/spiegel/0,1518,461828,00.html, accessed October 13, 2009.

19. Ibid.

20. James Pomfret, "Hundreds in South China Oppose Waste Incinerator," Reuters, November 23, 2009.

CHAPTER **5**

With the Appetite
of a Dragon

LAND AHOY!

In the winter of 2005, I met a vice mayor of a Chongqing township, deep in China's interior, in his voluminous but austere office in the countryside. The official seemed young for the position, in his mid-40s, affable if not disarming in his distracted greeting. He was casually dressed in a cheap pullover sweater and black faux-leather jacket. He said he would personally drive me out to the area where a client of mine could build a factory. The mountains in this part of the country are terraced rock where brick-wall shacks perch precariously above dusty shelves of vegetable plots. We drove 30 minutes from his office, then turned onto a dirt-and-pebble road. The vice mayor stopped the car between two hills. On one hill, a huge backhoe combed a bald pate smooth. On the opposing hill stood one of the ubiquitous ramshackle shacks, someone's home. A mother was out front of the shelter consumed with a backbreaking chore while her son scrambled around in the front yard. It seemed to me there had once been an entire village where I stood, with the solitary hovel now the only evidence. The vice mayor spread a map on the hood of the black Volkswagen Santana. He gestured toward another backhoe more than about 800 meters away that was scrabbling at the land. He announced: "From here to that machine can all be yours." He was offering up five times the space at 20 percent the cost my client was considering. Certainly, it was a better deal than officials in other parts of China had offered me on other projects, with their "two-for-one" deals: two large plots of land for industrial development for the price of one. Clients and I took none of the deals, as all were illegal under Chinese law, and overkill for what the projects required. Such is the length some local officials are willing to go, though, in China's land bonanza.

For all its long history, China has a very poor track record of conservation of its own natural resources. For the past 600 years, it has mismanaged its land, forest, oil, and water wealth. The trend accelerated when the Communist Party took control of the country in 1949. A pillar of Maoist policy and sloganeering was: "Humans must conquer Nature!" Unfortunately, there is only a limited amount of Nature to vanquish, and China's push to modernization over the next 10 to 15 years will see a dramatic increase in consumption of the precious resources that give all of us sustenance in this world, with no sign of reversal of the trend on the horizon. Urbanization and a growing middle class will require land, mineral, and water resources in quantities that Chinese geography is already finding difficult to yield.

China only has seven percent of the world's arable land and nearly 20 percent of its population. The continental United States is about the same size as China, and yet nearly 20 percent of its land is fit to grow food for a population about a fifth the size of China's. Nevertheless, as a result of the reckless acceleration of the destruction of farming land for commercial and infrastructure purposes, China's arable land dwindled to 122 million hectares in 2007 from 130 million hectares in 1996. If all the remaining arable land in China was collected into a single region, the area would only be slightly larger than the state of Texas. China is losing its crop land at the rate of about a million hectares a year, or an area roughly the size of Delaware.[1]

Despite the central government announcing a lower limit of 120 million hectares—below which it will not provide land for commercial or residential investment, or what it calls its "red line"—Beijing has found it difficult to curb the enthusiasm of local government officials in second-, third-, and fourth-tier cities who create illegal investment zones to lease land to domestic and foreign companies. Beijing considers 120 million hectares the bare minimum amount of land with which China can grow just enough food to sustain its population. The temptation to grab land and sell it onto commercial interests, though, is difficult to resist for poor districts and for low-paid government employees working in China's boondocks. Some local governments fix public auctions of land and take commissions from "winners". Local land bureaus may also take a cut of land-transfer fees. Taxes on real estate transactions are often the only way many towns have to finance local infrastructure projects and social services.

In 2007, the Ministry of Land and Resources (MLR) found 32,000 "irregular" land transactions in the first 60 days of a 100-day land-supply enforcement campaign.[2] According to the figures released by the MLR, 2.3 billion square meters of land—nearly one and a third the size of the state of Alaska—had been involved that year in such irregular transactions, including illegal expansions of land and occupying land before the approval of a lease. From 2001 through 2007, the Communist Party penalized nearly 9,000 officials while more than 1,000 others were criminally punished over illegal land-title transfers.[3]

The squeeze on China's arable land coupled with rising demand for food as Chinese consumers become richer have forced China to become a net importer of foodstuffs, and to buy farmland in other countries. In 2004, Chinese farms were no longer able to meet domestic demand through their own efforts, and had to import grains such as rice, corn, wheat, and barley to offset production deficits. Increased meat consumption contributed to the grain deficit, too, as Chinese farms fattened their prized pigs with cereal.[4]

China began in earnest investing in farmland in Africa after it was clear Chinese farmers would continue to be unable to meet the increasing domestic demand for grains and meats. China signed 30 agricultural agreements with African countries from 2007 to 2009, ensuring crop yields would be destined for Chinese tables, along with setting up about 11 research stations in Africa to study how to boost crop yields.[5] By 2009, China had invested in 2.5 hectares of farmland across five sub-Saharan countries at a cost of nearly US$1 billion. Chinese purchases in African arable land, though, are hardly unique, with twenty-first century food-security investments in Africa also made by the Saudis, the South Koreans, the Kuwaitis, the British, and the Germans.[6]

FORESTS FOR THE TREES

However, China's mismanagement of its land resources extends far beyond whether it will be able to feed itself. For instance, the Great Northern Wilderness that once blanketed the northeast of the country along the Russian border is nearly gone. China's central government in 2008 designated a former lumber processing area in the region called Yichun in northernmost Heilongjiang Province as one of China's "resource-depleted cities." The city simply has no more wood to cut.[7] As China became the furniture-manufacturing platform for the world, consumption of lumber increased without parallel, despite a 1998 restriction on domestic logging. Log imports increased nine folds from the time the ban was put in place until 2008, with factories in wood-manufacturing centers such as Nanxun, in Zhejiang Province, able to process one log every minute of every day. Nanxun is the wood-flooring capital of China; while Dongguan, in Guangdong Province, is the center of furniture manufacture. Other cities specialize in chopsticks, while still others whittle timber down to toothpick size.[8]

With government restrictions on domestic logging, it was only inevitable that China would look to other countries to feed its manufacturing sector's appetite for more wood. By 2005, Chinese buyers were importing more than 100 million cubic meters of wood a year. Nearly a third of the wood was illegally cut down in eastern Russia, Brazil, Burma, and Indonesia.[9] Indonesia alone loses a swathe of forest every year the size of the island of Puerto Rico.

Most of the more exotic wood imports enter Zhangjiagang, a major port on the Yangtze River, near the outlet to the sea. Zhangjiagang is about a two-hour drive to the west of Shanghai. A visit to the port one rainy spring day revealed huge lots of timber from around the world: African hard wood, Indonesian blood-red merbau, and rich Brazil wood. Most of the wood, though, is illegally exported from their countries of origin and illegally imported into China. Agents at the shipyard that I visited blithely pointed out the origins of the illicit shipments. Government officials on both ends of the trade either find the volumes of timber crossing their inspection stations too great to bother with, or too personally lucrative to deny, while middlemen who operate in the shadowy world of forged documentation and ill-gotten licenses take their cut as well. For example, smuggling rings pay about US$200,000 bribes to ensure each shipment can leave Indonesian jurisdiction.[10]

However, Zhangjiagang is not the only port that is in part or completely dedicated to the import of wood from other countries. Fujian Province has entire city districts devoted to the manufacture of wood products. Putian, in central Fujian, in the deep south of China, is a very small town with no high-rises to speak of. Its two main attractions are that it has a healthy trade in tea—with the most teahouses per square kilometer of any city I have visited in China— and a vibrant furniture-making market. The local government in 2007 had arranged for the port at Putian to be one of the few in the country that could certify the health of the timber imported from other countries. Men like Mr. Chen had positioned themselves to reap the benefits of the region's expanded trade in lumber. A slight man with steely eyes in his mid-60s, Chen's business card sported six different titles, some corporate and some related to wood-manufacturing industry associations in the area. We met in his son's office at a family furniture-making factory. The son looked little like the father: tall, portly, and busy. However, both had the composure of local bosses that most deferred to, even if visitors were out-of-towners.

The Godfather—as I came to refer to him—was bullish about Putian's role in China's wood-processing sector, and outlined the developments the local government was making in the area to consolidate and coordinate the fragmented local marketplace. The family factory—one of a handful the family ran—was clean and well-organized. Timber lay unshorn in a large lot open to the elements, while processed timber awaited craftwork in a large warehouse bright with natural light. Machines in the workshops on the compound were clean, well-maintained, and workers were neatly clad in matching work-jumpers.

The Putian Godfather and local government officials were most proud of the new wood-processing park that would prove the center-piece of Putian's economy. The local government had cleared several square kilometers of forest, farmland, and residential areas to build new factories, a state-of-the-art exhibition hall, and high-rise apartment buildings to accommodate the new rich that they were sure would congregate in the area.

Chinese proficiency in its consumption and processing of wood went far beyond wood centers like Putian, I discovered. Manufacturing hubs such as Zhenjiang, near Nanjing, and in other cities along the east coast, had created an ecology of consumption that ensured that even the smallest scraps of wood were saved and sold on at a profit to other shops that required the waste for their own production lines. Even sawdust was saved and sold to other companies. Factories that processed more expensive tree imports would collect and categorize wood leavings by species, since the isolated sawdust of finer trees fetched more than a sloppy mix of wood dust.

Central leadership has not cracked down on the illegal importation of precious woods from other countries to buoy its wood-manufacturing industry. The government is also acutely aware of the extent to which it had denuded the country's forest cover since the 1950s. In 1978, two years after the death of Mao Zedong, the central government began building its so-called Great Green Wall. Beijing plans for the wall of trees to stretch 4,480 kilometers from Xinjiang Province in China's extreme northwest to Heilongjiang, where the Great Northern Wilderness used to lie. When completed in 2050, the forest will cover 500,000 square kilometers—an area the size of Spain. It would be "the largest man-made carbon sponge on the planet," as described by the U.K. newspaper, *The Guardian*.[11]

The forest is also meant to slow the encroachment of the Gobi Desert, which has been expanding several inches a year since the early 1980s. The North loses 66,000 hectares of farmland to desertification each year—an area the size of Singapore—to a combination of water mismanagement and deforestation. Another of the drivers behind the desertification are Chinese goat herders in Inner Mongolia who have overgrazed the grassland. China's grasslands have shrunk every year at a rate of 15,000 square kilometers, an area about the size of the U.S. state of Connecticut, since the 1980s.[12] The fur from the goats goes to the factories that make the cheap and comfortable Merino wool sweaters sold by retailers in the West. Now all that is left of the wilderness is a fine dust that barely qualifies as top soil. The fine grains of the barren ground blow away easily. The resulting dust storms blanket Beijing every year in tons of sand, reducing visibility and making it difficult for residents to breathe.

Environmentalists say the Great Green Wall will do little in the near term to stop the desert, as the biodiversity of underbrush and moss has been lost and will require decades to return. In addition, the Chinese are planting mostly two kinds of trees: poplar and birch. The monoculture of trees can expose the vast forest to near catastrophic destruction through blight or blizzard, as was the case in the winter of 2008, when 10 percent of the forest succumbed to heavy snows.

OILY DAYS

Mao Zedong always had a vision of his country being self-sufficient and energy independent. China turned from being a thrifty, self-sufficient, if closed, society to a net importer of oil in 1993. The rejuvenation of its export manufacturing sector was a major factor in the role reversal. Since 2000, the growth of a middle class with American-style aspirations of consumption has wildly increased the country's requirements for crude oil, as well as implementation of infrastructure projects of a scope and scale that dwarf the Marshall Plan's efforts to put Europe back on its feet after the mass destruction of World War II.

In 1993, China was producing and then using nearly three million barrels of oil per day. Domestic production hasn't increased much since that period, approaching 3.8 million barrels of oil a day in 2008. Meanwhile, China's oil consumption came in second only to the United States in 2007, expanding to more than 7.5 million barrels of oil a day from 4.5 million in 2001. The United States in 2007 consumed about 21 million barrels.[13] The International Energy Agency projected in 2009 that China's net oil imports would top 13 million barrels of oil a day by 2030, more than China's total output in 2008.

The stark reality is that at the end of the first decade of the twenty-first century, China has only one percent of the world's proven reserves of oil, with nine percent of the world's oil demand and growing. Consumption increased seven percent from 2007 to 2008—and that was during the global economic slowdown.[14] By the beginning of 2010, the International Energy Agency predicted China would need nearly nine million barrels of oil a day by the end of that year.[15] With oil consumption in China having already doubled in the past 10 years, it is conceivable that with the country's double-digit annual growth in automobile ownership, oil consumption will again double by 2020.[16] In 2010, China accounted for one-third of the world's growth in oil consumption. Still, while China is the fastest-growing consumer of oil in the world, it will take some time before the average Chinese consumes as much oil as the average American; Americans use about 22 barrels of oil per person, while Chinese use about 2.4 barrels.[17]

China's western territories and their mineral wealth are strategically important to the sustainability of China's plans for rapid growth. The Tarim basin in northwest Xinjiang Autonomous Region holds both oil and gas.[18] Xinjiang's reserves of natural gas in particular have become preeminent in China's plan to ease its dependence on coal, a much dirtier supply of energy. Central authorities spent US$15 billion to bring online a natural gas pipeline that stretches from Lunnan, near the Kazakhstan border, all the way to Urumqi, 4,000 kilometers away. The Xinjiang gas fields supply 12 billion cubic meters of gas a year. Development of a second pipeline in 2008 from the same desert area will bring in an additional 30 billion cubic meters of gas a year by 2015.[19] China knew years before the turn of the new century, though, that it was going to have to range far from its borders to secure sources of energy to realize its national aspirations.

GLOBAL BUYING SPREE

The U.S. Energy Information Administration estimated that by 2025, foreign oil supplies will provide China with more than three-quarters of its domestic needs, compared with just under half in 2007. Chinese forays abroad in search of secure sources of oil now find the country with interests in the Middle East, Central Asia, Africa, Southeast Asia, and South America.[20] About half of China's oil in 2008 came from the Middle East, 30 percent from Africa, and 17 percent from other regions—such as South America—while only three percent came from Southeast Asia. Saudi Arabia and Angola are China's top providers of petroleum, making up about a third of China's supplies. Iran provides another 15 percent of China's imports.[21]

China began expanding its international oil prospecting at the end of the 1990s, near its borders in Kazakhstan where it had begun to buy oil fields.[22] Central Asia's mineral resources and pliable authoritarian regimes are the prime motive behind Beijing's bonhomie in so enthusiastically promoting the Shanghai Cooperation Organization (SCO), which discusses issues surrounding national security, management of Muslim populations, and natural resource exploitation and distribution. The SCO includes China, Kazakhstan, Kyrgyzstan, Russia, Tajikistan, and Uzbekistan. China's central government has taken advantage of the neighborly good feelings by building a pipeline directly from Kazakhstan's oilfields to the doorstep of Xinjiang, where China has built one of the largest petroleum refineries in the world. The Kazakh project represents nearly a quarter of China's total foreign production, at nearly 300,000 barrels a day. Total Chinese overseas production, however, meets just 14 percent of China's domestic requirement for oil, according to the energy consultancy Wood Mackenzie.

Instead of buying its oil on the open market, Beijing has dismayed Washington by taking tips from the largest oil consumer in the world—the United States. China has been buying up and investing in oil fields in countries around the world that the U.S. has either ignored as geopolitically inconsequential to promoting its own interests, or the governments of which the U.S. has found too unsavory to defend in the world court of public opinion, or has been barred from dealing with through self- or United Nations-imposed embargoes. China accelerated its international forays after the U.S. Congress foiled its bid for the U.S. oil producer Unocal in 2005. Since then, its dances with dictators have earned it Western opprobrium.

For instance, China buys most of Sudan's oil.[23] The international community severely criticized China for supplying arms, fighter jets, and training to the Sudanese government in 2008 while Sudan's president Omar al-Bashir was clearing the Darfur region of its inhabitants. The UN estimated that about 300,000 people died through what it termed a campaign of genocide, while more than two million others were forced out of the region to surrounding countries between 2005 and 2008. China also supported Sudan in the UN by refusing to cast a vote condemning the Sudanese government's actions as genocide. Throughout the early 2000s, China also was loathe to criticize the Muslim oligarchy ruling Iran through UN declarations and sanctions for its efforts to develop nuclear weaponry, abstaining during crucial votes.

Such blatant support of distasteful regimes eventually found countries tagging China with the "neocolonialist" label, accusing China of mercenary and mercantilist activities that sought merely to exploit the natural resources of other countries, especially in Africa. In 2009, China actively sought to buy one in six barrels of oil that Nigeria produced—which would make up six billion barrels of China's reserves. The U.S. business magazine *Fortune* quoted Tanimu Yakubu, an economic advisor to the Nigerian President, as saying China was "really offering multiples of what the existing producers are pledging [for licenses]." Yakubu added: "We love this kind of competition."[24] The China National Offshore Oil Corporation went head-to-head against oil and gas giant ExxonMobil for drilling rights in Ghana to take over nearly a quarter of Ghana's Jubilee field. Jubilee is China's largest offshore oil field, estimated to hold 1.8 billion barrels of oil. Also in 2009, China National Petroleum Corporation attempted to buy Canadian producer Verenex Energy's Libyan operations for US$357 million, a deal scuttled by the Libyan government, which wanted the assets for itself.

One of the biggest issues the country faces in dealing with countries with economies even less developed than itself is that the oil sellers have little infrastructure with which to pump out and then transport production. Chinese overseas infrastructure-investment projects also serve developing world aspirations by boosting local economies without the stringent conditions for fiscal policy reform the International Monetary Fund often requires, and the leadership changes that rich countries encourage. For instance, Sudan's oil industry benefited handsomely from Chinese investment totaling US$15 billion from 1996 through 2008. The Sudanese government's treasury also benefited mightily from the productivity boost given its oil fields, which eventually produced 500,000 barrels a day from the negligible amount it had originally been producing.[25] In 2007, China committed US$12 billion dollars to build or renovate the railways, roads, and mines of the Congo. China would receive rights to mine copper ore in the country to an equivalent value. The Chinese investment in Congo is more than three times Congo's annual national budget.[26] Meanwhile, Nigeria signed a contract with the China Civil Engineering Construction Corporation in 2009 to develop Nigeria's railway system.[27]

OUT OF THEIR ELEMENT

It's no wonder that with every city in China ramming up apartment blocks, malls, and entire highway systems ringing towns and dissecting city centers that China uses half of the world's cement, a third of its steel, and more than a quarter of its aluminum. From 2004 through 2008, shipments of iron ore to China grew by more than a quarter each year.[28] By 2009, China purchased half of all iron-ore exports in the world, and ushered in a four-fold increase in iron-ore prices between 2002 and 2008.

China's appetite for iron ore has seen it buy up half of all Australia's exports of it. China, to reduce the prices it pays foreign mining companies, has been investing in mines and in mining projects, especially "Down Under" in Australia.[29] Chinese state-owned enterprises began to aggressively take interests in Australian mining concerns when Chinese buyers found themselves having to absorb huge increases in the cost of iron ore after 2005 due to massive demand in Chinese infrastructure projects. Chinese steel mills had to accept a price hike of more than 75 percent. The China Railway Materials Commercial Corporation, for instance, bought an 11.4 percent stake in Australia's United Minerals Corporation and a 12 percent stake in FerrAus in 2009. Other Chinese grabs at Australian mining stakes included Ansteel's purchase of additional shares in a Gindalbie iron ore project at the Karara mine in Western Australia and a plan by Baosteel—China's largest steelmaker—to purchase a 15 percent stake in Aquila Resources, an iron-ore and coal-mining company.[30]

However, Australians themselves have drawn a line in the outback with their resistance to unabashed Chinese investment in their mining companies. Many Australian groups, especially the Australian military, consider the ore mines a strategic sector that requires security guarantees from the Australian government. One of the most high-profile refusals of Chinese state-owned money was the refusal of shareholders of Rio Tinto, an Australian mining conglomerate, to sell more shares to Chinalco, the state-owned aluminum company in China. Chinalco wanted to increase its holdings in Rio Tinto to 18.5 percent from 9.3 percent in 2008 during the nadir of the global economic downturn. Rio Tinto declined the offer when the ore markets and the global economy began to pick up. Australia's military was instrumental in gutting a US$1.8 billion dollar Chinese bid for Fortescue, another Australian iron-ore mine. The Australian military noted that part of Fortescue's holdings were near an aerospace test site. Australia's foreign investments review board ordered the Fortescue deal exclude the operation near the test range for national security reasons, which would reduce the total investment value to US$840 million. In another setback for Chinese overseas investment efforts, China Nonferrous Metal Mining Company ditched plans to take a 51.6 percent stake in Australia's Lynas, the second-largest producer of rare earth minerals in the world, in a deal valued at US$500 million. The foreign investments review board insisted the stake be reduced to less than 50 percent, at which the Chinese side balked.[31]

The most dramatic conflict between Chinese steel-making companies and Australians culminated in the autumn of 2009, during the annual negotiations with Australian mining concerns to set the benchmark prices for bulk purchases of iron ore by foreign buyers. In years past, South Korean and Japanese buyers would negotiate with Australian mining giants to set the price at which iron ore would be bought the following year. China took a back seat to the negotiations until 2005, when Baosteel took the helm on behalf of Asian buyers. In 2009, the China Iron and Steel Association took over from Baosteel and demanded a 40-percent cut off benchmark prices; South Korea and Japan, though, took the 33 percent reduction the Australians offered, effectively freezing the Chinese out of discussions. The Chinese retaliated that summer by arresting four employees of Rio Tinto in Shanghai, one of whom was an Australian citizen. The Chinese government initially charged the Rio Tinto staff with espionage, alleging they had illegally acquired steel-making cost structures from Chinese steel makers. Before the end of 2009, the government reduced the charges to bribery of Chinese businesses, and put the employees on trial in early 2010. The arrest and the trial itself sent shivers through the foreign investment community in China as well as through international markets.

Despite investing billions of dollars in infrastructure-development projects in African and Southeast Asian countries, China is increasingly finding that the national sovereignty of other countries— their laws and their mores—sometimes outweighs any amount of money on the table. In 2006, the African nation of Gabon stopped a Sinopec oil-drilling project in one of its national parks after discovering Sinopec—one of China's largest state-owned oil companies—did not have the requisite environmental permits. The Zambian government interceded on behalf of employees in several instances in mines in the country owned and operated by Chinese interests.[32] Zambian miners accused Chinese companies of overworking and underpaying them in harsh conditions. In 2009, Angola insisted Chinese mineral investments in the country use more local labor as a condition for further expansion of Chinese resource-extraction projects.[33]

Meanwhile, in 2009, China turned very protective of its own rare earth minerals, tightly restricting export of the limited resources that are fundamental to the manufacture of computers and clean-energy products. Chinese mining of rare earth minerals accounts for 95 percent of global production.[34] China-based manufacturers consume about 60 percent of the supply of rare earths, which include such minerals as dysprosium, terbium, thulium, lutetium, and yttrium, according to the U.S. Geological Survey.[35] In the early 2000s, China had used export quotas and taxes on rare-earth metals to lure foreign production to the Mainland. By the end of the decade, a more-confident China projected its intent to corner the markets that depend on low-cost production of new technology. The Geological Survey in 2006 reported 43% of the world's rare earth minerals are outside China, however, it takes several years to bring new mines into operation.[36]

INFLAMMABLE WATER

In early spring 2009, I hung over the rail of a plaza in Chongqing that overlooked the intersection of two great rivers, the Yangtze and the Jialiang, in China's mountainous interior. I was a bit puzzled. The two rivers were all but dry. I remembered how even five years before, the channels flowed strong and muddy. Now, I could walk across the mud flat if I wanted, and wade knee-deep through the remaining dribbles of water without incident. I shared the view with a couple of American friends, Pat and his wife Dana, who had lived in the city for three years. They were packing up to return to the U.S. for good. Pat said with a Southern drawl: "Yeah, even the locals say they've never seen it this low before." It was truly frightening to me to see how the mighty Yangtze had been drained of its vitality and how the land around it was less for the theft of its water.

China can import oil, minerals, and even land, in a sense, in the form of food and timber. But it cannot import more water from other countries. This is China's Achilles' heel in the most acute way. James Kynge wrote in his book, *China Shakes the World*, an insightful synopsis of China's historical focus on water-management policy and activities. Frequent flooding of China's great rivers—the Yellow and the Yangtze— brought both the wealth of fertile land and the devastation of annual floods that sometimes killed millions in a single swelling. A Confucian insistence on subduing nature was made into state policy to tame the rivers, which led to technological revolutions in China that were centuries ahead of engineering projects in the West and contributed to population explosions that made China the most populous in the world.

However, with having so much water in abundance, China never developed water-conservation habits and techniques to manage this most precious resource. China's cultural blind spot has historically been that water is, and will always be, abundant. Now, though, China is battling encroaching desert from the north and west. Cracked and dried river- and lake-beds are becoming more the norm in northern China, with water tables sinking so low that roads and homes are collapsing into sinkholes that spontaneously appear. Fishing industries in a northern swathe of countryside the size of Western Europe have dried up; farmland is unusable and industry is rationing the water it needs to manufacture many of the low-commodity products for which China has become known. The water that is available is highly polluted, undrinkable, and unusable even by industry without extensive processing. Nearly 70 percent of China's rivers and lakes are unsuitable for drinking or human contact.[37] About 30 million people in the countryside and more than 20 million city dwellers suffer shortages of potable water. In the north especially, drought has hit nearly 20 million hectares of arable land—nearly a sixth of China's remaining inventory of land that can be used to grow food.[38]

China supports nearly 20 percent of the world's population with just a quarter of the water available per person in the rest of the world. Meanwhile, the country's extensive water-pollution problems reduce water availability to just one-thirtieth of the global average.[39] Decimation of the forests, land erosion, unconcerned waste of water, and climate change have all contributed to the dearth of water resources. Deutsche Bank estimated that average water prices in China were four to 10 times lower than in Europe in 2009. Shanghai and Zhengzhou, near Nanjing, plan to raise their water prices by 25 percent in 2010 in a bid to enforce conservation. In Luoyang, in north-central China and home of the famed Shaolin monastery, government officials met with the public to argue for a rate increase of nearly 50 percent.[40] Many city administrations also are considering whether to charge residents tariffs of anywhere from two to five times the standard water rate if households use more than their allocation. Beijing's water rates do not even cover utility costs, resulting in the city piping water in from other provinces.[41]

The cost of agricultural use of water in China in 2009 was a mere one U.S. cent per cubic meter, compared with 15 cents per cubic meter for city dwellers and 16 cents per cubic meter for industrial use. The agricultural sector in the country uses water at 23 cents per cubic meter—still considered cheap by international standards. Cheap water has only encouraged farmers in the north to use water in abundance— and to waste accordingly. Only 45 percent of farmers' water allocation in the region ever reaches the farm plots, lost to poorly maintained irrigation infrastructure. Farmers waste nearly three-quarters of the water they use to irrigate their farms by employing crude methods such as water hoses, plastic buckets, and leaky PVC piping to nourish crops.[42]

So, although efforts to raise water prices will help somewhat with conservation, sustainable models of agriculture need to be developed and implemented. Success will lie in educating farmers about how to use the water, applying appropriate amounts and kinds of fertilizer, and understanding the kinds of crops that are appropriate to a geography that is changing more quickly than local habits and government policy can keep up.

Factories in China are also to blame for the extraordinary waste of water during their manufacturing processes. Only 15 percent of Chinese companies recycle their water, compared with 85 percent in developed countries, according to Probe International.[43] For every US$4 of economic output the country produces, factories and farms use one cubic meter of water, nearly three times the world average.

Actually, most of the water upon which China has built its cities and its societies over thousands of years has been an import. The glaciers of the Himalayas have been the source of the two largest rivers in China: the Yellow River in the north and the Yangtze to the south. Glaciers in the Himalayas also provide water to the Ganges—the holy river in India—and the Indus, which runs through Pakistan, as well as to the Mekong River, which blasts through western China to provide farmers and fishermen in Burma, Laos, Thailand, Cambodia, and Vietnam their livelihoods. Many of the feeder-glaciers have been melting as much as 30 meters a year, according to Indian and Chinese scientists.[44] Sometime during this century, it is entirely feasible that climate change will render the glaciers mere ice cubes, and the meltwater will be barely able to fill a bathtub, let alone support the megacities that China is building.

Chinese leadership has been working to top up the arid north's water supply by creating several pipelines that will transport water from the Yangtze River to Beijing and surrounding provinces. The projects have taken years to design and build, initially conceived by Mao Zedong himself, who suggested it was all right for "the north to borrow a little water from the south". However, in 2008, the city of Beijing was unable to wait for the completion of the pipelines, so it "borrowed" a little water from the neighboring province of Hebei, a province that itself is not very rich with water resources. Beijing commandeered water that had been stored in a Hebei reservoir for nearly two years, slaking the city's thirst through a straw nearly 320 kilometers long and costing US$2 billion to build. Farmers in the drought-stricken region felt the nation's capital was unjustly crippling their livelihoods in the countryside so that the officials and the rich of Beijing could continue to play in their well-watered golf courses and admire phalanxes of water fountains. Party officials were well aware of the peasants' grumblings, and so did not trumpet the engineering feat at the pipeline's opening. To further adorn the city, the Beijing government in 2009 announced it would turn the Olympic "bird's nest" stadium complex into a winter sports park, which would involve covering the grounds in nearly 200 thousand square feet of man-made snow.[45]

The grand scheme to pipe water hundreds of kilometers through three separate waterways—from the west, center and east of the country—has met with similar popular discontent, albeit in the hundreds of thousands—as entire ancestral villages have been razed and locals relocated to make way for the engineering projects. The central project begins on the Yangtze River, where the Three Gorges Dam site ends downstream, and extends northward nearly 1,500 kilometers through three provinces. The water that Beijing "borrowed" from Hebei in 2008 is from Beijing's connection point to the central pipeline. Forty giant pumping stations along the 1,500 year old Grand Canal usher water along the eastern route, from the Yangtze River near Shanghai. Tianjin is meant to be the final destination for the water flowing northward; however, Tianjin has said it does not want to receive delivery as heavy concentrations of industry near the mouth of the Yangtze River have polluted the water.[46] Both routes are due to be completed in 2013. The western route, which is supposed to stretch from the Tibetan plateau into China's arid northeast, came under reconsideration in 2009 as the true costs and engineering effort involved in the project were fleshed out. The project also is haunted by the monumental failure of another water-diversion project built 50 years before, called the Red Flag Canal. One hundred thousand peasants labored from 1960 to 1969 to build a canal that ran from Shanxi Province to the northern Henan Province. The canal has since dried up as the water levels of the rivers from which it draws on have dropped. Dai Qing, a middle-aged Chinese conservationist and political activist who has been imprisoned for her outspoken views on China's environmental issues, believes: "Just as there were unforeseen and detrimental consequences to the Red Flag Canal, so will there be with the south-north water diversion, which will be considered a disaster within 20 years."

Even when the pipelines come online in 2014, northern China's water problems will merely be mitigated, not solved. The source of the water for the pipelines is still China's great Yangtze River, which is fed by the very Himalayan glaciers both Indian and Chinese scientists have agreed are melting, though at what rate is still a point of contention. Conservation, as well, will only stave off the inevitable desiccation of the north, as it will have no effect on the source of water for the Yellow and Yangtze Rivers. According to Ma Jun, a well-known critic of China's policy toward water resources, piping water from the south to the north will simply buy the northern provinces some time, but not much, given the wasteful ways of farmers and the melting of the very source of the river waters, the Himalayas.

WHEN THERE'S NOT MUCH LEFT TO CONQUER

Modernization, as the Chinese assimilated it from the West, is ultimately a greedy way forward for a society's development. Britain and then the U.S. lit the way in the world for the application of scientific discoveries to technological innovations that would make our lives easier. Now, post-World War II man defines his existence by the ease with which he is able to acquire stuff, and using these possessions set him apart from his neighbors. The production and consumption of material wealth, though, is requiring increasing amounts of the very things that make life possible on Earth: its land, its forests, oil and natural gas, iron, and, most importantly, water. China's economic rise is not only significant in the extent of humanity has it raised out of a one-dollar-a-day existence, but has also made the manufacture and acquisition of material goods so much more readily accessible to billions who didn't even dream of such wealth 20 years ago. China as "the Workshop of the World" has provided the impetus to the country's cities and factories that sprout from the ground in a matter of months, requiring iron and concrete superstructures, stunning amounts of power generation, and even increasingly profligate use of a substance even more precious than oil: water.

Though the bulk of China's urbanization will have wound down by the year 2025, its middle class will have grown to nearly a billion people. Jared Diamond wrote in a *New York Times* editorial that the industrialized societies are at a consumption rate of 32.[47] Analysts have observed countries in the developed world generally consume 32 times more materials and expels 32 times more waste than do countries in the developing world. So, the United States through its meat-heavy diet, its car culture, and its large houses that require all manner of heating and lighting, uses and then discards about 32 times more resources than the Bushmen of the Kalahari in Sub-Saharan Africa, who would rate a "1" on Diamond's scale. That used to be the case between the Western developed countries and China, too, at least until the mid-1990s, when China's economy kicked into high gear. Diamond cited China in 2007 at 11 on the consumption/waste scale, and rising.[48] The Chinese government and its citizens have their sights set on achieving the American dream of the "good life," *tout de suite*. There seems little in the way of lessons learned from the economic rise and dramatic falls of the Western nations that China considers relevant to its own development. Diamond writes: "China's catching up alone would roughly double world consumption rates. Oil consumption would increase by 106 percent, for instance, and world metal consumption by 94 percent."[49] If China and catch-up India were to acquire and consume in the same quantities as the U.S., the "real-feel" of the world would be as though 79 billion people were living on the face of the Earth, not the six billion currently residing in its fragile ecosystem.

Common sense dictates that there is only so much to go around in the way of oil, minerals, land, food, and especially water. Of course, science says, there is always a solution to be found, and the human race always has proven resourceful and inventive (as long as funding is sufficient, resources plentiful, and the political climate supportive). However, with the entry of China and, increasingly, India onto the global consumption stage donning the same models of unsustainability as their Western counterparts, nations and the global environment are entering a new stage of existence.

China in many ways is the world's "canary in the coal mine"—the caged bird that miners would use in historic times to indicate when gas and noxious fumes emitted underground would be able to overcome a worker, or become explosive. When the bird died, it was time to run to safety. China, representing nearly 20 percent of humanity, is pressing into unknown environmental territory that is unprecedented, at a rate never before seen in other countries. The stresses the country is placing on its resources and on its environment are particularly harrowing in light of the paucity of land available for the population pressures within its geographic borders. China is on the leading edge of humankind's consumption model of existence. Where it goes in its bid for Western-style modernization the world will have to follow, feeding her appetite in return for ecological deficits. For no matter the extent to which China is able to invest abroad to supplement its surfeit of land, food, oil, and iron, there will come a time when the world will simply be unable to give up any more to the country.

Joseph Tainter, an American historian and anthropologist, points out in his book, *The Collapse of Complex Societies*, that energy is the fundamental currency that finances a complex society. As long as a society has an abundant amount of energy in the form of food, labor (human and animal), and fuel, the society can invest in becoming more complex. However, complexity becomes less affordable as energy supplies reach their limit or actually decline. A prime example of this is Britain in the 1700s, which used wood as its primary source of energy. With the discovery of readily accessible and exploitable sources of coal, and the technologies to process the fuel into energy, Britain was able to consolidate industry in the British isles and extend its hegemony to half the known world at the time. Kerosene complemented coal as a fuel in the 1800s, replacing whale oil to heat buildings and manufacture products. China, however, chose as early as the fifteenth century to turn inward, increase its population, and ignore the technological achievements revolving around the acquisition and harnessing of new energy sources with which to take a society to a new level of complexity. China is just now digging itself out of that historic hole to catch up with the West.

China risks reliving its cycle of decline as natural resources within its borders and around the world dwindle and societies require ever more energy to maintain their complexity. Population pressures, middle class expectations for the affluent life, and scant resources may drive China to search for and develop an economically viable energy source that will allow it continued, uninterrupted existence at or above the level of modern consumerist societies. The source would have to be as dramatic a leap in energy output as coal is to wood, as a nuclear bomb is to a shipload of liquefied natural gas. The wind farms, solar panels, wave energy and biomass technologies that China is engineering now will merely allow China—and the rest of the world—to run in place, but not necessarily make a social, intellectual, and creative leap as dramatic as The Age of Enlightenment in the 1600s. Social and business models of sustainability will have to reshape China, too, to make more efficient use of old-world and new-world energy technologies.

Environmental political activist Dai Qing once told a reporter: "Under Chairman Mao, we often heard the slogan 'Humans must conquer Nature!' and that is still the mentality of so many people today—but gradually we are learning that human beings cannot conquer Nature and that this philosophy inevitably leads to disaster."[50]

A disaster that is avoidable.

END NOTES

1. "Chinese government names and shames land grabbing officials," *People's Daily*, December 11, 2007.
2. "Land Authority Inspects Irregular Cases," *China Economic Review*, November 21, 2007.
3. "Crackdown on Illegal Land Transfers," *China Economic Review*, September 18, 2007.
4. Zhao Huanxin, "Crop Deficit Recorded for 1st Time," *China Daily*, August 20, 2004.
5. "Outsourcing's Third Wave," *The Economist*, May 21, 2009.
6. David Smith, "The Food Rush," *The Guardian*, July 3, 2009.
7. Jonathon Watts, "China's Loggers Down Chainsaws in Attempt to Regrow Forests," *The Guardian*, March 11, 2009.
8. Jonathon Watts, "China Consumes Forests of Smuggled Timber," *The Guardian*, April 22, 2005.
9. Ibid.
10. Ibid.
11. Jonathon Watts, "China's Loggers Down Chainsaws in Attempt to Regrow Forests," *The Guardian*, March 11, 2009.
12. Andreas Lorenz and Wieland Wagner, "China's Poison for the Planet," Spiegel Online, January 2, 2007, http://www.spiegel.de/international/spiegel/0,1518,461828,00.html.
13. Derek Scissors, "China Imports Half its Oil," *BusinessForum*, Issue 6, 2008.
14. Ibid.
15. "Oil Prices May Rise on Chinese Demand," *China Economic Review*, January 29, 2010.
16. Carola Hoyos, "Burning Ambition," *Financial Times*, November 3,
17. Jad Mouwad, "China's Growth Shifts the Politics of Oil," *The New York Times*, March 19, 2010.
18. "Go West, Young Han," *The Economist*, December 21, 2000.
19. "In the Pipeline," *The Economist*, April 24, 2004.
20. "Energy for China," The Economist Intelligence Unit ViewsWire, July 12, 2007.

21. U.S. Energy Information Administration website report on China oil, http://www.eia.doe.gov/cabs/China/Oil.html, accessed November 9, 2009.

22. Carola Hoyos, "Burning Ambition," *Financial Times*, November 3, 2009.

23. Hilary Andersson, "China Is 'Fueling War in Darfur," BBC News, July 13, 2008, http://news.bbc.co.uk/2/hi/africa/7503428.stm.

24. Bill Powell, "It's China's World (We Just Live in It.)," *Fortune*, October 8, 2009.

25. "No Strings," *The Economist*, November 10, 2009.

26. "A Ravenous Dragon," *The Economist*, March 13, 2008.

27. "News in Brief," *Shanghai Business Review*, November 2009.

28. "A Ravenous Dragon,"*The Economist*, March 13, 2008.

29. "Testing their Metal," *The Economist*, October 22, 2009.

30. "News in Brief," *Shanghai Business Review*, September 2009.

31. Michael Wines, "Australia, Nourishing China's Economic Engine, Questions Ties," *The New York Times*, June 2, 2009.

32. "No Strings," *The Economist*, November 10, 2009.

33. Carola Hoyos, "Burning Ambition," *Financial Times*, November 3, 2009.

34. Patti Waldmeir and Peter Smith, "China Predicts Rare Earths Shortage," *Financial Times*, September 3, 2009.

35. "News in Brief," *Shanghai Business Review*, September 2009.

36. Ibid.

37. Sophie Taylor and Alison Leung, "China Attracts Private Companies to Provide Clean Water," *The New York Times*, March 27, 2008.

38. Emma Graham-Harrison, "China Drought Leaves 670,000 without Drinking Water," Reuters, April 13, 2009.

39. Andrew Batson, "China Cities Raise Water Price in Bid to Conserve," *The Wall Street Journal*, July 31, 2009.

40. Ibid.

41. "A Shortage of Capital Flows," *The Economist*, October 9, 2009.

42. Christine E. Boyle, "Understand Northern China's Water Crisis," GreenLeapForward,.com, January 30, 2009, http://greenleapforward .com//understanding-northern-chinas-water-crisis/, accessed December 15, 2009.

43. "A Shortage of Capital Flows," *The Economist*, October 9, 2009.

44. "The High Stakes of Melting Himalayan Glaciers," CNN.com, October 5, 2009.

45. "A Shortage of Capital Flows," *The Economist*, October 9, 2009.

46. Jamil Anderlini, "China: A Blast from the Past," *Financial Times*, December 14, 2009.

47. Jared Diamond, "What's Your Consumption Factor?," *The New York Times*, Jan 2, 2008.
48. Ibid.
49. Ibid.
50. Jamil Anderlini, "China: A Blast from the Past," *Financial Times*, December 14, 2009.

CHAPTER **6**

China 24/7

CONSTRUCTING THE FUTURE

"What if you hosted a parade and nobody came to watch?" I considered, nestled snuggly in the back seat of a local government sedan. About half a dozen government officials had earlier in the morning come to greet me when I landed at the new, hi-tech airport at Yantai, which is at the northernmost tip of Shandong Province. On a clear day, beachcombers can see the Korean peninsula to the northeast. That January morning in 2004, though, was not clear. A light mist swirled near the ground and seeped through my heavy coat. I was cold, and simply wanted to fly back to Beijing to the warmth and comfort of my hotel room.

The local government honchos represented local business interests and foreign investment promotion. Any Westerner they could entice into investing in the area would likely mean a promotion to greater political heights; hence, the four-car caravan that awaited me at the exit of the airport. No other cars were in sight. I settled into the back seat of the third black Volkswagen Santana from the front. The moment the doors slammed shut the cars lurched forward, police sirens blaring. The cars sped out of the airport grounds only slowly enough to keep to within the curve of the traffic loop. The escort hit the straightaway and accelerated. The cars' flashing lights parted the cold mist before us.

We drove along kilometers of newly finished highway. The only audience available to appreciate the spectacle was the phalanx of lamp posts that lined the road awaiting traffic. There were no cars on the road, though, no drivers to yank their vehicles to the side to make way for the screaming caravan, no passengers to gape at the performance. Yantai had built the highway, and now was waiting for the cars to come, the industry to support the cars, and the employees who would have enough disposable income to buy the cars and shop in the planned shopping centers that had yet to be built. Yantai was waiting to catch up with its cousins to the south, in the Yangtze River and the Pearl River Deltas—chassis for the two largest engines of economic development in China—Shanghai and Guangzhou, respectively.

Yantai would only have to wait another three years for its infrastructure investments to begin paying off. More foreign companies were moving into the area on a monthly basis—mostly Japanese and South Korean automotive and appliance makers. The central government had begun encouraging the migration of industry from east coast hubs to the interior through a combination of tax incentives, regulatory prohibitions, and improved transportation infrastructure. Commercial and residential high-rise construction projects by local developers studded its once pristine seashore, with jack hammers, dump trucks, and cement mixers kick-starting at dawn, then retiring near midnight. Vanity projects, and construction with strong government interests involved, worked round the clock in an exhausting pattern familiar to every Chinese citizen in the run-up to the year 2020.

Yantai, it seemed, was on the vanguard of an infrastructure development boom that by 2009 had enveloped every city and possible transportation route in China, with the prospect of continuing nonstop for the next 15 years. New highways, airports, sea ports, and even entire cities were rising to meet the looming century. The country was working seven days a week, 24 hours a day, to build the modern infrastructure it needed to graduate from being "the Workshop of the World" with most of its wealth concentrated on its east coast to a consumer-driven economy in which the bulk of its citizens enjoyed a middle-class lifestyle, no matter where they lived in China.

The implications for Western companies that invest in China's interior—as China's cities grow up and are laced together with a transportation infrastructure that Chinese intend to become the envy of the world—are manifold. It will mean greater and less costly access to unskilled labor, a more affluent population which benefits from the new industries in their area and is able to buy more domestically made products, and a logistics infrastructure that will make moving products and components throughout China and into the rest of Asia more cost-effective than it is today.

The central government's manic efforts to bring economic prosperity to neglected regions of the country to match the vitality of its east coast are Herculean. Yet, for the country's leadership to deny modernization to overlooked parts of the nation would be to widen even further the gap between rich and poor, and the east coast and the rest. Withholding government-financed infrastructure development, job creation, and market liberalization to the remaining 80 percent of the country would be to encourage discontent among hundreds of millions of disenfranchised citizens and foment mass protest—if not out-and-out revolt—against the Communist Party.

However, regionalism, parochialism, local cronyism, and the overall lack of sophistication among the local citizenry and government administrations collude to baffle coordinated and efficient use of resources and funds. It also means challenges loom ahead for foreign companies seeking immediate profitability in China's interior. Corruption, cultural inertia, fluid investment policies, and an untrained, collusive judiciary that believes in promoting local interests over protecting foreign investment rights present significant obstacles to Western companies that want to reap the benefits of the new economy rising.

It has taken the tectonic shock of the global economic downturn of 2008–2009 to kick-start China's makeover of its undeveloped regions. Ground zero for the transformation was southernmost Guangdong Province, where capitalism was once again able to take root after decades of political suppression.

Fouls and Strikes

The air was barely breathable when I left the confines of Dongguan's city limits to visit the outlying manufacturing districts. Dongguan is a major manufacturing center in Guangdong Province, near Hong Kong.

The municipality produces about 70 percent of the furniture exports to the international market. There are literally thousands of wood-product factories that stretch for kilometers in the outlying districts of Houjie and Daling Shan. The area is also well known for the manufacture of home appliances and the production of bootlegged DVDs. For the few days that I traveled among these districts, my eyes burned and my throat scratched from the constant pollution. In another district, the sand and grit from deforestation and the rubble that lined the avenues made it difficult to see my surroundings. Yet, Dongguan and all of Guangdong Province served as the first model for modernization ushered in during the early 1980s by Deng Xiaoping, China's leader from the late 1970s to early 1990s.

Guangdong has become famous as the center for production of shoes, toys, and electric appliances. The first factories in the region were originally Hong Kong and Taiwanese enterprises, which operated in an environment of lax environmental and labor regulations. The cavalier approach that the Hong Kong and Taiwanese businesses adopted became known as the Hong Kong model, synonymous with exploitation—of people, of resources, of society at large. As the test model for foreign direct investment into China, the region did not know to put into place policy controls that would regulate the stresses on the infrastructure and environment. Traffic jams created hours-long delays on the roadways; rivers, ponds, and lakes became foul with toxic waste; and the air became almost unbreathable in some areas. Mainland Chinese investors quickly learned the Hong Kong business model and appreciated the *laissez faire* environment that Guangdong offered, and followed suit with their own factories.

The Hong Kong model for Guangdong had effectively run its course by 2008. For 25 years, Chinese from the poorer, rural southern provinces had been flocking to Guangdong to work 16 hours a day for less than US$10. Hong Kong and Taiwanese investors reaped great profits from the lower costs of labor, preferential tax treatments for foreign investors, and lax regulation of pollutants.[1]

Chinese New Year in 2008 ushered in China's Perfect Economic Storm, which pounded the Hong Kong model until only the strongest factories were left operating. While I was huddled in Suzhou—a manufacturing center near Shanghai—snuggled warmly against the

60 centimeters of snow that assaulted central China, nearly a million migrant workers were trapped by the same elements in and around Guangzhou train station near Hong Kong. Guangzhou is the capital of Guangdong Province, and as such serves as a major manufacturing hub in South China. It was China's worst blizzard in 50 years and it happened during the busiest travel season in the world in absolute numbers. Outside of Guangzhou, there were hundreds of millions of more workers on their annual trek home for the traditional two-week holiday, who found themselves trapped in bus and train stations as well as on the road and rail. The meager savings that many of the factory workers had been able to scrape together since the last Chinese New Year holiday dissipated as they bought food during their nearly week-long wait at the stations or as they bought new tickets to find a way back home.

The deteriorating local economy compounded the region's challenges. Chinese factories were struggling with the decline of the American and European household purchasing power, as the collapse of the housing bubbles in the West began to evaporate individual wealth in the last quarter of 2007. Oil prices shot up to more than US$80 per barrel, forcing an increase in transport prices as well as in the prices of the plastics and chemicals upon which many of the Chinese low-end manufacturers depended.

Provincial governments in 2007 raised the minimum wage 20 percent to nearly US$100 per month. The rise in the wage floor put a further squeeze on low-cost producers, whose only comparative advantages with Southeast Asia were developed transportation and utilities infrastructure, and an abundant supply of labor from the countryside. Foreign investors in China—both Western and Asian— knew that with the advent of a new labor law to take effect from 2008, companies that had invested in China solely for its low-cost workforce would have to severely revise their low-margin business models. The Labor Law in China effectively made it illegal to hire workers without a contract, made it more expensive to fire workers, and put the onus on employers to find cause for termination. The new Labor Law severely tightened the noose round the necks of operators who squeezed out profits by exploiting workers whose every waking hour was nearly all spent working on the factory floor.[2]

The strands of other long-standing trends came together during the 2008 Spring Festival to finally tie the knot that would choke off businesses based on low-cost labor. Local governments along the eastern seaboard that wanted to upgrade the value of their industries increasingly denied entry to low-end manufacturers and began refusing renewal of business licenses for industries that were heavy polluters. The primary target for China central administrators and the provincial government was to upgrade the business environment in Guangdong Province, and to force out many of the businesses manufacturing low-end commodities such as shoes, textiles, toys, and cheap appliances. The central government had designated Guangzhou and Shenzhen as Services Outsourcing Hubs in 2007, two of only 10 others in the country at that time. Local governments wanted to capitalize on the higher corporate tax bases and lower resource consumption levels of information technology, research and development, and service sectors.

Other factors bolstered the strength of the Perfect Storm for Chinese manufacturers. For one, there was a backlash against poor-quality Chinese products bought in the United States and Europe. American and European buyers were realizing that cheaply made products from China came with a hidden cost—or, at least, a cost they were willing to ignore until it was too difficult to any longer keep at arm's length. There were also quality issues that resulted from a lack of buyer-implemented quality systems. Hence, by mid-2008, U.S. plaintiffs had launched scores of lawsuits against Chinese suppliers in the Pearl and Yangtze River Deltas seeking damages on products such as tainted toothpaste, poisoned pet food, lead-laced toys, fake milk products, and more. Just months before, the Chinese government had executed the former director for the Chinese equivalent of the U.S. Food and Drug Administration, Zeng Xiaoyu, for taking kickbacks and certifying products without proper testing.

The business environment worsened for export manufacturers throughout China as the West's economic downturn became a global economic catastrophe. In late 2008, the U.S. financial system froze, American companies laid off staff, and a sizable portion of homeowners in the U.S. saw the value of their homes plummet to less than what they were paying in mortgages. Americans could no longer afford to buy much of the goods produced in China. China's own export sector froze in response and Chinese consumers hoarded their cash. Millions of the migrant workers who had been able to retain work on the east coast suddenly found themselves out of a job—some, for the second time around that year. Protests flared up in Chinese cities—low-level, with only hundreds rallying at any given time—but central government saw the potential for mass unrest as the greatest in 20 years since the Tiananmen Square protests. Through 2009 and into 2010, the Chinese government ordered its banks to loosen their lending policies to state-owned enterprises, local governments, and private citizens. The fiscal stimulus accelerated development of transportation infrastructure and property development around the country, especially in the historically poor regions. Heavy construction projects unprecedented in ambition and numbers provided jobs and income for hundreds of millions of disenfranchised Chinese.

By late 2009, factory workers who used to travel to the east coast for work no longer had the need. About 70 percent of the migrant workers who lost their jobs earlier that year did not return to the coast.[3] Jobs and business opportunities abounded in their own small towns and counties. Income from the infrastructure projects, wages from mom-and-pop factories in outlying areas, as well as profits from small farms dramatically raised living standards in the countryside. Why, then, travel far away from family and likely into a form of slave-wage labor when one could more easily make as much, if not more, money nearer home? If there is one cultural secret foreign investors should know about Chinese, it's that Chinese like to be very near home.

Guangdong factories, in particular, were hard hit, often with only one worker available for every two jobs; contrast that with four workers competing for every three jobs in the heady days of 2007. Migrant workers, long marginalized in manufacturing hubs far from their hometowns, had gained a new freedom—the right to stay home to make a decent living. They grabbed their new opportunities with an inexhaustible gusto. They set about building airports, roads, ports, railways, and apartment buildings that would increase their wealth and help propel their society to superpower status.

THE ARTERIES OF A NATION

The flood of funds into the development of China's transportation infrastructure accelerated a master plan to develop regions outside the Yangtze and Pearl River Deltas that had been on the drawing boards of central government and local administrations since the beginning of the twenty-first century. China's leadership had been for some time aware that the country would need to invest heavily in roads, rail, air, and water ways to modernize the poorer parts of China. Transportation infrastructure, in particular, was the key to enticing investment into neglected regions and to giving locals the opportunities they needed to take jobs and build businesses in their otherwise isolated hometowns. One of the cities most isolated from the east coast throughout China's economic boom was Kunming, the capital of Yunnan Province.

Kunming is tucked in a mountain plateau with an average year-round temperature of a pleasant 24 degrees centigrade. Established more than 2,000 years before as an *entrepôt* for the portion of the Silk Road running through Burma and India, Kunming came back on the central committee's radar in 2007 as the future logistics and distribution center for goods traveling across China into Southeast Asia. Kunming became a prime target for an infrastructure makeover on a scale and pace that would see the city realize the economic vibrancy of its east coast cousins within a handful of years.

Kunming's main airport, originally built in 1923 and expanded multiple times, was small, worn, and congested with travelers when I first visited the city in 2007. Departures for many flights required passengers to descend dark, worn staircases with heavily scuffed walls to the ground floor of the airport, where the ceilings were low and the smell of jet fuel so strong in the lobby that I had to gasp for breath a minute at a time. In 2008, Kunming began building an international airport, which aims to become China's fourth-largest hub (after Beijing, Shanghai, and Guangzhou) and one of the world's top 80 airports in terms of the number of flights as well as passenger capacity and cargo handling by 2020. A light-rail network spidering the municipality would tie the airport to the downtown by 2015. The local government plans to have the first phase of the airport complete by the end of 2011. The Kunming airport project is just one of 15 airport-construction projects the Yunnan government plans on launching in the province. The airports will create an international transport network supporting the transshipment of goods from North Korea, Japan, and the interior of China into Southeast Asia.

The development of Yunnan's air network is part of a national effort to advance air travel throughout the country. In 2008, China planned to spend US$62.5 billion on building 97 new regional airports by 2020. Chinese planners also received orders to expand 73 airports and to relocate 11 more hubs. Northwest China's Xinjiang Uygur Autonomous Region planned an increase in the number of its airports to 20 from 16 in 2010. Meanwhile, north China's Inner Mongolia Autonomous Region, which is also included in the country's "Go West" Development Strategy, was to have 12 airports in 2010 and 18 by 2020. Infrastructure plans also involved expanding and improving the airports of Dalian, Shenyang, Changchun, and Harbin, as well as building new airports in the Changbai Mountains near the border with North Korea, the northwestern part of Jilin Province, and in the frigid reaches of the northern cities Mohe, Daqing, Jixi, Yichun, Arshan, and Erenhot.

The jump-start in Kunming's economic development is also bringing with it a host of challenges for its environment and its local society. Each time I tour Kunming, I am surprised at how poor the air quality is. Millions of cars without catalytic converters belch the noxious exhaust of leaded gasoline into the air. Kunming traffic is slow moving, congested, and often times blocked by incessant construction at what should be off-peak hours. During a visit in 2009, I had the misfortune of staying in a hotel that was near one of the many construction sites that pockmark the city. I found myself at 2 a.m. inserting plugs into my fatigued ears to block out the droning of machines and trucks in a pit nearby. China cannot find sleep even in its pristine mountains.

"Kunming still is the place Westerners come to when they want to get away from someone, or something," Matti told me. Matti was a Canadian-Finn who had lived in Kunming for 10 years. We were sitting outdoors at an open-air cafe called Salvador's. Salvador's sits at the crossroads of Wenlin Street and Wenhua Lane, a main center of activity for students who go to nearby Yunan University, and that is popular with the trendy Chinese as well as the youthful expat community. The cross streets are reminiscent of San Francisco's hip Haight-Ashbury district, with Chinese characteristics.

The two streets support numerous cafes, tea houses, restaurants—Sichuan, Xinjiang, Kunming local cuisine, Korean, Japanese, and American—and rather expensive boutiques catering to Western tourists. Next door to Salvador's at the time was a grunge and hip-hop clothing and accessories shop that was open air, like so many of the neighboring boutiques. Chinese skateboarders sporting dyed hair, baggy pants that slid down their narrow hips and outsized T-shirts with flaming skulls, endlessly practiced turns and jumps on skateboards the size of small ironing boards.

Kunming as a growing logistics center for manufactured goods was also a favored hub for the drugs trade into China, Matti and a couple American teachers explained to me. "A favorite drug around here is *tao pao,*" one California Bay Area native explained to me. "It's cheap, a few *mao* (毛, pennies) for a handful. It's an amphetamine that makes you super-aggressive and also hallucinate."

Kunming is very close to the Golden Triangle, a major narcotics-manufacturing region that encompasses Burma, Thailand, and Vietnam. Most of the drug lords in the region are tribesmen in isolated hills and mountains. They have their own armies, and factories in thatched huts hidden away in jungles. Government authorities in each of the countries have an uneasy alliance with the tribesmen, who are all but impossible to quell without an all-out war. Besides, the trade is just as lucrative for the authorities. Other popular drugs that come out of the area are heroin and ketamine, a pet tranquilizer apparently popular at Chinese discos ("I don't know how much fun that could be, though," a Kunming expat joked. "Everyone asleep on the sofas and the floors from doing too much pet tranquilizer!")

By 2015, Kunming will be a major thoroughfare and logistics hub between China and Southeast Asia. In 2009, the city was frenetically building 15 new bridges or overpasses to ease traffic congestion, as well as a 163-kilometer-long light-rail network to connect outlying towns with the downtown area. Plans at the time saw a high-speed rail link between Kunming and Shanghai, nearly 2,000 kilometers away. Westerners who had lived in Kunming for several years already found the slow pace of life that had drawn them to the city ebbing away because of the urban upgrade. "One day," one American resident told me while we sipped beers on the raised patio of Salvador's, "they're going to tear all this down." He gestured at the boutiques, cafes, and casual strollers around us. "Where to next, then?" I asked. He took another swallow of beer "Don't know," he said. "Kunming's unique."

Or rather, "was unique," I considered, and settled back in my chair to savor the moment.

ROAD WARRIORS

In the mid-2000s, Kunming began building new highways and improving older roadways in earnest to facilitate transport between Kunming and the South China coast (and ports such as Shenzhen and Shanghai), and in 2008 completed the Chinese stretch of the New Burma Road to India.

In 2009, China had roughly 3.5 million kilometers of road. More than half of that was low grade, however.[4] With only 53,000 kilometers of expressways in 2007, China's grand "interstate" highway plan involved having 80,000 additional kilometers of expressway built by 2020, surpassing the length of the continental United States interstate highway network. Two-thirds of national financing for roadways is slated for expansion into the central and western regions of China through the central government's so-called "Go West" program, launched in 2003. The aim of the program is to jump-start the economies of central China through massive infrastructure investment. The roads-infrastructure project has the aim of connecting all the towns and cities with populations greater than 200,000 throughout the provinces of Chongqing, Gansu, Guangxi, Guizhou, Inner Mongolia, Ningxia, Qinghai, Shaanxi, Sichuan, Yunnan, Xinjiang, and Tibet by 2020. The central government aims to have 82 percent of the population living within a 90-minute drive from an airport by 2020.

One of the most heavily populated yet most isolated regions in China has historically been Chongqing, stamped in the steep mountains of central China. Chongqing has served as the platform for the country's "Go West" economic development program since 2003, with the intention of making Chongqing a kind of Chicago of China's interior, linking the developed east coast with a forbidding interior. The city is perpetually shrouded by clouds and fog. It was the combination of rough terrain and lousy weather that made the area such an important post as China's capital during the Japanese invasion in the late 1930s through the mid-1940s. Japanese bombers found it near impossible through the impenetrable clouds to identify strategic targets to cripple.

Chongqing, despite its isolation, is the most heavily populated region in China at around 31 million people, giving it greater political leverage in its plans for economic development than other cities in

China's interior. The downtown area is perched at the intersection of the Yangtze and Jialing Rivers. At night, the city is beautifully illuminated along the Yangtze River with a rainbow assortment of lights, and the warm weather—even in winter—allows one to sit outside at one of the numerous restaurants that line the river and eat delicious fresh food cooked in the mouthwatering hot spices that make Sichuan cuisine so famous. Perhaps because of the juxtaposition of this city in the mountains or maybe because of its dynamic history, I have always enjoyed traveling to Chonqing. However, I have found doing business there challenging. Chongqing seems to exist in its own time-space bubble, probably because of its historic inaccessibility.

The most apt description of the Chongqing business environment that I have ever heard came from the president of a South Korean subsidiary of a U.S. company in the automotive industry while we were working on an investment project in the city. The American boss asked the president what it was like doing business in Chongqing. The Korean quipped: "Chongqing has twenty-first-century hardware and nineteenth-century software." Though China's transportation and information infrastructure was quickly developing, the insularity of the local culture had bred habits of doing business in ways that ran counter to international standards of transparency and fair play.

In 2009, Chongqing's mayor, Bo Xilai, supervised the arrest of more than 2,000 businessmen and women, judges, government administrators, and police who were all colluding with local gangs. The super-mafia controlled businesses in the province as wide-ranging as wholesale seafood to nightclubs, a privatized bus network, as well as the usual drugs and prostitution rackets. The news cemented Chongqing's reputation as the Wild West of China.

An American friend—I'll call him Jim—with whom I had worked in an advisory capacity on a project in Kunshan several years before, built a manufacturing operation in Chongqing in late 2008. Jim is a chaw-chewing, towering 1.9-meter Texan who cut his teeth as a general manager for an American *Fortune 500* manufacturer in the Taiwanese jungle of Kunshan, a 45-minute drive from Shanghai. During his time in the small city, he became hardened doing battle with entrenched government interests that had been lulled by the gray zone of business dealings by the overwhelming number of Taiwanese companies, many of which had been there since 1984. He quickly realized the Kunshan project was the proverbial walk-in-the-park within weeks of moving to Chongqing. I asked Jim why his new U.S. employer chose to put its factory in a township in the Chongqing municipality. He answered simply: "Natural gas." Then explained: "Natural gas in those parts is much less expensive than on the east coast." That seemed to be the company's primary concern during the site selection, which it had conducted before Jim had joined the company.

"The township [in Chongqing] in which they had chosen to locate the factory actually ran out of its allotment of natural gas halfway into the year [2007]," Jim continued. The promise of a wealth of natural gas had been the *only* reason the company had located the operation there. "It was even in the contract that the company would receive supplies of natural gas without interruption," Jim said. "So when the local government told me: 'So sorry, no more gas,' I was angry. One of the vice mayors of the township told me that if my company gave him nearly US$300,000, the local government could look the other way so that I could hook up to the lines of the next town over, which still seemed to have supplies."

"So I wrote letters directly to the Chongqing provincial government complaining about the township government reneging on the agreement and asking for kickbacks. I told them we were going to have to 'Come to Jesus' on this one, or I was going to advise the owner of the company to pull the investment out of Chongqing if they didn't live up to their end of the bargain." "Come to Jesus" in American parlance means to have an open and frank discussion, usually emotional, hopefully revealing, of the thoughts and intentions of all involved in the confessional.

"The meeting was pretty tense," said Jim. "I think these guys figured they could just mumble some apologies and I'd go away happy, since they'd given me the opportunity of an audience with them. But sometimes, there comes a point in time here in China when you have to jump up, kick the table over, and shout expletives to get things moving."

"Just don't do it very often!" he laughed.

The threat of pulling the investment out of Chongqing seemed to have been enough to get the quota of natural gas the company required. With just a couple weeks before he was to move to the newly built facility at the end of December 2007, Jim sent me an email: "My costs (other than labor) are no different here than in east China. If you want to save money out here, it is doable but you sacrifice your ethics and pay bribes—which I will not do."

The Wild West will live on for some time through Chongqing.

PORTS OF CALL

A major barrier to getting goods manufactured in inland cities like Chongqing out to China's coast for export is the country's lack of sea ports. The central government found the lack of ports a sizable bottleneck in sustaining the export sector's booming business for the five years in the runup to the global economic downturn, which started in 2008. International buyers had become frustrated by the lead times it would take to receive their goods from Chinese manufacturers. The same lack of ports and transshipment capacity for imports bedevils manufacturers and consumers in China's newly developing interior. The central government made port development a major infrastructure construction priority for provincial and city administrations in 2009.

Back along the east coast, though less than an hour's train ride from Beijing, Tianjin remained one of the orphans of China's rapid development for nearly 30 years after China opened itself to the world for business in the early 1980s. Each time I visited the huge city in the mid-2000s, I left with the impression that its place in central government planning as an ore-processing center, depot, and *entrepôt* for the country's mineral-rich northern reaches would be difficult to shake. Always gray with pollution, the rusted skeletons of factories too-long in use always left me depressed at the end of trips, despite the open and friendly character of the people. Once a colonial treaty port during the late 1800s and early 1900s—and later occupied by the Japanese during their incursion into China—Tianjin was an industrial powerhouse during Mao Zedong's reign over China. The center of the Bohai Region, Tianjin is one of the few municipalities in China that has provincial level consideration, along with Beijing, Shanghai, and Chongqing; that is, the city administrators report directly to the central government as a province—or state—in and of itself. Many theories have circulated about the moribund economic state of Tianjin and the Bohai Rim, including a political elite in Beijing that did not want Beijing's own development overshadowed by its northern neighbor, and Tianjin's own people preferring to live life a little more slowly than its uppity neighbor, Beijing. Whatever the reasons for its decades-long dormancy, in 2007 infrastructure investment kicked off mightily with the construction of a railway passage that linked Tianjin Port directly to west China. In 2009, Tianjin began expansion of its port to handle an additional 23 million tons of cargo annually in addition to the nearly 200 million tons it managed in 2009. The docks in the US$600 million project will be able to take on 300,000-ton bulk carriers.[5]

Northeast China, as the traditional rust belt of the country, was a hive of port construction activity. Qingdao, southeast of Tianjin on the coast of Shandong Province, facing South Korea, announced plans in the summer of 2010 to build the world's largest iron-ore handling terminal at a cost of US$50 billion, to be completed by 2030.[6] Hong Kong investors made a deal in 2009 to plow more than US$2 billion into Yantai's infrastructure development, including the Yantai West Port Construction Project, San Tuti Container Wharf of Yantai Port, as well as two 50,000-ton berths in the Penglai Port Area.[7] Dalian, which lays opposite Yantai across the Bohai Sea, had under construction in 2010 a container terminal and crude oil terminals in Dayaowan and Changxing Islands that could manage 300,000-ton deadweight vessels.[8] In the south, in Guangdong Province, Shenzhen began construction of six ports: Liantang Port, Longhua Railway Port, Fujian Guangzhou-Shenzhen-Hong Kong Passengers Port, Dachan Gulf Harbor Port, Nanao Tourism Port, and a port connecting the airports in Shenzhen and Hong Kong via an undersea tunnel.[9]

In mid-2008, I visited one of the most ambitious port projects I had ever seen in China: the Meishan Free Port, which involved the remaking of an entire island to service some of the largest cargo ships and cruise liners in the world. The last few kilometers into China's newest free trade port were spent slowly driving on a temporary bridge tiled with thick steel plates followed by winding gravel roads. Visitors driving along those last tortuous bends had to make way for the constant stream of dump trucks returning from filling the surrounding ocean with landfill. By 2010, the small island off the northeastern coast of Zhejiang, an hour's drive east of Ningbo city, would transship cargo for Zhejiang Province, Anhui Province, Jiangxi Province, and Fujian Province. Meanwhile, Yangshan Free Trade Port just to the north of Meishan would handle many of the containers coming down the Yangtze River from river port towns, and north China, including Jiangsu Province, Shandong Province, and Henan Province. Yangshan port is based on a small island off the coast of Shanghai, connected by a 32-kilometer-long bridge, the longest sea bridge in the world when it was completed in 2005.

Ningbo Meishan Free Trade Port Area was the fifth free trade port area that China's central government approved to be built, following Yangshan, Tianjin Dongjiang, Dalian Dayaowan, and Hainan Yangpu, all completed by the time Meishan began construction. Though the island is only about 27 square kilometers, with seven kilometers of coastline, its shores are naturally deep waterways that require little dredging, and a logical supplement to Beilun Port, a network of ports on the northern shore of Zhejiang Province. Beilun ranked second of all ports in China since 2000, and fourth place in the world, in terms of the total capacity of cargo that moved through its berths, according to Ningbo administrators.

Through an extensive landfill project, the local government plans to enlarge the island to 36 square kilometers. The island already had a population of 150,000 when the project began shortly before my visit. The primary industries had been fishing and salt processing. I saw the footprints of old salt-processing facilities along the rough route to the government offices, on the east coast of the island.

"The advantage of free trade ports is that ships can dock, offload their cargo and processing can be done right at the port, then reloaded on other ships without customs duties paid and VATs [Value Added Tax] tabulated," according to Jeffrey Casper Yu, a senior administrator in the Promotion Bureau for the Free Port. I had met Jeffrey nearly five years before in the Ningbo Free Trade Zone, and already knew he had a great deal of experience in developing such bonded zones in China. We were eating seafood caught nearby and served up in rustic surroundings at a restaurant near the government office—the only eatery for miles around. "Another point is that domestic companies that sell into a free trade port can apply for a VAT rebate," he explained, "while those that sell into free trade zones are not eligible."

Ultimately, the island was to have three bridges spanning the half kilometer of water that separated it from the Mainland. The makeshift bridge over which I had passed would disappear, Jeffrey said: "The island will serve several roles: as a port logistics hub; to support service industries such as customs, port affairs, ship inspections, finance, law firms, audit firms, and the like; tourism—including the development of an international cruise ship port in the north of the island; and an exhibition center to show off import and export commodities, among others." The island's authorities also planned to entertain commercial and logistics real estate projects.

The first phase of the port was put into operation in 2010, which included two 100,000-ton container berths, as well as the completion of Meishan Bridge, the construction of a main thoroughfare Meishan Boulevard, and the Container Truck Highway. By 2020, the port would be complete and in full operation, with an expected annual throughput of about six million twenty-foot equivalent units (TEU), accelerating the export of Chinese manufactures to world markets. Port infrastructure development has not only stimulated the local economies and brought hundreds of thousands of jobs for able-bodied dock workers, but also has served as direct interface between Chinese manufacturers and international buyers, and, increasingly, between Chinese consumers and international sellers. Without port development, China would have little chance at developing the wealth and access to markets it needs to become a superpower.

RAILROADED

A major impediment to getting goods from the interior of China to the ports are transport links that make the conveyance of cargo into and out of the country fast and efficient. The rail links also will prove over time to become important in distributing goods from international markets—and even other regions of China—to would-be buyers. Despite the huge economic boom China experienced after acceding the World Trade Organization in 2001, its entire rail system since then has been less than adequate in circulating people and cargo throughout the country. From 2010 through 2012, the central government plans to spend more than US$1 billion upgrading its rail system and building new infrastructure, according to Vice Railway Minister Wang Zhiguo. By the end of 2009, China had 86,000 kilometers of railway, second only to the United States; by 2012, that will have increased to 110,000 kilometers. The United States has 260,000 kilometers of rail. The U.S., however, does not yet have the high-speed tracks that China's state-owned railway construction companies are laying, which included 13,000 kilometers of tracks serving 42 passenger lines.[10] The average speed of the bullet trains was clocked at 350 kilometers an hour; Japan's *shinkansen* rapid rail travel at 300 kilometers an hour by comparison. The bullet train linking Wuhan in Hubei Province with Guangzhou in 2009 compacted a 10.5-hour train ride into one lasting less than three hours. High-speed trains originating in Beijing will be able to reach most provincial capitals within eight hours. The central government plans involve the high-speed railways covering 80 percent of China's domestic flight network by 2020, connecting 70 percent of its key cities.

Not only would the Western regions see the rail network nearly double to 40,000 kilometers by 2020, but a bit of high-speed track laid between Shanghai and Hong Kong also would reflect a further, significant thaw in relations between the Mainland and Taiwan.

One of the most significant rail-line upgrades in 2010 took place in Fujian Province, the middle of which was once an economic no-man's land born of *realpolitik*. Over small cups of dark, rich Pu'er tea picked from a nearby tea grove, local officials of the small town of Putian gave me a lesson in geopolitics and its relationship with macroeconomics. Putian is on the coast, centrally located between the provincial capital Fuzhou in the north and Xiamen to the south. Xiamen is about 650 kilometers to the north of Hong Kong. On a clear day, one can see Taiwan from the shore. At the time of my visit in 2007, Putian's most notable claims were of being a major wood-processing center, and of having the highest density of tea shops of any city I have ever been to in China, most of which were open-air, mom-and-pop concessions that could seat no more than five or six people at a time.

Putian government administrators pointed out to me that the economy of Fujian Province was purposely ignored for more than 50 years by the central government in Beijing, which refused to plow billions of dollars in infrastructure development into a region that had a high probability of becoming a war zone should the Mainland and Taiwan take up arms against one another. Approval for economic development of the region had to come from the highest level of power in China in 2006 as relations with Taiwan began to thaw. Projects to build high-speed railways, new and expanded ports, and a highway system in the mountainous interior all kicked off, with little time to waste. The hindered economic development of the region was why Fujian people made up such a high proportion of Chinese illegally trafficked to the West's Chinatowns. The slave wages they would be making in sweatshops and restaurants in the West were still higher than any standard they could imagine in their hometowns—even after subtracting loan payments to mafia gangs and to family members who awaited their return. By 2012, passengers should find that a train ride from Shanghai to Hong Kong along China's southern coastline will take only eight hours, instead of the 20 hours the trip used to require during the Cold War between the Mainland and Taiwan.

The development of China's rail system will integrate China's east coast with the rest of the country to distribute wealth and resources in a way the country has never before experienced in its long history. Factories that are finding the economic and environmental stresses of remaining on the east coast will decide moving inland will be good for business—for both the export and domestic markets. With more workers staying closer to home, where salary levels are a fraction of those on the coast; and with logistics costs falling as transport links mature, China's manufacturing sector will receive an unexpected boost in profits as they adapt to the new lay of the land.

CHINA SHELL GAME

Despite the excitement surrounding transportation-infrastructure development that will tie China together like never before in its history, Chinese people hold residential property ownership closest to their hearts. If there is any sort of infrastructure-construction project in China that literally runs round the clock, it is real estate construction, residential and commercial, mostly high-rises.

An apartment-complex manager in Suzhou explained to me about the high-rise units just in front of us. "Those sell for more than 10 million yuan each [US$1.2 million]," he said, his round face excited at the prospect that the neighborhood was on Suzhou's high-value property map. Suzhou is an hour-and-a-half drive to the west of Shanghai. The apartments faced a medium-size lake, around which scores of other high-rises had gone up. He pointed at the new construction just a few hundred meters from where we stood, where high rises in various stages of completion saw a hum of ant-like activity. The site had awoken me the last year every morning at 6 a.m. as heavy machinery prepared the site for the work of the day. The construction site quietened around 10 p.m. every night, unless the workers had concrete to pour, which was an all-night affair. "Those have all sold out, and were even more expensive," the manager droned on. Some of them did not even have lake views. It would be years before anyone ever moved into the concrete husks—if they would be occupied at all.

Even one of China's leading property developers admitted the property market in the country was distorted. "Real estate prices should only go up because people want to actually use the space, but at the moment we can see more and more empty buildings across the whole country and in every real estate segment," Zhang Xin said. Zhang Xin is Chief Executive of Soho China, one of the country's most successful privately owned property developers. She built her fortune in China's explosive real estate market.

"In Manhattan, they have vacancy rates of 10 to 15 percent and they feel like the sky is falling, but in Pudong [the business district in Shanghai] vacancy rates are as high as 50 percent and they are still building new skyscrapers," she said in an interview with *Financial Times*. "If you look at GDP growth, China looks like a new engine driving the global economy, but if you look at how growth is being created here by so much wasteful investment, you wouldn't be so optimistic."[11]

The property-development virus with which the central government inoculated the economy in the summer of 2008 quickly spread to the parts of China that had been neglected during the boom leading up to the global economic downturn that year. In every city I have visited in China since the outbreak of Severe Acute Respiratory Syndrome (SARS) in late 2002, I have seen stretches of empty, newly built property, some of which still remains unoccupied. Overcapacity has resulted in swathes of residential and commercial real estate remaining empty for years and that will become part of a growing inventory of city blocks and entire districts that are devoid of people, of businesses, and of government services.

Some of China's more remote areas even have entire cities, newly built, that are in want of residents, businesses, and government administration. Just outside Kunming, construction of a new town called Chenggong began in 2003. Now, the city sports every sign of Western modernity that an urban center could boast: office high-rises, residential apartment blocks, banks, a high school with an indoor swimming pool, and government offices.[12] However, the town is completely empty of people. Kangbashir, the city center of Ordos, a coal-mining center in Inner Mongolia, is 25 kilometers from the city proper. Kangbashir is nearly empty, too, though many have bought apartments in the city as investments.[13]

Many analysts have argued that with the central government's emphasis on moving its 800 million citizens from the countryside into urban centers, it is inevitable that towns like Chenggong will one day show signs of life. However, that is no guarantee, as no one—including both Chinese government officials or international observers—are sure of just how much empty capacity the country has. Many of the projects that local government officials and property developers hatch between them have little to do with placement and durability of structures that make sense from a livability and longevity point of view. Many local government officials are rotated out of their positions to other cities within five years of their posting, leaving any fiscal messes due to a lack of return on the investments to future administrators. Little thought goes into the utility of new property in China, with high-rises rammed up next to loud, polluted elevated highways, and cities erected far from people's work and businesses.

Nonetheless, many families pool their personal savings to invest in second and even third apartments in their hometowns and other cities, which then lie vacant. Property developers throughout China construct the buildings but leave apartments as empty concrete shells without power and water. Strict Chinese financial regulations mean investing in property and the stock markets are the only activities in which Chinese can make their money work for them. Families intend to "flip" the apartments at the height of specious market valuations to make money off the empty shells. Most of the real estate property that developers prefer to build are relatively expensive for city dwellers—costing as much as 20 times an annual salary—and are out of reach for the hundreds of millions of people that the central government is culling from the countryside to take up residence in the cities.

Li Daokui, a professor of economics at Tsinghua University and a member of the Chinese central bank's monetary policy committee boldly announced in the summer of 2010 that the Chinese property market was even more dangerously perched than the U.S. market had been before its housing bubble collapsed. He argued that while Americans were fulfilling the "American Dream" of buying a home, Chinese believe home ownership a necessity. The rapid and artificially stimulated inflation of housing property values in China had left the overwhelming majority of Chinese without the wherewithal to address that necessity. If housing remained so stratospherically out of reach of average, hard-working Chinese who were trying to play by the rules that clearly were bent to the advantage of those in power, the blatant inequity could ignite social discontent on a massive scale.[14] Of course, then, if the Chinese residential market was to see a correction in valuations as dramatic as what the United States and the United Kingdom experienced in 2008, new-money homeowners could find their investments turned to plaster-dust. A major housing recession in China before the year 2020, when it is expected most housing will be built, would be cause enough for China's growth to seize up. On the upside: early morning walks marred for years by the incessant din of construction would once again be sublime.

THE BIG GAMBLE

By the beginning of 2010, some economic and government analysts questioned whether the increase in infrastructure development throughout the country was warranted from the latter part of 2008 onward. They considered whether the economic fundamentals supported the more than US$2 trillion in loans that flew from banks during the global economic downturn in 2009 to early 2010, much of which went toward infrastructure and property development. During that time, infrastructure investment went from about 25 percent of China's GDP to nearly 50 percent, an investment-to-GDP ratio the same as Thailand's when it was on the brink of the Asian Financial Crisis of 1997–98.[15] Though China certainly has isolated regions in need of infrastructure development, a measure called the "incremental capital/output ratio" shows that Chinese investment has been highly inefficient. Japan's investment boom in the 1980s saw a ratio of three, while China's—during its less profligate period from 1991–2003—saw a ratio of about four. After the fiscal stimulus of 2009–10, the ratio went to over six, a warning signal that the heavy investment in infrastructure was not providing the returns the country needed to remain productive, according to Yu Yongding, an economist at the Chinese Academy of Social Sciences.[16]

No one seems quite sure when the country will see a payback in productivity gains from the new railways and highways, nor when enough cars will be on the roadways to pay the exorbitant tolls between cities and provinces to recoup costs, nor when there will be enough companies to fill the hectares of vacant office space so property developers would break even. Government vanity projects abounded at the close of the twenty-first century's first decade, such as the replica of the U.S. White House in a remote town in Anhui Province, meant to serve as a local district office. Eventually, the town mayor was subsequently arrested for graft and waste of government funds on the construction project, which cost 30 million yuan (US$4.5 million).

By any account, it will take China at least a decade to see an economic return on its extensive investment in transportation and residential infrastructure. The most difficult challenge for central and local governments will be to steer the economy clear of serious slack periods of activity, between the time when local projects are completed and when they can be monetized. Given that governments throughout the country started many of their infrastructure projects in mid-2009, when the central government ordered the banks to suspend controls on lending, a great many of them should wind down at about the same time, about mid- to late 2011. Should a critical mass of such projects come to fruition at the same time with minimal—if any— returns on investment, banks will find themselves under tremendous stress to recoup their loans. The rate of nonperforming loans could approach 30 to 40 percent of total assets under management, an insupportable condition that Chinese banks had experienced 10 years before. After breaking into the piggy bank to shore up the economy through the global financial crisis of 2009 by investing in transportation and housing infrastructure on a scale unprecedented in history, China's banks would have little room for maneuver should another dramatic economic downturn occur and its economy require successive jolts of fiscal adrenaline before 2020.

China may then have to grapple with an eternal economic lesson it has not had to confront during the boom times of the past 30 years of infrastructure construction: pay now, or pay more later.

END NOTES

1. Elaine Kurtenbach, "Rising Costs Squeeze Chinese Factories," Associated Press, February 22, 2008.
2. Tom Mitchell, "Factories Face Survival of the Fittest," *Financial Times*, February 25, 2008.
3. "Situations Vacant,"*China Economic Review*, November 2009.
4. Emma Graham-Harrison, "China says Needs Extra Million KM of Roads by 2020," Reuters, November 16, 2007.
5. Guo Changdong, "Tianjin Port Launches Ore and Coal Docks," *China Daily*, July 29, 2007.
6. "China Port of Qingdao to Build Largest Iron Ore Terminal," Dredging Today.com, August 30, 2010, accessed September 10, 2010, http://www .dredgingtoday.com/2010/08/30/china-port-of-qingdao-to-build-worlds-largest-iron-ore-terminal/.
7. Liu Yi Yu, "Yantail Gets $2.2 Billion from HK Investors for 33 Projects," *China Daily*, July 16, 2009.
8. Zhu Chengpei and Zhang Xiaomin, "Dalian Growing as Shipping Center," *China Daily*, January 7, 2009.
9. Zhan Lisheng, "Shenzhen Plans to Build Six New Ports," *China Daily*, September 1, 2008.
10. "Beijing's Rail Ambitions Right on Track," *The Malaysian Insider*, December 18, 2009, http://www.themalaysianinsider.com/world/article/Beijings-rail-ambitions-right-on-track/, accessed March 13, 2010.
11. Jamil Anderlini and Tom Mitchell "Fears of China Property Bubble," *Financial Times*, November 18, 2009.

12. Geoff Dyer, "China: No one Home," *Financial Times*, February 21, 2010.
13. Kevin Hamlin, "China's Desert Ghost City Shows Property 'Madness' Persists," Bloomberg, June 23, 2010, http://www.bloomberg.com/news/ 2010-06-23/china-s-desert-ghost-city-shows-property-madness-as-buyers-pay-in-cash.html, accessed June 25, 2010.
14. Geoff Dyer, "China Property Risk is Worse Than in US," *Financial Times*, May 31, 2010.
15. Geoff Dyer, "China: No One Home," *Financial Times*, February 21, 2010.
16. Ibid.

CHAPTER 7

China, at Your Services

SERVICES RUN-DOWN

Every night just a few hours after closing, patients and their families and friends queue in front of the Xiangya Hospital in Changsha, the capital of Hunan Province. It's considered one of the best hospitals in the city, established by a Yale-educated American doctor in 1906. Yang Yan had been waiting at the door with her husband and his mother since 2 a.m. They had to be in line early to win the race to the clerks' windows, where they could get tickets for her husband and mother-in-law, who needed to see doctors for their ailments. The hours of waiting outside in the November drizzle wore down Yang Yan's stamina, and the crush of hundreds of bodies pressing her into the locked glass doors began to hurt. At 5:30 a.m., the guards inside the entrance unlocked the doors and stood aside. Hundreds of people stormed the lobby, running as fast as they could to the ticket windows. Young, healthy men also competed for the coveted "passports" to see a doctor; it was their job. These gangs would always be the first at the windows to obtain as many of the precious few tickets as they could, and then force patients to buy the tickets for about US$40 each. Their customers were the ill, the handicapped, the indigent, and the elderly.[1] Yang Yan was not fast enough, nor strong enough to keep up with the crowd.

Someone shoved her from behind to catch up; another elbowed her aside to gain advantage. She fell, and the crowd continued to run for the windows. Around her, over her, on her they trampled. After a couple of minutes, the stampede subsided. A pool of indifference opened up around her. Yang Yan stood, wracked with pain, limped through the crowd looking for her husband and his mother. She found them near the window; they also had been pushed aside. Yang Yan told her husband her shoulder was broken. Knowing that they were defeated, Yang Yan's husband turned away from the ticket stations, escorted his wife with his mother in tow to the emergency ward. Neither he nor his mother would be receiving treatment that day for their own ailments.[2]

Many public hospitals in China—especially those considered to deliver the best care—are literally overrun with patients every morning. Conventions we take for granted in the West, like patient confidentiality, privacy, and customer-centered care, are far-removed from the realities of health-care delivery in China. It is little wonder that in such a frustrating system for patients and their loved ones, in 2006—the last year the nation's Health Ministry published statistics on hospital violence—attacks by patients or their relatives injured more than 5,500 medical workers, according to *The New York Times*.[3] Shenyang, in northern China, reported 152 "severe conflicts" between patients and doctors in 2009.[4] The Chinese health-care service industry is in sore need of reform. Indeed, most of its service sector requires an overhaul, if not outright development. Services broadly include any business activity that does not involve the manufacture of goods, such as health care, finance and banking, telecommunications, software development, consulting, retail, hospitality, and more.

The service sector in China has been growing on average about 10 percent a year since 2000. From 1990 to 2004, though, the service sector as a proportion of China's GDP increased only modestly from 34 percent in 1990 to about 40 percent in 2004, where it has held steady through the rest of the decade. The sector actually lost ground to manufacturing and infrastructure investment. Industrialized countries such as Japan, Germany, and the U.K. have service sectors that contribute upward of 70 percent of their country's wealth. The United States derives nearly 80 percent of its wealth from service industries (it is a nation of lawyers, doctors, and accountants after all), which, since 2003, have accounted for nearly 80 percent of the nation's employment.[5]

The group of Chinese *apparatchiks* that are keen on economic reform understand China requires a robust service sector to take the economy to the next level of wealth creation, and make the country less dependent on exporting goods to other countries. In particular, the service sector is more labor-intensive than the manufacturing sector, which is attractive for its low barriers to entry (a Chinese family only needs to pool its income to buy a plastics-injection mold machine to make toys), and ready buyers in both China and abroad. Services, however, requires education, skills gained through experience, and attention to customer requirements.

However, the Chinese leadership is averse to diminishing its prospects for keeping the economy growing at near or above eight percent GDP growth annually. The government believes that with the eight percent benchmark, it will be able to generate enough new jobs to keep its citizens satisfied with economic opportunities. For the past 20 years, the engines of growth have been manufacturing and infrastructure development. Infrastructure development in particular— especially after the injection of nearly US$2 trillion in bank loans during 2009 and 2010—is an easy way for a society in need of buildings, roads, bridges, railways, and airports to generate jobs. Expanding service-related jobs is more difficult and takes time.

So what's in it for countries such as the United States, Russia, or any of the nations of European Union for China to change its dependence on manufacturing to services? A better-educated workforce, greater wealth and mobility for its citizens, and broader social stability. Better-educated employees will likely know more about the outside world than farmers and machine operators, hopefully nudging its leadership in more constructive forms of engagement with the rest of the world. Meanwhile, in order for China to implement policies that encourage the development of a service sector, Beijing will have to dismantle government policies that give the country's manufacturing firms an unfair advantage over competitors in producing goods for its domestic and export markets. Elimination of export subsidies, revaluation of an artificially low currency exchange rate that defies market forces, and greater emphasis on enforcement of environmental regulations will force low-end manufacturers out of business. Factories will need to increase productivity to remain competitive on world markets, which implies using fewer workers to do more.

Meanwhile, a more developed service sector will absorb more people of working age than manufacturing ever could. Fields such as hospitality—hotels, restaurants, spas, tourism—and finance and banking, can potentially mobilize far more human energy than a company that can no longer make widgets the country has vast stockpiles of and no longer desires.

Calcified social structures, mercantilist business models, and a historic aversion to transacting intangibles like services have China struggling to create a service sector that understands and efficiently exploits economies of scale, provides its workers adequate skills training, and upgrades standards of customer service. Hospitality, retail, and banking and financial service offerings are in dire need of substantial investment and expertise in recruitment, training, and talent development of their most important asset, human resources. Chinese business, however, still considers staff to reside on the liabilities side of their balance sheets, an expense to keep as low as possible.

SCARY HEALTH CARE

Of all the service industries in China, health care arguably has the most intractable issues. The root of China's health-care problems is that China has too many people, too few hospitals, and too few doctors and nurses making too little money, within a business and management environment that harkens back to a Soviet-style bureaucracy born in the 1950s. The greatest disadvantage of the health-care industry is that it is state-run, making procedures a bureaucratic nightmare and every service provider a bureaucrat. At the same time, however, its greatest advantage is that it is state-run. When China's central government gets behind the reformation of one of its sectors, transformation is typically swift and wholesale.

"It would be sensational to say I witnessed a rape scene last weekend while waiting for a health checkup at a Beijing hospital," Chen Weihua wrote in his *China Daily* column.[6] "But what flashed before my eyes was truly horrifying. I saw a doctor conducting a rectal examination on a man in front of three of his colleagues, without any curtain drawn for privacy." Chen's experience was more the rule than the exception in the small, cramped doctors' offices in which most examinations in Chinese public hospitals occur. On more than a few occasions, I have gone for an examination and had an audience of as many as six Chinese crammed into a room no larger than five square meters commenting on the doctor's diagnosis of my ailment. The Chinese in general—with the exception of Chen—seem not to mind the intrusion on their privacy. The doctor pokes, prods, and asks questions of the patient at the head of the line. The patient duly answers, while all in attendance listen intently, sometimes commenting out loud to a neighbor their thoughts about the diagnosis. Privacy is the exception—or for the exceptional—in China. Typically, doctors' offices are also examination rooms they share with another doctor, desks in opposition. Sometimes there is an examination table tucked into an alcove—with or without the prized privacy curtain, depending on the medical specialty. Whitewashed walls are usually heavily scuffed with the traffic of time, while floors maintain the same level of grime over the years, despite—or because of—daily moppings with a solution that approximates used dish water, though with less soap.

One visit I made to the best public hospital in my adopted home of Suzhou—Suzhou No. 2, a designation made in the tradition of a central-planned economy—elicited amused chuckles from onlookers as I explained to the doctor in his cramped office that I was in agony whenever I turned my head or lifted my arm. He pulled at my arm, pushed at my head, and sagely announced I needed an X-ray. He scribbled something cryptic in a flimsy blue book—the same sort I used to write essays in college—that was given to me by the cashier after waiting in line for 15 minutes, and told me to return to the cashier.

The cashier in a Chinese hospital not only takes patients' money, but performs triage on patients as well (amazing what can be diagnosed through smeared plexiglass), directing them to the appropriate department after hearing what the ailment is. A different cashier than the first collected my fee for an X-ray and and gestured me in the general direction of the lab. Again, I was greeted by scuffed walls, a bemused audience (watching through reinforced glass), and disengaged technicians. After an hour's wait, they gave me the oversized films and told me to return to the cashier to pay for the doctor's diagnosis of the X-rays. After queuing, paying, waiting, watching the diagnosis of an elderly man who could barely speak and then a middle-aged woman who could barely walk, I presented the X-rays to the physician who had told me to get the X-rays in the first place. He pushed the transparencies into a light box affixed to the wall next to his desk, and jabbed a stubby finger at the point where two vertebrae were hunched toward each other. "You have a pinched nerve," he said, again, sagely.

"Uh, yeah," I answered, less than bemused, "I know. What can you do about it?"

He scribbled in my blue book, pushed it over to me: "You have to pay first, then I can tell you."

I wanted to say, "You're kidding!" or "That's ridiculous!" Instead, I just thanked him and pushed my way through my audience to get out of the hospital. The typical service cycle in a hospital involves a doctor at the end of the exercise prescribing drugs, anyway, a percentage of the cost of which he receives in his otherwise paltry paycheck. So, I opted for an American chiropractor who worked at a clinic in Shanghai that specifically serviced Western expats. I was up and about pain-free three weeks later, having paid only once, each time, at the end of each session.

Even after patients are able to see a doctor, cultural and social conditioning give rise to a surfeit of poor quality service. Culturally, Chinese are conditioned to obey authority, even if the advice goes against common sense ("Don't drink too much coffee," some Chinese doctors tell expectant mothers, "or your child's skin will come out black!") Doctors are effectively government workers, and every Chinese citizen has experience with eponymous government workers making their lives miserable through ignorance, nonchalance, impatience, or just because they're in a bad mood. Chinese citizens have no conditioning about managing their relationship with health-care providers, as many in other cultures do. In the West, while still revering health-care professionals, we are taught to question authority and to even walk away when we feel the doctor is wrong or ignorant of what really ails us. Also in the West, we are conditioned to get that ever-important "second opinion" from another doctor. In China, people do not even form the words "second opinion" in their minds, let alone express the sentiment to the primary doctor. The hierarchical aspects of Chinese culture preempt any ideas of questioning the declarations of the highly educated, even if those in authority trained in a latrine in the mountains of Sichuan to obtain their credentials.

China's new-found wealth has not been spent yet on reforming its moribund health-care services sector. Most hospitals in China have yet to automate their administrative systems. Patients must pay for every medical transaction because most citizens do not have medical insurance; even if they do, the hospitals are not equipped to process insurance claims *before* the patient sees the doctor. Some hospitals automatically deduct the amount of unpaid patients' bills from the paychecks of attending physicians whose charges skip out of the hospital without settling their bills. One Chinese doctor blogged the hospital for which he worked had already docked him three months' salary for the unpaid bills of a patient when yet another patient had stolen away without making payment. He lamented how, under such a system, he was unable to save money.[7]

China does have private alternatives to the government-run hospitals, however. Nearly three million patients were served by private hospitals in 2007—almost double the number served in 2003.[8] Most private hospitals in China's largest cities have been established to serve expats and rich Chinese; local residents, however, consider them exorbitant. For instance, the birth of my own son through VIP services in a public hospital cost about US$1,600, while the birth of a British friend's child cost 10 times that at a private hospital in Shanghai.

I went to one such clinic at Tomorrow Square in downtown Shanghai, to have a sports injury looked at. Tomorrow Square is a luxurious complex of hotel rooms, serviced apartments, conference and meeting facilities, boutiques, and anything else the developers could think of that was expensive to consume, which included the World Link clinic. Its lobby was more like that of a posh hotel than of a medical establishment. Young, attractive Chinese women neatly adorned in clinic garb sat behind a tall, marble reception desk. In the center of the small lobby, middle-aged Westerners and sophisticated Chinese sunk themselves into comfortable sofas and high-backed chairs. I sat down in a chair that faced the entryway. My feet sunk deep into long-haired shag carpet. Beside me, along the wall facing the reception desk, a Chinese husband and wife sat speaking with each other, voices muted.

I could tell they were not from the Mainland. The husband wore a button-down shirt and freshly pressed slacks; his wife was dressed in black. She wore a large diamond ring; the sort of ring that said the couple was happily ensconced in the world's corporate elite.

It took me only 20 minutes to discover how expensive the clinic and its specialists were: five minutes to wait for my name to be called by an attractive attendant; five minutes to be seated in an examination room to have the nurse take my blood; five minutes to meet with the Chinese specialist educated in the United States; and five minutes to collect my prescription. The visit cost me US$400, including the medicine, of course, which accounted for half the total price. One box of pills was to relax my blood pressure ("It's a little high, you know," the doctor announced discerningly), and another to eliminate infection. No other issues, as far as he could see, looking at test results from a previous clinic. So I was 400 bucks out, which, I suppose, was far cheaper than taking a flight back to the U.S. to be told the same thing.

The idea of customer service in Chinese hospitals is as new to the country as private property ownership, which effectively began in 1998. In the decades before, Maoist-style communism had created an overwhelming apathy best summed up by the Soviet-era expression: "They pretend to pay us, and we pretend to work." Most jobs in the cities, which were doled out by the state, were in huge, state-owned factories or government offices micromanaging the lives of citizens. Outside the cities was the excruciating poverty of the farm families, who were all equally poor, which was acceptable under communist ideology.

The development of a middle class, though, implies commensurate evolution of a service economy that will support middle-class aspirations for leisure, travel, lifestyle, and, well, vanity. In Chinese history, only a fraction of a percent of the population at any time had enough disposable income to afford a vanity lifestyle. A vanity lifestyle effectively makes people who have enough money feel as though they are kings and queens in their own right. Services in modern society are meant to make buyers feel special, exclusive, even. Customer service in a bureaucracy, on the other hand, is intended to put patrons in their place, belittle them even. The Chinese sense of service derives directly from the Confucian sense of hierarchy: the ministers are subservient to the king; the people are subservient to the ministers; the children are subservient to the parents; and the wife is subservient to the husband. The Emperor, as the Son of Heaven, is subservient to the whims of the gods. The big difference between the Confucian construct and the Chinese Communist Party's is that the Party is by dictate atheist, and so its leadership has no one to whom it owes obeisance.

FAWLTY CHINA

In the 1990s, when I first visited China, there were very few hotels that catered to Western expectations of customer service. Beijing's Friendship Hotel was the only place foreigners could stay until the mid-1990s. Very few staff spoke English, the rooms were always cold in the winter, when great thermoses of hot water were daily placed in rooms for tea and for washing up. The central government liberalized its policy toward foreigners by the late 1990s, allowing them to stay in a hotel of their own choosing. At a hotel in one of Beijing's famed *hutong* 胡同 districts, I called down for bottles of water to be brought up to my room for my guests from the Foreign Languages Institute. No response. After several minutes, I excused myself and went down to the main lobby to ask if I could buy some water at the front desk. The day manager, who was busily chatting with one of his coworkers, told me the service staff who typically manned the snack counter was gone. He pointed across the narrow lane at the outdoor grocery and told me to get it myself. I saw from the manager's slack expression that I would more likely win an argument with the plastic bust of Mao behind the main desk than with the manager himself. Reining in my exasperation, I crossed the lobby and bought the bottles of water I had promised my guests.

Fast forward 10 years to the mid-2000s, and Westerners were able to stay wherever they pleased: flea-bitten inns that cost a couple of dollars a night to six-star accommodation in Beijing and Shanghai. By 2005, as a business traveler, I was able to stay in a five-star hotel in pretty much any second-tier city in China—cities smaller than Beijing or Shanghai, but almost as rich per capita. One has to be careful, though, when researching star ratings of Chinese hotels. Chinese provincial governments have their own five-star rating, which may or may not conform to international standards. A Chinese five-star hotel in Nanjing, for instance, provides a higher standard than a Chinese five-star hotel in

Kunming, the capital of Yunnan Province. Chinese government officials learned early on in the country's economic development that the stars are a great marketing ploy for attracting out-of-towners and the ignorant. Meanwhile, an international five-star hotel in Ningbo will be head and shoulders above equivalent Chinese-run five-star lodging in the city.

My worst hotel experience was in Yantai, in Shangdong Province, across from the Korean peninsula. It was the sort of place where one had to put towels on the bathroom floor to keep one's feet from touching the slimy mildew that coated its surface. There was no service staff during my blustery January stay, and the front desk was less than cooperative. Still, the most harrowing stay ever recounted to me happened to an American friend who had been out late with government officials drinking and singing *karaoke* during a 2005 visit to northern China. He was feeling sick when he returned to his inn near dawn. The corridor stank, and he began to feel even more nauseous. As his vision adjusted, he realized that the corridor was lined with tubs of human waste, one for each room. He said he wasn't able to make it to the tub in his own room before his stomach violently responded to the assault on his senses.

Some of my most pleasant stays have been in cities such as Xiamen, Ningbo, and Dalian, where many of the front-desk staff spoke English, service was fast and pleasant, and the rooms tastefully decorated. Indeed, most new or newly refurbished hotels in China since 2007—no matter what the rating—come equipped with flat-screen televisions and free broadband service (with the exception of international hotels, which usually charge for Internet connectivity).

The Beijing Olympics was a huge magnet for new hotel start-ups by both domestic and international players. By 2006, the city boasted 4,761 hotels, inns, or hostels for visitors, 658 of which were star rated.[9] By the time the Olympics launched in 2008, there were more than 800 star-rated hotels in Beijing, 50 of which were five-star, up from fewer than 20 just five years before.[10]

In 2008 alone, the Chinese market saw 856 new hotels open and 784 more projects in the works—comprising 58 percent of total projects in Asia and 67 percent of total rooms in the region, according to Lodging Econometrics, a U.S. research company.[11] The 28 confirmed four- and five-star hotels, including the Four Seasons Pudong, Ritz-Carlton Pudong Shanghai, Peninsula Shanghai, and new Shangri-La, would contribute an additional 11,340 new rooms in Shanghai alone between 2009 and 2011. According to the global hotel-consulting company HVS, the top five luxury-hotel markets in China—Sanya (on Hainan island), Beijing, Shanghai, Lijiang, and Tianjin—reached a supply-and-demand balance in 2006 and 2007, and had a surplus of luxury hotels by 2008. From 2006 through 2009, the supply of five-star hotels in these cities increased by 15 percent, while demand only grew by 10 percent. The increased competition between luxury hotels themselves and their less-than-luxurious counterparts has proven to be a boon for customers as prices have fallen. In the first half of 2009 alone, the average daily rate for a luxury hotel room in Shanghai dropped to 1,225 yuan (US$180) from 1,552 yuan (US$225).[12] Total transaction volumes for China's hotels, however, trended downward from US$1.6 billion in 2006 to US$1 billion in 2007 to US$300 million in 2008, according to Jones Lang LaSalle, the U.S.-based real estate consultancy.[13]

The greatest benefit to customers from the heightened competition, though, is the promise of better service. After all, a service provider's greatest advantage is the service experience it can offer its customers, and word-of-mouth commentaries in China spread faster and wider than in the United States. But with the explosion of hotels in China set off by the the 2008 Summer Olympics, finding qualified management talent and recruiting and training junior staff— from housemaids and room attendants to chefs and registration attendants—who are eager to embrace a service culture is difficult. For one, there are only about 10 hotel schools in China, and even fewer courses at universities. The dearth of educational opportunity is in large part due to cultural stigma. "Given the choice, many parents would rather see their children in business than serving other people," according to Ed Dean, director and founder of JETT, a Shanghai-based service-industry consultancy.

Also, as is the case with Chinese patients' hesitation in seeking a "second opinion," Chinese consumers have little sense of what to expect from a service provider. In a culture that seems welded to the concept of "good enough" in its manufacturing practices, "good enough" and "cheap" have the upper hand in service requirements. Another obstacle to developing the armies of quality-service workers that the hospitality industry requires is a sense of mutual respect that service providers expect from customers. Chinese customers—especially if they are cash-rich—expect to be waited on hand and foot, and believe they have the right to ill-treat service staff, often in the form of talking down to them, humiliating them in front of others, and generally trashing a venue without reproach. Though, of course, Western consumers can be equally uncouth—stories of British tourists behaving badly in the Spain are legion—Chinese visitors spitting, smoking, yelling, and fighting in hotel lobbies can be expected, though of course not permitted. This sort of behavior relates to the lack of experience many Chinese have with international standards of decorum and with a form of Emperor's syndrome that has permeated so much of Chinese society and history: when Chinese are in a position of power, they tend to exercise it without boundary and without shame. It's only within the past 10 years that many Chinese have come from the countryside to the cities, or that luxury hotels have begun opening up in second- and third-tier cities. However, no service industry in China relies as much on the patronizing attitudes of customers for staff than one of the country's most famous entertainment venues, KTV.

SERVICE WITH A SMILE

Karaoke Television—or KTV, as it is called in Asia—is a major focus of relationship building in China, both socially and for business. Westerners, by and large, take some time to warm to it. KTV requires exploring extraordinary levels of humiliation as pop-star wannabees struggle to keep in tune singing the latest hip tunes or drippy romantic classics while watching music videos with lyrics for subtitles. The Carpenters goes over great with Chinese. Whatever the age, most Chinese know the English words to at least one Carpenters song. For most of the young male wait staff and female attendants, KTV parlors are the nearest escape exit out of farms and poorer towns.

An old Chinese buddy named Peter gave me a phone call one night. I hadn't seen Peter in some time. "Hey," he shouted over the phone in Chinese, "Why don't you come out and play!" I could hear very loud music thumping in the background. He invited me to join him and his friends at a *karaoke* parlor. I decided to take him up on his offer. The baroque façade of the multistory building at which he greeted me was a telltale sign that this was KTV of the highest—and most expensive— order. It wasn't the kind of place at which teenagers gather to sing the latest Taiwan pop tunes; instead, it was where the monied locals, South Korean, Japanese, Taiwanese, and Hong Kong businessmen retired for ritual bacchanalia.

Another reason Westerners tend to be uncomfortable in KTV is that you must leave your resume at the door. Everyone becomes equal in the KTV room: the tycoons, presidents, and the juniors. Everyone except the hostesses. Westerners, especially Americans, tend to identify themselves so completely with their roles in the corporate world that it is difficult for them to just cut loose and sing silly songs, even if they sing off-key, and to dance, even if they can't even keep rhythm to save their own lives.

Then there are the young ladies, the hostesses. They are supposed to be pretty enough to encourage male customers to buy the establishment's food and drink, and perhaps even invite additional young ladies to join them (which, of course, costs more money). When the *mama-san* (the woman who manages customer satisfaction) trotted out a handful of young ladies to keep us company, Peter imperiously commented to me: "They aren't very pretty, are they?" He turned them away—which is what customers who want to show they are discerning do as a matter of course. The *mama-san*, disappointed, explained there were no other girls available. Peter said we'd take one of the more homely young ladies if the *mama-san*—attractive in her own right—would party with us. She accepted.

This style of partying—which can be interpreted as exploiting these young ladies as chattel—can be uncomfortable for Westerners, myself included. The Chinese, and many in other parts of Asia, do not see it that way. Instead, Chinese society accepts the young ladies have signed up for a job that involves extensive drinking, chatting, drinking games, and squeezing-of-the-knee by the fellow who has chosen her to be his companion for the evening. The money isn't bad for the hostesses, and opportunities abound for them to find boyfriends (whether married or not does not have to be a problem for either side) and potentially husbands that will take care of their and their parents' financial requirements.

As accommodating as staff at KTV parlors can be to their customers, home-appliance repairmen in China can be downright insufferable.

THE TV REPAIRMAN COMETH

Subservience is the last thought that comes to mind of appliance and utility technicians who come to Chinese homes to repair systems that have broken down: air conditioners in the summer, heaters in the winter, gas while you're showering. All service staff who visit Chinese homes share one common characteristic; they are all "experts" in their field. There is no question they cannot answer without great authority about the mechanism they have been called in to repair. They are "Lord of the Air Conditioner," or "King of the Gas Stove," or "Earl of the TV." The attitudes that service staff adopt when they visit homes are meant to assure customers that they are completely in control of the situation, master of the inconvenience, and—in Confucian tradition—commander of the customer. As China is a more hierarchical society than that in the U.S., the U.K., or Australia, Chinese willingly fall into place, and question none of the mumbo jumbo that technicians often spout when they are clueless as to the cause of a breakdown, or when they simply do not want to do anything about the problem. Many are the times I have interrogated repairmen who have come to my home in China about what they are doing to my appliances, much to my Chinese wife's embarrassment. She would rather I simply defer to them and later call the company for another repairman. Repair service staff simply do not have it in them to say: "I don't know what the problem is. I will call in a colleague who does." It all comes down to the repairman preserving face, that is, presenting oneself in an admiring light to others. The repairman knows he doesn't know what he's talking about, the Chinese customer knows the repairman doesn't know what he's talking about, yet both work to preserve the façade that the repairman is the "expert" and has everything under control. Hence, my wife's displeasure at my expressed displeasure with these fellows: I'm breaking taboo at exposing the repairman's ignorance.

One American friend—I'll call him Frank—got into a scuffle with the TV repairman who had gone to his apartment to repair the speakers on his flat screen TV. The first encounter involved the repairman inflating the price of the parts that needed to be ordered, assuming my friend did not know the pricing of the components. As Frank dealt with Chinese suppliers of similar electronic bits, he directly called the company to obtain the real price. When the technician returned to my friend's home, he took apart the TV, then said the parts would not work, without even having put them in place—he was signaling his dissatisfaction with Frank interfering to find out the real price of the parts, thus deflating his "service fee". Instead, he lit up a cigarette, packed his tools and started to make his way to the door.

Frank blocked his exit and demanded the repairman finish the job. My friend, who admits he is no electronics whiz, saw that replacing the components was as simple as snapping the electronic boards into place. The repairman tried to push past Frank, who kept his ground. The two began wrangling with each other like *sumo* wrestlers intent on dominating the ring. Eventually, the repairman relented—without bloodshed—realizing my friend was not going to let him out of the apartment until after he had finished the job, which he did, within minutes.

While the appliance-repair business sometimes forces customers to practically beg service providers for adequate service, China's wedding industry will bend over backward to do almost anything to ensure their customers' satisfaction.

DEARLY BELOVED

An organizational secret that Chinese government firms and privately held companies have learned and employed is "beauty tames the savage beast". For instance, in the fast-developing bullet-train services that are lacing Chinese cities together, most attendants are in their mid-20s, fair-skinned, attractive, and wear smart uniforms. Indeed, job descriptions for attendants on the trains read: "30 years old and younger, 1.65 meters and taller, 50 kilograms and lighter, dignified appearance, high personal character—what Chinese people would characterize in Chinese as *wenrou* 温柔, "gentle and willowy."[14] Government officials literally have beauty pageants to choose the most young, charming, and attractive ladies to lead crowd control on the super-fast trains. Typically, as well, each train will have a least one burly police officer backing up the bevy of bachelorettes. However, it's extraordinary to observe the tranquilizing effect the "gentle and willowy" attendants have on people who, just minutes before boarding the trains, were boisterous, chewing watermelon seeds, and spitting the shells on the floor as they roughly pushed past others to make way for themselves to their assigned seats.

Truly, sexism in China goes a long way toward effective crowd control in public spaces, from flight attendants to restaurant wait staff to coordinated private security at gated communities, strategically dispersed estrogen in China commands respect, if not attention.

One service industry in China from which all others can learn is the wedding industry and, by extension, the many women's vanity services such as plastic surgery and spas. Few other customer care industries in China can match the level of quality of service, attention to detail, and professionalism that makes buyers—usually, fiancees and husbands—buy more despite their limited budgets. I speak from personal experience on this count, as the groom *cum* husband in 2009 to a lovely Chinese bride who felt completely understood and cared for by the staff employed to make her wedding day the happiest and most memorable day of her life. Though in the end, the final bill was steep—in the five figures (and we're talking—deep inhale—U.S. dollars, not yuan) and though the entire process was trying at times, I have to admit that the bride and groom business in China strongly impressed me.

Marriage in China is very important. There is very little choice in China as to whether a child will marry. From childhood, finding a good husband or a good wife is a primary value that Chinese parents impress on their children. Whereas in North America or the U.K., a daughter or son can choose to not get married—or, if married, not to have children—such an alternative lifestyle is nearly unheard of in China, even in the more cosmopolitan cities such as Beijing and Shanghai. Typically, the first boyfriend or girlfriend is the betrothed; there's not as much experimental sleeping around as there is in the West. Marriage is about survival of the group first, that is, the extended family; selfish pursuits that exclude the welfare of the parents are severely frowned upon.

Hence, in a country in which hundreds of millions of couples get married each year, the multibillion-dollar marriage industry is seldom in the doldrums, with competition for customers fierce. Hence, service levels tend to be high, as every schoolgirl knows that an unhappy bride will tell her girlfriends what a frightful experience she had with photographers, makeup artists, seamstresses, caterers, car services, master-of-ceremonies, even the guy she buys fireworks from (families launch fireworks when the groom and bride exit the their new home after the groom "convinces" the bride it really is in her best interest to marry him). Wedding-related service providers know this, and bend over backward to accommodate the bride's caprice. During wedding preparation, the groom pretty much humbles himself and shells out whatever amount he can afford if the families are not helping with expenses.

Chinese brides are beset by four persons' opinion. The first two she has a great deal of time for—the account manager at the local photography studio and the account manager of the catering service. She tries to ignore the other two sets of opinions: her mother's and her mother-in-law's; though, if the fathers are of retirement age (60 for men in China,) they will get in on the act as well. The photography company is important because every Chinese wedding is accompanied by photos of the bride and groom that were taken months before the wedding ceremony during a full-on 14-hour marathon session that stretches credulity and patience. Typical middle-income couples pay anywhere from a few hundred U.S. dollars to a few thousand, depending on the number of indoor and outdoor settings and costume changes. Couples will change costumes anywhere from four to six times during the day-long session. Most of the costumes are standard wedding fair: maybe two styles of wedding dresses with the groom wearing a white tuxedo and then a black suit. The bit that begins to stretch imagination involves choosing costumes that range from the clothing worn by young Chinese maidens 100 years ago to the bright-red traditional Chinese robe with heavy, winged hat to 1930s Shanghai gangster-moll posturing. (My favorites were the Chinese scholar's look—a long, dark, green robe over pants with a white scarf intelligently arranged around my neck—and the Shanghai gangster look, albeit sanitized for family consumption. I sternly refused to wear the rhinestone disco costume, much to the disappointment of all the Chinese involved that day.) All good fun (in hindsight), and terribly exhausting for the couple and for the crew that had been assigned to photograph and primp the bride and groom. Day in and day out, the female staff—and it's all women running the show—are polite, patient listeners as the brides-to-be fret about the stiffness of their hair, the dark rings under their eyes, the color of their lipstick and the tightness of their shoes. The staff at the salon that my wife had chosen wore neat black dresses with black pumps. They were all in their 20s, and almost all attractive. The more matronly types in their late 30s and 40s tended to be custodial workers.

Eighty percent of the time, the grooms just sit and wait for the loves of their lives to change costumes. For the men, of course, there is little effort expended during the ordeal. A quick change of clothes, an attractive attendant to powder the shine from his nose, and long stretches of waiting for his soulmate to be satisfied with her appearance. The grooms watch TV or black-market action movie DVDs, or surf the Internet in private booths. Account managers will even bring box-lunch sets to sustain the bride and groom through the grueling session. Photographers—nearly all young men—are lively, talkative, and try to encourage couples to look their best. It's easy to conclude that the industry really seems to have learned that word of mouth matters in growing their businesses—and in staff keeping their jobs.

The day-long wedding festival is filled with a variety of other service providers: videographers, hair dressers, wait staff, even hotel-floor management. My Chinese bride and I had our 10-course wedding banquet at a five-star European hotel in downtown Suzhou. The chain has other hotels in other first- and second-tier cities throughout China. At least three hotel managers were assigned to our banquet, each of whom was likely responsible for at least two other wedding banquets on the expansive premises. A master-of-ceremonies introduced this nervous couple to the crowd of well-wishers that had come to eat, play games, and pass red packets of money to the appreciative groom—and his bride, of course. A master-of-ceremonies at a Chinese wedding banquet officiates over the event, prompting the couple and the crowd at each stage of the nuptials: the exchange of vows, the cutting of the cake, the diving into the first course of the meal, and even the rounds of *karaoke* singing. High levels of service that day resulted in a happy bride. Thankfully.

SERVICE WITH A FROWN

China, despite the length of its rough-and-tumble history, only has now arrived on the international stage to present to the world its own interpretation of service and customer satisfaction. As with so much of the society, some parts of the sector are extremely refined, while others remain mired in a past throttled by vested, petrified political interests and Confucian tradition. The dividing line between effective service businesse and disaffected service organizations in China lies in the amount of competition within an industry forcing companies to excel, and the extent to which a lack of customer service will deny business growth.

For instance, China does not have many hospitals per capita despite its large population and growing wealth. Patients (as customers) have few alternatives, thus suffer from corruption, ineptitude, rudeness, and a patronizing attitude during most visits to hospitals. Patients who spend five to 10 times more for VIP services at public hospitals for the most part receive greater attention and care than the average patron. The growing wealth of a new middle class, however, has seen the demand side of VIP services increase and the supply side of well-trained doctors and nurses schooled in medicine and bedside manners decrease per capita. As a result, customer-service levels of VIP offerings have dropped dramatically since the mid-2000s. Western-style care in China has Western-style pricing structures and palazzo-style trappings, indicating an extremely wide gap between the price that international insurance companies are willing to pay for services and the true cost in China of running a tidy but competent establishment in modest surroundings. Ultimately, the value-add the high-end clinics offer is peace, space, and decorum in a country short on all three.

Likely the greatest revolution the service sector in China can expect is the evolution of mutual respect in a business transaction: the seller and buyer exchange services for payment based on consideration. Certainly, the customer is king in the KTV industry; but then, the service staff are treated as mere vassals. In contrast, in Chinese health care, the service provider is king—even the janitors in hospitals can give patients grief if they have had a bad day. The health-care industry is the epitome of a bureaucracy gone mad with self-interest—of government administrators who prefer their power position of control over the comfort and lives of others. In neither nightclub nor hospital is there a sense of mutual respect: service providers who learn and meet the requirements of customers, and customers who hold in high regard the abilities and professionalism of caregivers.

International brand hotels in China go to great lengths to inculcate self-respect and customer consideration in their staff, since what they otherwise offer (food and lodging) is easily reproducible by an increasingly crowded marketplace in China. High levels of customer service are the only competitive advantage many luxury brand hotels have to offer, just as in the case of China's wedding industry. Competition is fierce in both industries, and staff in both businesses are aggressively considerate of the needs of their customers. Health-care reform, however, will require more than just a smile from caregivers for patients to feel properly attended to; consumers will require laws and an impartial judiciary that will support and enforce valid claims of malpractice. The health-care industry will take a step closer to consumer emancipation when a patient requests a second opinion on a diagnosis without fear of losing access to medical treatment.

Reforming China's TV repairmen, however, may prove a tougher nut to crack.

END NOTES

1. "Chinese Hospital Rushed by Patients and Ticket Scalpers," chinaSMACK, August 31, 2009, http://www.chinasmack.com/videos/chinese-hospital-rushed-patients-ticket-scalpers/.
2. "Waiting All Night Outside a Hospital Hoping to See a Doctor," chinaSMACK, November 2, 2009, http://www.chinasmack.com/pictures/chinese-waiting-hospital-crowds/.
3. Sharon LaFraniere, "Chinese Hospitals Are Battlegrounds of Discontent," *The New York Times*, August 11, 2010.
4. Ibid.
5. Wu Yanrui, "Service Sector Growth in China and India: A Comparison," *China: An International Journal*, March 2007.
6. Chen Weihua, "Need for Medical Privacy," *China Daily*, November 15, 2008.
7. "Worker Cannot Pay Hospital, Doctor Suffers," chinaSMACK, December 21, 2008, http://www.chinasmack.com/stories/migrant-worker-cannot-pay-hospital-doctor-suffers/, accessed March 30, 2010.
8. "Caring for Profit," *China Economic Review*, May 2009.
9. "More Hotels Needed for 2008 Olympics," *China Daily*, March 20, 2006; accessed March 10, 2010, http://arabic.china.org.cn/english/2006/May/168938.htm.

10. Loretta Chow and Jason Leow, "Beijing Hotels Face Glut of Rooms," July 18, 2008.
11. "China New Hotel Projects," *China Economic Review*, December 18, 2009.
12. Ibid.
13. "Luxury Hotels Facing Difficulties in China," *China Economic Review*, August 24, 2009.
14. "Train Attendant Selection Process or Beauty Contest?" chinaSMACK, October 20, 2009, http://www.chinasmack.com/pictures/train-attendant-selection-process-beauty-contest.

CHAPTER **8**

The Global
Sugar Daddy

A BIG STICK

Stern Hu was one of the few people around the world *not* surprised by the court's verdict: guilty of bribery and industrial espionage. Before he walked into the Chinese courtroom, sequestered from his family and his government for more than half a year, he already knew his accusers had signed, sealed, and delivered the judgment to the Chinese court. Hu was a Chinese, a naturalized Australian citizen sent to China to be the lead negotiator representing the interests of Rio Tinto, one of the largest producers of iron ore in the world. For much of 2009, Rio Tinto and other major mining players had been in intense negotiations with Chinese steel manufacturers represented by the China Iron and Steel Association about discounts on the global benchmark price of iron ore for large buyers in 2010. The association demanded a cut of 40 percent off benchmark prices; the miners offered only a 33 percent discount. Stern Hu was Rio Tinto's man in China, talking with the general managers and heads of China's top steel producers almost on a daily basis. He and his top lieutenants knew their competitors from top to bottom, their businesses, and their personal foibles. In October 2009, state enforcement officials arrested Hu and three of his Chinese associates, who were Chinese nationals. The police confiscated Rio

Tinto computers from the company's Shanghai office, bundled the Rio Tinto employees off, and held them seclusion, where no one—not family, not lawyers, not their employer, not even the Australian embassy—could access the accused. The highest authority in China incarcerated the Rio Tinto negotiators for allegedly committing one of the worst crimes conceivable in China: theft of state secrets. Chinese investigators claimed they had found on the Rio Tinto hard disks classified costing information of the Chinese steel companies involved in benchmark negotiations with the Western iron miner. The central government accused Rio Tinto of using the information against the Chinese negotiators. Rio Tinto countered that databases and reports on the computers were in the public domain. Nevertheless, three Chinese general managers of domestic steel mills were taken into custody by the authorities at the same time Stern Hu and his staff were arrested. Eventually, state authorities scaled down accusations against the four Rio Tinto employees to mere bribery. Seven months later, in the spring of 2010, Stern Hu confessed to a tribunal of judges he had indeed taken nearly US$150,000 in bribes from Chinese steel producers. The Chinese court sentenced Stern Hu to 10 years in prison on bribery charges.

While Stern Hu and his associates may have confessed to having been bribed, the consensus within the world business community was that China was an adolescent and vindictive participant in the international marketplace. Preempted in bids by Japanese and South Korean iron-ore purchasers, and stonewalled by a foreign company that only months before nearly accepted a rescue package of cash-for-shares from a Chinese state-owned enterprise, China had clearly been outmaneuvered and left looking amateurish. The arrest and subsequent conviction of Stern Hu and his coworkers in a country rife with institutional corruption and theft left China only looking more immature in the face of the complexity and sophistication of today's global financial transactions. Four thousand years of history had left the leadership few tools with which to operate in a complex international financial environment. The tools it did have at hand were blunt instruments, which it used against the four Rio Tinto executives.

Yet China has no choice but to further integrate its economy with that of global commerce, trade, and financial networks. The expectations, livelihoods, and even survival of its own citizens depend on the degree to which the Chinese elite are able to balance the expediencies of an economy in hyperdrive with the expectations of a society intent on sharing the same benefits of the "good life" as many of their Western counterparts within a lifetime. For China to turn its back on globalization would be to undo several generations of work and sacrifice by countless millions and transport the country back to the bad old days of politicized self-reliance programs such as the Great Leap Forward and the Cultural Revolution. The keystone of China's globalization strategy has been the manipulation of its currency, the yuan.

A YUAN FOR MORE

If China's economy was a nuclear reactor, one of the few moderators of the momentum of its hyper-kinetic development is the value of its currency, the yuan. No trade issue between China and the United States is more explosive than the peg China has maintained between the yuan and the U.S. dollar. From 1995 until 2005, China kept the value of the yuan steady in relation to the dollar—at about 8.3 yuan to the dollar. As the dollar decreased in value, the yuan's own value remained the same, making goods exported out of China cheaper for Americans and Europeans to buy with their currencies. But just how much does the value of the yuan relative to the dollar contribute to unfair trade between the countries?

The best way to gauge the extent to which a currency is under-valued or overvalued is through a measure called Purchasing Power Parity (PPP). PPP compares the cost of a basket of goods in a standard country—typically the United States—with the price paid in the same currency in a different country. *The Economist* uses—somewhat tongue in cheek—what it calls its Big Mac Index, which compares the cost of a McDonald's hamburger—its signature Big Mac—with the purchasing price of the same burger across a range of countries. In early 2010, *The Economist* determined a Big Mac in America cost US$3.58 compared with the same Big Mac in China costing US$1.83, implying the yuan was nearly 50 percent undervalued compared with the dollar. The Peterson Institute for International Economics estimates that the yuan is undervalued by between 20 and 40 percent.[1]

The hidden "subsidy," is an undervalued yuan that makes products sold into America cheaper than they would otherwise be. As they are relatively inexpensive, Americans—always up for a good bargain—snap up the products. China, however, does not buy as many goods from America as America buys from China for a variety of reasons, including the artificially higher prices of American goods because the dollar seems expensive to Chinese. China, then, had a trade surplus with America of almost US$230 billion in 2009, according to the Office of the U.S. Trade Representative. The U.S. Congress threatened tariffs of 25 percent against Chinese imports in 2005, and again in 2010 to force China's hand on allowing its currency to trade at its real value. Some in Congress believed that pressing China to increase the value of its currency would help protect remaining manufacturing jobs in America, and even bring jobs back to the United States: if a revalued yuan makes Chinese products more expensive, congressional wisdom goes, then American manufacturers will be able to compete more effectively with China in terms of production costs.

The problem with that thinking, however, is while the Chinese exchange rate does affect the cost of goods that flow from China into the U.S., the value of the yuan is only one part of the cost structure of products. Deutsche Bank estimated that a five percent appreciation of the yuan reduces the profits of low-end China manufacturers, such as textile and electronics makers, by five to 10 percent.[2] Chinese low-end manufacturers generally have profit margins of less than two percent, according to China's Vice Commerce Minister Zhong Shan. Downward pressure on supplier profit margins by buyers such as U.S. retailer Walmart gives Chinese exporters little room in which to adjust prices upward when the yuan's value increases: a sudden devaluation of the yuan would drive manufacturers who make relatively inexpensive commodity products—such as toys, shoes, and clothing—out of business.[3]

Still, other, more inflexible costs in the supply chain go into the price structure of a product, including the cost of materials, labor costs, manufacturer markups, middlemen, and retail markups. Effectively the only costs that Chinese producers can influence are labor costs, assuming their margins are as thin as the average Walmart supplier's. The costs of materials that go into product manufacture—plastics, metals, and chemicals—tend to be the same around the world, though a stronger yuan would tend to make the import of some materials cheaper for Chinese producers. The cost of material inputs in China still rose annually in the double digits from 2004 until 2008, despite the yuan strengthening as much as 20 percent during the period.

If there is any component on the Chinese side that would have a marked impact on the cost of products coming out of China, it is labor costs. Extremely low labor costs in China relative to the country's wealth as measured by GDP are the main factor behind lower prices for Chinese exports. Chinese labor costs from 1980 through the mid-2000s averaged about three percent of the average worker salary in the United States; while the average worker salary of Taiwan, South Korea, and Japan during comparable periods in their respective economic development averaged 30 percent of U.S. salaries, according the U.S. Bureau of Labor Statistics.

Labor costs in China, however, are something Chinese company owners and local governments can control through the level of minimum wages and benefits to which workers are entitled. Manufacturers in China, however, were able to hold down labor costs throughout the 1990s until 2008 because of a demand for jobs from people who live in China's interior who flowed to factories along the east coast. However, even as salary levels began to rise in 2007 and then again in 2010 by anywhere from 20 to 50 percent in some cities along China's eastern seaboard, jobs in the low-end manufacturing sector in the U.S. did not return. In other words, Chinese manufacturing had become less competitive during these peak salary periods; however, no American industries became revitalized as a result of China's salary inflation. Globalization had already restructured jobs and entire industries out of existence in America in the 2000s: textile production, toys, shoes, plastics, and a great deal of machining and tool-making had all but become industries of the past. The east coast of China began to see just such a decimation of the same industries in early 2008, as labor and environmental policies reset the richer regional economy and the work migrated to China's interior. One day, those jobs will migrate out of China completely to Bangladesh, Southern India, and Cambodia. Export businesses will always seek out the lowest salary levels globally to offer international buyers the cheapest goods possible.

Ultimately, at the center of the relationship between the value of the yuan and the dollar is the dollar's role as both a foreign reserve currency and a national currency. America has what's called a "currency hegemony." For all intents and purposes, the fates of the currencies of most countries in the world rise and fall in accordance with U.S. fiscal and monetary policy. The U.S., as the strongest economy in the world, uses its prestige and economic might to give assurance that it will always pay its debt back to international investors, including the governments of other countries. The dollar substituted gold as a safe shelter for the savings of most countries. The dollar's place in the world as a currency refuge keeps U.S. interest rates on its debt low; instead of the U.S. having to pay three percent interest on the loans it takes out through its own purchase of U.S. Treasury bills, it only has to pay 1.5 percent, in general, because of international demand for the bonds. The difference in the interest rates can be seen as a "shadow tax" other countries have to pay in order for the U.S. to keep its interest rates low, which made it easier for Americans from 2002 to 2008 to purchase houses, to pay for its wars in Afghanistan and Iraq, and to buy cheap products manufactured in China.

When China pegged the yuan to the dollar in 1995, China's central government ordered its state-owned banks to fork out as much as 20 percent of their dollar deposits to China's central bank. The dollars came from revenue from Chinese export-driven companies doing business with American buyers, from foreign direct investment flowing into the country to set up new factories and other operations, and from the speculative flows from overseas Chinese who wanted to catch the China economic wave. China's central bank would then reinvest the money in U.S. Treasury bonds, a kind of debt that American citizens, institutions, and foreign governments buy to finance the debt the American government carries.

The 1997 Asian Financial Crisis had seen the strongest economies of Asia—Singapore, Thailand, Taiwan, and South Korea—devastated by a flight of capital by institutional investors calling in their dollar-denominated debts. China, however, survived the economic tsunami that laid the other Asian economies low over the next eight years. It saw it was better to be a dollar-denominated creditor than dollar-denominated debtor. China chose to be an Asian country calling in payment on debts as it increasingly exposed its economy to the international markets, instead of being set upon by governments and institutions that wanted their money back when times got tough. From the beginning of 2001 until the spring of 2009, China's foreign exchange reserves went from practically zero to an incredible US$2 trillion, making the country by mid-2009 the largest holder of foreign exchange currency—and American debt—in the world.

The Chinese central government was committed to ensuring the U.S. economy's success by continuing to buy Treasury bills to help keep American interest rates low. Higher costs for the American government to pay down its debt would otherwise ripple through the American economy to make the cost of borrowing for companies and individuals more expensive overall, as well as ramp up inflation—a surefire way to stall a restart in the moribund U.S. economy. Inflation also would devalue the hundreds of billions of dollars of Treasury bills in which the Chinese had invested.

As John Maynard Keynes, the famed British economist from the early twentieth century, once said: " . . . If you owe your bank manager £1,000, you are at his mercy. If you owe him £1 million, he is at your mercy." China, in other words, had to continue buying dollar-denominated Treasury bills from America for the foreseeable future to maintain the value of the debt in which China had already invested. At the end of the first decade, any dramatic indication China gave to the rest of the world it no longer had faith in the U.S. economy would create a selloff of the Treasury bills that would quickly devalue China's own international investments. A lack of faith also would further weaken the dollar, which, since 2002 had already lost 35 percent of its dollar-index value against the yuan.

The Chinese central government, however, has historically been loathe to allow its currency to simply float on the currency markets, vulnerable, as it sees it, to the whims of international institutional currency traders who would have greater sway over the country's domestic market than the Chinese leadership would prefer. China had already seen that the final nail in the coffin of the Asian Tiger economies in 1997 was allowing their currencies to float after strongly pegging them to the dollar. Rapid devaluation of the currencies in the markets led to central banks trying to buy up their currencies to help their countries avert bankruptcy. Central bank attempts at manipulation may have even accelerated the collapse of the currencies, since the actions smacked of desperation and succeeded in spooking even the most daring foreign investors. Still, the Chinese leadership has long understood the need to let the steam out of its economy while at the same time restructuring its trading and financial systems, albeit slowly. In 2005, China released the yuan's specific peg to the dollar in favor of the massaged value of a basket of currencies that included the dollar, the euro, and the Japanese yen. In 2009, to help its exporters at the *nadir* of the global economic downturn, it returned to the strong dollar peg: the yuan by that time had strengthened to 6.85 yuan to the dollar. By the end of 2009, though, American cries of currency manipulation started growing again. The Chinese pushed back at America, claiming the problem was with the dollar's dual role as a reserve currency and a trade-settlement currency.

The huge debt that the U.S. incurred to rebuild confidence in its banking system in 2008 and to reduce job losses during the Great Recession of 2008–09 rattled the Chinese leadership into understanding that it needed someplace else to park its dollar reserves. In mid-2009, China began pushing the International Monetary Fund (IMF) to issue its own reserve currency—a "super-sovereign reserve currency"—which many considered mere political noise on China's part. In other words, neither the U.S. dollar nor the European Union's euro nor even the yuan itself could be a currency that other countries would buy to use for a rainy day. They instead would use a super currency that would cross international borders. For decades, the IMF had been using a "fake" currency internally to keep track in its accounting books of the loans it gives out to countries. The IMF calls the internal currency Special Drawing Rights (SDR). The book value of SDR is based on the value of a clutch of currencies, including the U.S. dollar, the euro, and the British pound. The Chinese began mooting the option of an alternative reserve currency because of their nervousness that their U.S. Treasury investments would decrease in value because of the huge debt the American government racked up to stimulate its economy during the global economic downturn.

In addition to serving as a reserve currency, the Chinese also proposed the SDR could serve as an alternative settlement currency for transactions between countries. Basically, the Chinese by mid-2009 were looking for a way to stabilize their own currency on a peg that was no longer as exposed to the strained policy and economic conditions of the United States, as well as to protect the dollar-denominated investments they had in the U.S. Treasury bills. But China also knew the yuan's peg to the dollar was straining its economy at home, too.

BALANCING INTERNATIONAL AMBITIONS WITH DOMESTIC REALITIES

In July 2009, the Chinese leadership agreed with U.S. Secretary of State Hillary Clinton and U.S. Treasury Secretary Timothy Geithner that China needed to develop a more consumer-based economy to supplant a large portion of its manufacturing sector—what's called "rebalancing" its economy. A key component of consumption-based economies is a service sector that employs more people than the manufacturing sector, in which productivity and profits are gained through more efficient use of fewer workers. A growing service sector implies that fewer dollars will enter China's financial system, allowing China to use more of its finances domestically, rather than internationally through its purchase of dollar-denominated assets.

China, then, would need to rebalance its economy away from the sort of trade surpluses that was compelling its central bank to buy dollar assets to keep the yuan low in value and that were creating bubbles in its real estate market and stock exchanges. Many Western economists and European and U.S. policy makers throughout the 2000s agreed the key to closing the trade gap between China and other countries was for Chinese citizens to buy more goods—domestic and imported—to become consumers in the American mold.

The real problem in opening up consumer pocketbooks, though, was not that citizens were too conservative in their spending habits, but that they did not have enough money in their purses to begin with to buy the sorts of durable goods that present themselves as sizable upticks in the growth of an economy, such as cars, washing machines, TVs, and stereos. The lion's share of the glut in savings had not been at the individual level, but, instead, at the corporate level, with money pouring into the coffers of private companies and state-owned enterprises

(SOEs). SOEs made up 80 percent of the increase in savings in China from 2000 through 2009. In other words, most Chinese families had not shared in the wealth that the country's economy had generated; their incomes had stayed close to stagnant in real terms. Instead, company profits had in most instances been pocketed by bosses, put into the Chinese stock market, invested in property, or spirited out of the country. The result was that the average Chinese citizens on balance were no richer than they had been 10 years before. The cost of health care in China as well as the lack of a national pension system force Chinese families to maintain high levels of savings in case of catastrophic health issues and to prepare for old age. What that means for American businesses is the market for wares that the Chinese may actually like and could use is much smaller than it would be in a more balanced economy. It also means that even if the Chinese government successfully rationalizes health care, strengthens its social security net, and bolsters education, Chinese will still feel poor because company and SOE bosses will still speculate with profits, instead of reinvesting surpluses into increasing productivity or developing new, even more profitable industries.

The national government's task in distributing its society's newfound wealth is monumental. Beijing doubled spending on health care, education and social security between 2005 and 2008. However, by 2009, spending on the welfare of its citizens only totaled six percent of GDP, compared with an average of 25 percent in richer countries. During the depths of the global economic downturn in early 2009, central government authorities pledged to provide basic health-care coverage to 90 percent of its citizens by 2011; still a paltry half-percent of GDP.[4]

In other words, the Chinese government will have to force SOEs to remit their profits back to the state, and perhaps even give up some of its own control over the economy to the marketplace to rebalance its books and to deflate the speculative bubbles that could destabilize Chinese society and world financial markets.

MODERNIZATION OF CHINA'S BANKING AND FINANCE INDUSTRY

China has ever so slowly been rationalizing its stock market and internationalizing its insular banking system. By the close of 2009, foreign governments were accusing China of being a mercantilist—some may even say mercenary—economy that needed to accept its role as a responsible trading partner in a world of international checks and balances. Leading economists in the West propounded that gambling in Las Vegas was a safer bet than gambling on the Chinese stock market; at least, analyses proffered, the House in Las Vegas was not going to change the rules mid-game, which the Chinese had done several times since the establishment of stock exchanges in Shanghai and Shenzhen. Properly regulated stock markets are meant to be an effective way for money to flow to worthy investments that help keep the entire financial system in balance and grow economies; much like water that you run from the tap to fill an ice tray moves from one deficit hole to another until all the holes are filled and the tray is full of water. The Chinese government, however, tips the tray to suit its needs and imperatives as it sees fit, so the water flows to the holes that meet its political expediencies. It doesn't allow anyone outside a closed clique of cronies to know how it wants the water to flow and in what direction the water is flowing. Central government policy also favors obscurity of corporate structures, governance, and reportage to suit political needs.

China established its stock markets in 1990 to finance its failing SOEs. Essentially, the government had no more money in its state-owned banks to lend to the SOEs so that the firms could continue to manufacture widgets that nobody wanted or needed. The central government wanted only Chinese residents and Chinese institutions to be able to buy shares on the bourses, so-called A-shares. By the mid-2000s, Chinese SOEs made up 70 percent of the 1,200 or so listings on Chinese stock markets; while the central government and other SOEs remained the majority shareholders of those listings. In 2004, only 20 companies listed produced half the profit reported on the bourse.[5] Though China has its own version of the U.S. Securities and Exchange Commission—called the China Securities and Regulatory Commission—it only promoted policy that would continue to be in the best interest of the SOEs. In other words, the Chinese government listed state-owned companies on government-sponsored bourses that a government agency promoted as safe investments. The central government essentially asked investors to trust in the SOEs because—at the end of the day—it was not going to allow very much to be written and published about SOE business activities, losses, and profits. To ensure a captive pool of punters on the stock exchanges, the central government placed capital controls on Chinese banks to keep companies and individuals from moving yuan into offshore vehicles to limit Chinese investment to domestic opportunities.

The lack of information about listed companies seemed to have not deterred speculation on the market at all. Despite the odds of winning on the Chinese stock markets being less than beating the House in Las Vegas, hundreds of millions of Chinese since 2005—as inveterate risk takers—have been depositing their money into the bourses and into property. Chinese residents and institutions put their savings into the stock market because it is the only place, other than the property market, where they can achieve annual investment returns higher than one to two percent. They believed that whereas the value of their paper money might decrease, property values and stock prices would only increase above the principal amount they had invested. So, even if values dropped by half, they would still come out with a profit. Chinese held the same sentiment about the stock market, despite the lack of policing of the bourses and the lack of quarterly and annual reports to shareholders. (Any company reports that were submitted for public inspection were highly suspect.) Still, the Chinese did not necessarily feel they were investing in the dark. As one Beijing lawyer who had invested tens of thousands of yuan into the stock market told me at the height of the Shanghai stock market rally in 2007: "I know a woman who works at one of the big banks in Beijing. She is one of the first to get information about the stocks. She will call me when I should sell." Every Chinese who plays the stock market believes his special personal network of friends, family, and associates—called, *guanxi wang* 关系网, in Chinese (literally, relationship net)—gives him an inside track on the thinking and decisions of any of the bureaucracies that have interests in inflating or deflating the value of the stock market.

Government gerrymandering and the lack of company information and transparency are just a couple of the reasons there are so few foreign investors in the Chinese stock markets. The Chinese government moving into the second decade of the new century continues to prefer its stock market to be near-hermetically sealed. Some international investors can buy A-shares through a program for Qualified

Foreign Institutional Investors (QFII—pronounced "Q-fee"), launched in November 2002. Most foreign investors who want to trade the shares of Chinese companies have to deal on the Hong Kong stock exchange in what are called H-shares; many companies whose shares were traded on the Shanghai and Shenzhen exchanges list on the Hong Kong exchange through "the back door." That is, they took over the shell of a company that had once successfully listed on the Board but for any variety of reasons had become inoperative but not delisted. Despite the lack of company and trade transparency, the Shanghai stock market in 2009 overtook the Japanese stock market as the second-largest stock market in the world, with a total capitalization near US$4 trillion, compared with US$10 trillion in equities listed on American boards.

In 2009, China's state-owned banks released a record $1.4 trillion of new loans as part of a stimulus package aimed at bolstering growth through the global financial crisis. Much of the lending went to local governments for infrastructure-development projects, and to SOEs, which invested the money in the stock market and in real estate.[6] The banks performed little in the way of qualifying the customers for the loans, as most of the borrowers were government entities themselves, such as the banks. Near the end of 2010, the banks had pumped a nearly US$1 trillion more into the economy through the same state-owned channels. By that time, however, central government officials were voicing concerns that the default rate on the loans could be as high as 30 percent, which would put a major strain on government finances already stretched to bail out the banks. Loans that customers do not repay that the bank carries on its books are called non-performing Loans (NPLs). NPLs cripple entire economies when the banks no longer have more money to finance investments with real returns, such as in research and development and infrastructure. In 2001, more than 20 percent of the loans on the balance sheets of China's four largest banks—all nationalized—were NPLs. By creating companies that essentially bought the bad loans on the bet that they would be able to recoup some of the losses, as well as the government mandating the banks carry larger financial cushions in case of future gargantuan losses, the banks were able to whittle the percentage of NPLs to 1.6 percent of total loan value.[7] Two of the banks—Bank of China and Industrial and Commercial Bank—were able to put their houses in order to a degree that they could list their institutions on the New York Stock Exchange.

As China approaches 2020 with its overriding mandate for social stability, the country's leadership will find it must eventually burst the financial dams of its own making that have kept the super-surplus of yuan pent up behind regulatory walls. Ready convertibility as well as de-pegging the value of the yuan from the U.S. dollar will see the yuan's value increase as more countries snap up the currency as a reserve currency and a trading currency. Though the increase in the yuan's value will affect companies (Chinese and foreign) that export from China's shores, it will also give Chinese consumers greater power to buy foreign goods. China will come closer to its desire for social harmony when it dis-bands the opacity and cronyism that currently infect dealings and operations of its state-owned enterprises, which share tangled crosshold-ings, do not give enough of their surplus revenue back to the government, and use the stock market as a rigged roulette wheel with financing from the state banks. Financial deregulation will see the SOEs forced into activities that make the companies more competitive in the global marketplace, instead of just idle speculators in domestic land deals and the stock market. The stock market itself requires greater opacity, and a true watchdog agency that has a mean growl and actually can bite compa-nies that misbehave without fear of retribution from government-vested interests. Without rectifying these issues, the next decade has the potential to be fraught with social instability as its financial system is beset by asset bubbles that, if they pop, may wipe away the bit of wealth the average Chinese has accumulated, while exacerbating the gap between rich and poor. Beside the out-and-out corruption of government officials, nothing else ignites the Chinese temper like the sense that someone is getting away with what should rightfully be theirs, whether its property, money, or a great bargain. China's leaders, however, have been taking baby steps to release some of the speculative pressure from the economy by allowing some countries to trade with China in yuan.

The government in 2008 created agreements with countries to settle transactions in yuan. That year, the central authority allowed payments to be made between companies in the Pearl and Yangtze River Deltas with those in Hong Kong and Macau. China also carried out currency swaps with a host of countries on the order of about US$120 billion.

In 2009, China signed currency-exchange agreements with Argentina, Indonesia, South Korea, Malaysia, Belarus, and Hong Kong. The smaller countries could use their yuan reserves to trade with China. In the same year, the State Council permitted exporters in Shanghai, Guangzhou, Shenzhen, Dongguan, and Zhuhai—major export centers in China—to settle transactions with international buyers in yuan. Further deregulation saw the China units of HSBC and the Bank of East Asia China to be the first overseas banks to sell yuan-denominated bonds in Hong Kong in 2009. Still, these initiatives to open up its financial market come nowhere near solving China's greatest international finance conundrum: what to do with its stash of dollar-denominated savings held abroad?

OUTBOUND INVESTMENT

China's "Dollar Trap" is of its own making. Nobel-winning economist Paul Krugman coined the term to sum up China's inability to dump its U.S. Treasury bills onto the international market. By the end of 2008, China had nearly US$2 trillion in U.S. Treasury bills, overseas direct investment, and other holdings as the American economy was sliding into recession. The Dollar Trap preempted China from yanking its dollars from the bond market; certainly, it did not want to buy those dollars with its own currency, which would overnight pump up the value of the yuan, hurting its manufacturing-export sector. Nor did it want to take its Treasury holdings and sell them onto other countries. Both moves would signal a lack of confidence in Washington's ability to keep inflation down at home, thus devaluing China's savings. It could also trigger concerns that the U.S. would not be able to repay its creditors on the debt Uncle Sam took out to subsidize everything from the Iraq War to Social Security pensions.

So, China had to play a more measured game internationally than it was able to get away with domestically. It could not make sudden moves in the international financial markets with its great stash of Treasury bills, nor rock the boat geopolitically. Still, it had to diversify its interests—take many of its eggs out of the American basket—without getting yoke on its face. The country gave primacy then to foreign direct investment (FDI) as a way for China to release the funds gathered through its trade surplus back into the international financial stream. FDI involves companies crossing national borders to make an equity investment in another country by setting up an operation, or entering a joint venture with another company, or outright merging and acquiring businesses in foreign lands. Though far from adequate in quickly drawing down its precariously large pile of dollars, it was a viable and effective means for China to release some pressure from the bubbles it had created within its own economy. But how big is China's Dollar Trap, really? Will the Trap close on America, instead?

America has little to fear from the notion that China will "buy the world." By the end of 2007, U.S. holdings in foreign reserves were more than US$7 trillion, compared with China's US$1.5 trillion in reserves. While America's official foreign reserves grew by more than US$1 trillion in the same year, China's grew by only half that amount.[8] The Dollar Trap, however, still froze a great deal of the capital that China had worldwide in dollar terms. So China, as early as 2005, began encouraging its state-owned enterprises to begin actively and aggressively acquiring dollar-denominated assets in other countries.

The odd thing about China's FDI, though, is it has everything to do with *not* making a profit on those investments in other countries. Its gerrymandered financial system cannot deal with greater inflows of capital in the way of further profits from its SOEs offshore acquisitions. Certainly, China does not want to lose money on its investments, as news of a string of bad investments—or even a single, one-off loss on a huge investment—could add to the derision most Chinese hold for their leadership. Indeed, one of the primary reasons for China's economic stewards to reduce the country's dependence on Treasury bills is that America's weakened economy brought the Chinese leadership in for hard criticism by its own citizens. Chinese bloggers accused government fund managers of being "running dogs" (that is, traitorous collaborators) of the Western governments for keeping Chinese money in Western assets that were in danger of depreciating. Taking a conservative tack with its foreign cachet, China uses its cash reserves and the surpluses of its SOEs to gain technology from Western companies it would be hard put to develop on its own, and to gain political favors with countries that are mineral rich.

From 2003 through 2008, China invested about US$43 billion in metals assets, mostly iron and steel in Australia. China committed about US$40 billion in energy investments over the same period, peaking in 2006, after which oil in particular began to become prohibitively expensive. China favored energy-sector deals with African nations, Russia, Brazil, and Central Asian countries. China also took about US$26 billion in stakes in financial institutions, including investments in Morgan Stanley, Blackstone, Fortis, Barclays, and Standard Bank of South Africa.[9]

In 2003, Chinese FDI flows into the United States were a mere US$65 million. By 2008, Chinese FDI into the U.S. had multiplied nearly eight times that value. Chinese FDI into South Africa in 2003, meanwhile, was a slight US$9 million, which ballooned in 2008 to more than US$4 billion, mostly in the mining, construction, electronic appliances, and automobile sectors capped with some activity in financial services. Australia—because of its vast mineral deposits—was the focus of a great deal of Chinese FDI attention in 2008, with more than US$2 billion passing into Australian coffers—a far cry from the tentative US$30 million China invested in the country five years earlier. In 2003, Hong Kong was China's largest target for "foreign" direct investment with slightly more than US$1 billion dollars passing into the Hong Kong property market and stock exchanges. By 2008, nearly 40 times that amount flowed out of Mainland China into Hong Kong, which still served as a platform for speculation and as an *entrepôt* to other worldwide destinations.[10]

China's first, high-profile move into the world of foreign direct investment came as a wake-up call for America. In 2005, the China National Offshore Oil Corporation (CNOOC) was blocked by the U.S. government from acquiring Unocal, a U.S. oil firm. Certainly, CNOOC's case was not made any easier by the fact that the company was a state-owned enterprise, and considered of strategic importance to China's own survival as a post-industrial country. Further, China defends its own domestic oil exploration industry with a state-run monopoly, which leaves foreign countries wondering why China should have access to their markets while they cannot penetrate those in China.[11] So, though the deal was valued at only about US$18 billion—relatively small in oil-conglomerate terms—U.S. legislators considered the attempted buyout enough of a security threat that regulatory hurdles thrown in front of the deal all but scuttled the transaction before serious mergers and acquisition talks could even begin.

The West, too, whether it likes to admit it or not, still suffers from a particularly virulent form of plague called "The Yellow Menace". From the mid-1800s into the twenty-first century, America in particular, and Europe to a lesser extent, has entertained fantasies of being overrun by Chinese. Indeed, laws in America were made in the late 1800s and not repealed until the mid-1960s that made it illegal for Chinese to bring women and family members to settle in the United States. Now, with the horde of foreign currency reserves China is holding in the new century, and is dying to offload—however surreptitiously—the sense of threat in the West has resurged.

Though Chinese investment in U.S. companies totaled about US$100 billion in mid-2008,[12] the amount is minuscule compared with the total US$11 trillion value of American companies listed on American stock exchanges in 2008.[13] Sensitive to American "sinophobia", however, some Chinese companies discarded their Mao jackets and donned dark-blue pinstripe suits and red "power ties" and attempted to invest in the U.S. with the help of other American companies. For instance, in 2008, the Chinese Internet-equipment maker Huawei partnered with Boston-based private equity firm Bain Capital to acquire 3Com, a technology company. However, Congressional rebuff of the acquisition spoiled the attempted buyout, and sent China back to its shores to try to figure out another way to make sizable acquisitions in America.[14]

In 2008, British government auditors caught out the Chinese financing arm of the State Administration for Foreign Exchange (SAFE) investing upward of US$16 billion in sectors ranging from banking to utilities. SAFE regulates foreign exchange policy and flows into and out of China, and also manages the lion's share of U.S. Treasury bonds; in 2008, SAFE had at least US$1 trillion in U.S. bonds in its portfolio.[15] SAFE invested in more than 50 companies in Britain with stakes that were each less than three percent the value of each company—the maximum amount a foreign stake can take in the United Kingdom without disclosing the purchase to British authorities.[16]

Though China has been investing in mining rights in South America, Africa, and Australia, most of its non-minerals, and nonenergy-related investments have been going to Southeast Asia. Countries such as Indonesia, Malaysia, Singapore, Vietnam, and Thailand took in more than US$13 billion in FDI in 2008.[17] Investments in wood, rubber, and construction contracts were main targets at the time. Indeed, of the top 10 cross-border Chinese mergers and acquisitions in terms of dollar value in 2009, eight were in Southeast Asia.[18] An affinity between Asian cultures as well as a population of overseas Chinese who are typically top merchants in these countries will see an increasing trend toward China investing more in non-mining projects in places that may present less resistance to Chinese investment than Western countries.

INTEGRATION, NOT DOMINATION

America has little to fear over the next 10 years in China's buying the United States, much as Americans had needlessly worried just before the Japanese bubble burst in the early 1990s that Japan Inc. was buying the American Dream. Even if the U.S. does not put its financial house in order after the near meltdown of its financial sector and economy in 2008–09, China will not be pulling its bond investments from the U.S. Treasury wholesale because of "the Dollar Trap" it has created for itself. Even though it already has US$2 trillion in foreign currency reserves at the beginning of 2010, it will not suddenly stop buying U.S. Treasury bonds, because it needs to consider the possibility of a rapid devaluation of its gargantuan nest egg. America may lose its "hegemony" over the currency reserve market, with countries around the world falling into line behind China, saying enough is enough; the U.S. should no longer have debt so cheaply if its government and its people can no longer balance its books.

On the world stage, China will continue to diversify its international holdings into the next decade. It will continue to push for an alternative reserve currency into which to park its savings, and it will continue to use a portion of its dollars to buy the ores and energy it needs to further develop its economy and meet the consumer requirements of its growing middle class. It will find most of the mining rights and purchase agreements in other developing regions in the world, though—and not in America and the European Union. Western national security considerations and cultural proclivities will resist seeing the world through red-tinted glasses.

Going forward, it will appear to most of the world that China is muscling in on prime investments abroad, and will seem to many to play the part of unwanted sugar daddy. It will also continue to be accused of stealth tactics in buying up assets abroad without flagging local regulatory controls, especially in Africa. However, China will remain a relatively new entrant in a global financial system in which the Western powers have already been engaged for nearly 400 years. Already, its huge foreign reserves, unprecedented in history, have created imbalances and opportunities for the country that will make its transition to financial superpower status controversial and fraught with conflicts.

Despite China's increasing attentions abroad, the country's leadership will continue to play a delicate balancing act in managing returns on investments and domestic demands that will become more onerous over time. A large and still growing population, a graying "bulge" of citizens that will reduce the country's productivity, and a mushrooming middle class with high expectations for wealth and consumption will all conspire by 2025 to draw Chinese financial investment abroad back nearer to China's borders. Foreign companies invested in China will increasingly find that greater, unwanted attention is placed on their activities in the runup to the next decade. The regulatory regime for Western investments in China will become increasingly restrictive for all but the richest multinationals as state-owned enterprises continue from 2010 to cordon the domestic market from international investors. Like many of its own government workers, the Chinese economy will have retired to anemic middle age about 55 years after Deng Xiaoping officially announced in 1978 as supreme leader of China that the nation was once again open for business. After its economic boom, China will hold much of its wealth nearby—just as its retirees do—through overwhelmingly Asian networks with which it has historical and cultural affinities.

END NOTES

1. Paul Krugman, "Taking on China," *The New York Times*, March 14, 2008.
2. Michael Schuman, "The Yuan Effect," *Time*, July 25, 2005.

3. Andrew Browne, "Chinese Official Warns of Risk if Yuan Rises," *The Wall Street Journal*, March 18, 2010.
4. "The Spend Is Nigh," *The Economist*, July 30, 2009.
5. "We Are the Champions," *The Economist*, March 28, 2004.
6. Shelly Smith, "China Defaulting Loans Soar, Insolvency Lawyer Says," Bloomberg, February 5, 2010.
7. Ibid.
8. Derek Scissors, "Monetary Flows: Chinese Investment—How Much and Where?" BusinessForum China, July/Aug 2009.
9. Derek Scissors, "Drowning in Cash," BusinessForum China, May/June 2009.
10. "China's Thirst for Global Resources," *Financial Times*, March 22, 2010.
11. "Dealing with Sinophobia," *The Economist*, July 10, 2008.
12. Derek Scissors, "Monetary Flows: Chinese Investment—How Much and Where?" BusinessForum China, July/Aug 2009.
13. World Development Indicators, World Bank, http://data.worldbank.org/indicator/CM.MKT.LCAP.CD, accessed September 2, 2010.
14. "Dealing with Sinophobia," *The Economist*, July 10, 2008.
15. Derek Scissors, "Drowning in Cash," BusinessForum China, May/June 2009.
16. Derek Scissors, "Monetary Flows: Chinese Investment—How Much and Where?" BusinessForum China, July/Aug 2009.
17. Ibid.
18. "Hey, Big Spender," *The Economist*, June 4, 2009.

CHAPTER **9**

Hot Pot Nation

ALL IN THE FAMILY

David Chen is a Kunshan native with his own small business that refurbishes factories. Kunshan is a small city by Chinese standards—about 650,000 people—a 45-minute drive to the northwest of Shanghai, made rich by early investment from Taiwanese factories in the mid-1980s. David's dream is to emigrate to Canada. He's a successful entrepreneur, speaking English in a hurried, staccato fashion. David and his wife had a son, who was four years old when his wife found out she was pregnant with their second child. The nurse who performed the ultrasound scan in the first trimester was the wife's eldest sister. The sister agreed to keep the pregnancy a secret while David continued to pursue a visa to Canada to work. Then, their thinking went, when they emigrated to Canada, they would be able to have the child without harassment from local government authorities.

Ironically, David's eldest brother worked in the local government, in the department that monitors local citizens' adherence to the one-child policy, which limits the number of children that parents can have to a single birth. The policy does have its exceptions: parents who have a daughter as the first child may try again for a second child after two years without penalty. But if the first child was the ever-important son, the family must pay stiff fines for the second child, which can be as much as three and six times their annual income. People in the countryside and in smaller cities often resent that richer urbanites can buy their way out of the one-child policy to have as many children as they please. A Chinese government source once related the story to me about a Guangdong businessman who strode into a local birth-control office—wife and children in tow—and flung more than US$30,000 on the desk of an official, and told the official to take however much fine that the government required to leave him and his family alone. His wife had already given birth to three children.[1]

David, however, was not a rich businessman. He believed if he and his wife were unable to get permission to emigrate to Canada before his wife showed her pregnancy, his brother would help them keep the baby—or, at least, look the other way when it came time for the birth. Unfortunately, his brother had been stamped more deeply by government policy than the bonds of brotherhood could support. While David's wife was at the clinic with her elder sister for a prenatal checkup, David's elder brother appeared in the office with an order to abort the child. No amount of tears or argument could dissuade the elder brother's purpose and duty. The abortion went through. If his brother had allowed David's wife to have the baby, the brother would not have been able to keep his job. At this writing, David is still working on emigrating to Canada, more intent than ever to move from China "so he can be free," he said. He and his brother have become sworn enemies.

I first related this story in a post on my blog "This is China!" A regular Chinese reader responded in a way I've heard from other Chinese: "It is unfortunate certain families keep putting feudal thinking ahead of the good of the nation. Some Western people criticize it, mainly because Western countries don't have this kind of massive population pressure." Chinese may not like the one-child policy, in other words, but they understand its necessity in a society with such strong emphasis on raising large families and sustaining family lines even when the environment plainly cannot support such levels of consumption. China's birth rate stabilized at just above one percent growth per year in 1995, down from three percent at the inception of the one-child policy in 1980. However, because of the large base of population, there was still a net increase of about one million newborns each month by the year 2010; that's the total population of Shanghai added to the Chinese census every year for 15 years.[2]

China has nearly five times the number of people as America, crowded into a physical space the size of the continental United States. Some provinces, such as Chongqing in the interior of China, have more people than the entire population of many countries with its 31 million residents. If Chongqing was a country, it would rank thirty-seventh in the world for population size, just after Canada (population 33 million). Every year, China's population grows by an additional 12 to 13 million people; it's like tacking on another country the size of Belgium annually, or by U.S. standards, another Illinois, Pennsylvania, or Ohio.[3]

The clash of traditional values and the allure of middle-class affluence becomes titanic in the face of one of China's—and humankind's—greatest challenges: China's huge population and the pressure it is putting on its environment and natural resources. The complexion of the demographics is also shifting, with the population becoming increasingly homogeneous through developed transportation links and urbanization, and overwhelmingly elderly by the year 2050. The demographic shift will have a dramatic impact on China's ability to continue generating wealth for its society at the stratospheric rates it had been able to in the first quarter of the century, and will have to increasingly consider how to absorb the costs of supporting the largest graying population in history.

POPCORN POPULATION

Even 2,000 years ago, China had the world's largest population, with about 60 million people representing nearly one-quarter of the world's population at the time. Chinese cities, since in the days of yore, have been amongst the largest by population in the world. Chang'an (modern day Xi'an) was the largest city in the world two millennia ago, following in the footsteps of Thebes, Babylon, and Alexandria before that. Upstart Rome took the pole position for several hundred years, as power and wealth moved from Western Europe to Constantinople (modern day Istanbul), and along the caravan routes of the Silk Road back to Chang'an, around 600 AD. By the time Marco Polo visited China in the mid-thirteenth century, Hangzhou—a two-hour drive west of Shanghai—was the largest city in the world, with more than 300,000 inhabitants. One hundred years later, during the

Ming Dynasty (1368–1644 AD), Hangzhou, Beijing, and Nanjing passed the baton between them with populations that pushed 700,000. Beijing rocketed to the top with more than one million inhabitants at the beginning of the eighteenth century, until the Industrial Revolution at the start of the nineteenth century catapulted London into first place for the next 100 years.

For the nearly 5,000 years since the first Chinese societies established themselves along the Yellow River in the north and the Yangtze River in south-central China, the main crops had been low-yield sorghum, winter wheat, and millet. China's land and indigenous crops seemed unable to support more than 60 million people until the 1400s.[4] During the Ming Dynasty, American Indian grains introduced through trade with the Europeans by way of the Silk Road took root on Chinese farms. The Chinese found that corn, potatoes, and sweet potatoes could be grown in far-larger quantities across a more varied terrain than their traditional crops of rice and millet. From the start of the Ming Dynasty until its fall in 1644, China's population grew to 120 million from 60 million.

China saw a great, nearly exponential, population explosion in the mid-1600s during the Qing Dynasty. The new, foreign rulers from Manchuria brought a social stability that reduced the number of casualties due to warfare, famine, plague, and general thuggery. The Pax Manchuria ushered in a doubling of the population from more than 175 million around 1750 to more than 350 million within 60 years. By the time Europeans had kicked open the doors to trade with China in the mid-1800s, China's ecology was foundering. Massive denuding of the forests in the northwest, in central, and in the southeast of the country had expanded deserts in the north, increased the frequency of flooding along the Yellow, Huai, and Yangtze Rivers, and caused famines in the south. Internally, the country began to fragment under the weight of its own people and their needs for survival, while industrialized powers pried open the fractures further.

The population continued to grow through the 1800s and into the mid-1900s despite the millions of casualties due to floods and famines. Having large families was still—as it had been for thousands of years—an insurance policy for carrying on the bloodline and supporting elders in their old age. Some of the more remarkable floods and famines that were occurring with greater frequency included the Famine of 1907, just before the last gasp of the Empress Dowager's reign, in which nearly 25 million people died; and the 1931 flood of the Yellow, Yangtze and Huai Rivers, in which about three million people were killed by drowning, disease, and famine throughout the country. Still, Chinese managed to claim, in the country's first modern census in 1953, nearly 600 million citizens residing within its borders.

About 36 million people were estimated to have died during the famine of 1959 to 1962, created by the policies of Mao Zedong's Great Leap Forward. After the policy debacle, Mao declared the way to replenish the country's strength was through liberal birthing policies: a family's "insurance policy" was morphing into economic and defense policies. Also, Mao had come to believe through the Communist Party's victory over the Nationalists led by Chiang Kai Shek that the strength of the country lay in the sheer numbers of its people. If the Communist Party could mobilize the small activities of the people into one, great force, then the country was unstoppable militarily and economically. The strategy, part of Mao's "human wave", as he called it, resulted in an annual growth rate of three percent, taking the population to 900 million in 1974 from ~~from~~ 660 million in 1961. Women in China in 1979 were, on average, having six children.

Others though, including the president of Beijing University at the time, Ma Yinchu, proposed the country was overpopulated and needed to launch a nationwide program of family planning. Ma was forced out of his position by Mao's hardliners, which became the source of the Chinese expression: "We lost one Ma Yinchu but we gained an extra 300 million people."

With Mao's death in 1976, the emergent leader Deng Xiaoping ushered in the one-child policy in 1980, without which the country would have had an additional 300 million to 400 million people by 2000; birth rates plummeted to 1.7 children per woman through sometimes draconian enforcement of the policy. Without a measure as severe as the one-child policy, it would have been near-impossible for China to have realized the economic growth and social reformation it has experienced the past 30 years. Population pressures would have kept the country "treading water" to support the additional hundreds of millions of mouths to feed and heads to shelter. One Chinese taxi driver bitterly explained to me that if it hadn't been for Mao encouraging Chinese families to have as many children as possible, the country wouldn't have to have a one-child policy." I have seven brothers and sisters," the cabbie complained. "Too many people."

WHAT'S LOVE GOT TO DO WITH IT?

The first batch of "Little Emperors" and "Empresses" came under parental pressure to marry in 2005, and found the institution of sharing and mutual support rough going. An unintended knock-on effect of the one-child policy is that single children are pampered by their parents and grandparents, and made the center of their families' universes as "Little Emperors" and "Empresses". Increasingly in China, spoiled, overweight children can be seen with a sweet red-bean bun in one hand and an ice cream in another, happy grandparents trailing behind carrying the children's backpacks. These children tend also to be the least mannered of the generations, shrill in their protests for McDonald's burgers, KFC wings or marinated chicken feet from the nearest convenience store. As they have grown older, their requirements and demands have grown more selfish, and young people are finding marriage not to be the route they want to travel the rest of their lives.

As recently as 20 years ago, centrally planned work units would essentially assign a mate to an employee, preside over the marriage ceremony, and provide housing for the couple as well as employment. Before the Communists took power in the country in 1949, parents would either commit their offspring to marriages or work with a matchmaker to find a suitable mate for their child. Sometimes the boy or girl would be as young as eight years old when he or she was betrothed by their parents. That meant that a great many couples had little passion in their relationship to begin with, let alone common interests beyond parenting children. The Communist Revolution abolished the practice of marrying off children to older partners.

The Wangs in Beijing were such a Revolutionary couple. I first met them at the Foreign Language Institute in Beijing in 1999. The wife, in her late 60s at the time, was white-haired (unusual in China), vibrant, and loquacious. Even after retirement, she never stopped being a

Communist Party supporter, though she had not been active in the Party in decades. She had been a professor of Russian literature, literally plucked from the countryside just after the Communists had wrested power from the Nationalists in 1949. Her husband was a historian of Chinese history. Wang was the complete opposite of his wife: quiet, retiring, and good-natured. His wife originally had fallen in love with a soldier who she had met in the 1950s in Beijing at a local dance. They saw each other several times after the event, which would have been considered illegal in many other parts of China as all energies were supposed to be directed at the development of the Party and the reconstruction of the country. However, as the future Mr. and Mrs. Wang worked at the same university, administrators of the work unit believed them to be a good match. The Party believed the marriage was for the good of the people as the couple's skills, training, and intellects were comparable. Their relationship was, at best, amicable: Mrs. Wang led and Mr. Wang followed. They remained married for nearly 50 years until Mrs. Wang passed away in 2003.

Modernity has ratcheted up expectations for marriage beyond anything older generations could have dreamed of in China. Love, for instance—the unrequited version of which is quite popular in Chinese folktales and classics—is a growing factor in choosing who to marry. People who grow up in the same cities in many instances have been classmates in primary, middle school, or university, or their parents have introduced them. The relaxation of the *hukou* 戶口 residence-permit system has allowed many couples from different regions of China to meet in universities or workplaces for the first time. However, for young people in the large cities, in which locals and out-of-towners alike can feel anonymous, the Internet is becoming a common means for becoming acquainted and of determining the extent of a couple's shared interests and values.

But sometimes, traditional parental pressure and the growing expectations of the young middle class can be too much for a young couple to bear, especially for those born and raised as "Little Emperors" and "Empresses" under the one-child policy. Leonard and Lei Lei, born and bred in in the south-central city of Suzhou, are archetypal of the kind of pressure, expectations, and distractions that tear a young marriage apart. The couple seemed perfect by Chinese middle-class standards: both in their late 20s, both locals, both classmates, both sets of parents knew and liked each other, and both belonged to the same rising socioeconomic class. Lei Lei, the bride, was a pretty, wide-eyed, and intelligent young lady who but for her height would have gone on to be a professional model. Leonard, the groom, was a pudgy, good-natured bloke who frequented KTV parlors and partied at discos. Lei Lei was an elementary school teacher and Leonard a mobile phone salesman for a Taiwanese manufacturer. Within weeks after marrying, Leonard was back in the discos with a new girlfriend in tow. Within a year, he and his wife divorced, without even a grandchild to present to their anxious elders. Leonard later moved to Xiamen, in Fujian Province, just north of southernmost Guangdong.

It was clear that for Leonard, marriage in his late 20s was simply a check on the short list of parental expectations: university degree, marriage, grandchild. Once the children have married and produced a baby, they have fulfilled their parents' highest expectations. They can "check it off" and get on with their own lives. Sometimes, that involves simply getting divorced and starting over—if they haven't already picked up a girlfriend or boyfriend on the side—especially in the larger cities. Beijing and Shanghai, in particular, have the dubious distinctions of a 50 percent divorce rate; comparable to the United States.

Leonard's story is hardly unique in China. Marriage is increasingly a tough commitment to sustain in light of all the distractions—economic and emotional—that China's new society is affording youth of the one-child policy. For instance, 27-year-old Chen Juan divorced her husband just before giving birth to their child because he "talked dirty, did not buy her clothes, and seldom went with her for her pre-natal examinations." Beijingers Wang Jing and Chen Sen remained married for only 18 months because her husband Chen had become addicted to online games. She said her husband would miss meals altogether because of his gaming passion, and that he did not take care of her when she was sick. Single children Gal and Deng divorced because they could not agree over who was responsible for doing the housework.[5] But, then again, 35 years before, at the height of the Cultural Revolution, spouses would turn their partners in to local Red Guard units to be violently "struggled" against should they express contrary political views at the dinner table. Many did not survive the often brutal sessions. Divorce—Chinese style—may actually be an advancement on getting out of a marriage.

In Leonard's case, it was clear his divorce from Lei Lei was merely a symptom of the stresses of a society in perpetual motion, with dire implications not only for its youth, but for its elderly who, are increasingly looking to their married children to support them in retirement.

Meanwhile, the offspring of the one-child policy gravitate toward the larger cities for university education or simply to find jobs that pay more than they would make in their rural hometowns.[6] Meeting the family imperative of marrying and settling down once the children reach their 20s is becoming more difficult for young people in modernizing China. Youthful pursuits of career and perhaps even exploring a sense of identity independent of social mores are increasingly at odds with the familial imperative to extend the bloodline and shore up the social security of the older generations.

Parents who leave the marriage calendar up to their children are becoming frustrated with a trend with the younger generation to defer marriage—or perhaps even choosing not to marry at all. Young people are still under a great deal of pressure to find a mate—usually the first girlfriend or boyfriend that comes along—and marry. And not just to anyone. Of course, marrying a local is best, but if the son or daughter is living and working out of town, then an outsider will do just fine. But the prospective partner must be of the same socioeconomic status; at least, for the men. "Marrying down" is not supported. For women, "marrying up" is permissible, even preferable, if the woman's parents are from a small village or the countryside; the expectation for the new husband is that he will be able to help in the support of the woman's immediate family, and be able to, from time to time, lend a financial hand to extended family members. Some young Chinese who have moved from the countryside or small towns to larger cities dare not call home too often because of the grief family members—parents, aunties, uncles, and grandparents—will give them about getting married. The pressure to have a mate-in-tow is especially great during Spring Festival, when young people are expected to trek back to their hometowns to present their future spouse for familial review and approval.

Many young people have been turning to the Internet for respite. In the runup to Spring Festival, young men and women by the thousands post their requirements to rent a boyfriend or girlfriend to take back to their hometowns for the weeklong festival. One young man, for instance, took his new "girlfriend" back to his hometown in Yueyang, Hunan Province, on condition he would pay her 1,500 yuan (US$219.50) for four days. The renter is usually responsible for paying expenses as well.[7] Renters can be especially tight in their requirements. One girl's online criteria cited candidates should be educated, employed, well-behaved, and between 170 and 180 centimeters tall. Eye glasses were a plus, as her father considered men with glasses to be particularly smart. She also admonished candidates: "Don't be too skinny." The trend seems to be catching on, with enterprising individuals hosting "love for rent" parties. In smaller cities such as Xi'an and Huizhou, in Guangdong Province, young people pose as renters and candidates, both actually hoping they will be able to develop more permanent attachments after some time together.[8]

4-2-1 . . . BREAKDOWN

Children born after the one-child policy came into effect in 1980 now have an inverted demographic pyramid bearing down on their shoulders. The Chinese call it the "4-2-1 Problem"—one child supports two parents and four grandparents. When a couple marries and have their own child, the equation extends outward just a bit more to become a 8-4-3-1 issue, with the man of the house often the sole support of his nuclear family (three people) and parents (four more people) and grandparents on both sides of the family (eight additional souls). Of course, when a son or daughter marries, and assuming both partners work, then the married couple has a 8-4-3-2 challenge on their hands until relatives become ancestors: a working couple (two people) supports themselves and their child (three people), each of their parents (four people) and all related grandparents (eight people) until the elderly pass away. However you do the math, Chinese married couples in which both spouses come from single-child families are going to have it rough. Especially given that it is against a law established in 1996 in China to NOT support your parents. The law was a direct response to the mass firings that ensued when the central government began dismantling thousands of its underperforming state-owned enterprises, which had offered hundreds of millions of employees retirement benefits—or the "iron rice bowl," as it was called. Nowadays, some parents sue their errant children if their offspring have neglected their welfare. Though many elderly in China do rely on their children for financial contributions, many retirees from state-owned enterprises and government offices rely on government pension funds to supplement their income.

Shanghai administrators, however, were among the first in China to realize that one day there wouldn't be enough workers in the city to support the social security program for the elderly. Many parents who live in Shanghai began discovering at the turn of the new century what those in the post-industrial world had realized decades before—kids ain't cheap!—and of their own accord are stopping after one child, independent of state policy. In mid-2009, health administrators promoted a clause in the one-child policy that many had overlooked before: If both spouses in a marriage are from one-child families, the new parents can have two children, without penalty. Shanghai parents, however, remained nonplussed by the announcement.[9] Modernization is proving as effective as the one-child policy in accelerating the trend toward below-zero population growth in the larger cities, such as Shanghai, Beijing, and Hong Kong. These cities now are as expensive to live and work in as New York City (Hong Kong even more so in 2009). Economics, then, is trumping parental expectations for their children to marry and produce grandchildren. Buying a home in Shanghai has become so expensive that many young men are simply choosing not to have girlfriends. Courtship is too expensive, they are finding, especially when one considers that many young women expect their suitors to already own their own apartments. Given that the average salary for a young professional working in Shanghai is about US$9,000, and the average 40-square-meter apartment may go for about US$200,000, a young man needs to have saved a substantial amount of money to ponder catching a local girl. Not even the combined savings of the suitor's family is enough to buy an affordable apartment, with property speculation rife since the 2008–2009 global economic downturn.

Some couples who want to spend the rest of their lives together despite social mores are turning to "naked marriages". In the past 10 years, it has become common for couples in cities such as Shanghai and Beijing to marry without the apartment, without the expensive ring, without even a wedding banquet (which is downright un-Chinese). Though 80 percent of men supported "naked marriages" in a Sohu.com survey in 2010, 70 percent of the women polled thought such marriages were not reliable. "If a man does not give you the wedding you want, will he take care of you wholeheartedly in the future?" questioned one respondent. "Half-naked marriages", another trend, would at least net the girl a ring, but likely no flat and no wedding banquet.[10]

The fraying of the tight social ties that used to bind families and communities together is behind the rise of more than 10 million single people older than 35, according to *China Daily*. Modernization has made it more difficult than in the old days of arranged marriages for men and women to find mates. The social stigma of age makes it more difficult—unless one is quite well-off financially—to marry. In Chinese society, a man or woman who is not married by the age of 30 is considered a "leftover". "Leftover gentlemen", as they are called in Chinese, out-number "leftover ladies" by as much as two-to-one in smaller cities.

By the year 2020, the one-child policy will have contributed more than any other single social factor in the change of complexion of Chinese marriage. Simply put, China has 32 million more boys under the age of 20 than girls. Industrialized countries see a ratio of about 103 to 107 boys for every 100 girls. China, before the implementation of the one-child policy, had a ratio of 106 boys to 100 girls. With the introduction of ultrasound technology into Chinese clinics in 1986, many parents have opted to abort a female fetus over a boy, since it is the male in the culture who carries on the family line. By 2005, China saw a birth rate of 120 boys for every 100 girls; in Guangdong, Anhui, and Qinghai Provinces, the number has reached as high as 130 boys for every girl. For parents who live in rural China, the one-child policy is more liberally applied in the event that the first child born is a girl. Those bent on the second child being a boy will do whatever it takes to ensure just such a result, including abandonment or even infanticide of newborn girls. In some villages and small rural towns, the ratio of boys to girls is as high as 143 to 100.[11] Despite China making it illegal for medical technicians across the country to disclose the sex of an unborn child, bribery is rife in city hospitals and country clinics—old ways of thinking die hard.[12]

With Chinese women of marriageable age increasingly becoming a valuable "commodity", women are upping the "bride price," as the Chinese call it. Now, instead of a man having to just provide a sizable dowry (upward of US$30,000 in some parts of the country) and an apartment, he may also be on the hook to provide a car to a prospective bride and the promise of a lavish wedding banquet. One young woman from the countryside of Anhui Province explained to me that families of young women also get in on the negotiations with suitors. "The girls' families have discovered getting married is a great business!" she said.

At the same time, Chinese women are now finding considerable competition coming from Vietnam, Thailand, Cambodia, and Burma. The lack of brides, especially in the Chinese countryside, and the high cost of Chinese dowries has led to the booming business of buying brides from Vietnam. "My ex-girlfriends would always go to the big shopping malls to buy things, while this one [Vietnamese wife] now would be very pleased just going to a large market," a Chinese man in Nanjing happily blogged about his Vietnamese bride.[13] The process of obtaining a bride from Vietnam can be as straightforward as posting an advertisement in a Vietnamese newspaper stating one's intentions to find a wife, then traveling to Vietnam to meet the women who responded to the ad. In this case, the happy blogger's male friends were so impressed with the blogger's good fortune that they asked him to arrange wife-hunting tours for them to Vietnam.[14] Not all of the competition is legal, though. Some men in the countryside have taken desperate measures, going so far as to kidnap young Chinese women in cities and trapping them in the countryside, where extended family members will keep a constant eye on victims to ensure they do not escape. Young women from Vietnam are kidnapped from the Hmong tribes along China's border and sold to bachelors for about 5,000 to 6,000 yuan (US$730 to US$875), while North Korean women trafficked across the border with Vietnam fetch 2,900 to 9,700 yuan ($406 to $1,358).[15]

Some social commentators believe the national surplus of testosterone will result in higher crime rates in the country[16] and a greater sense of nationalism, as unmarried young men seek to channel their unrequited energies into other activities, including a greater proclivity to go to war with other states. However, Drew Thompson writes in *Foreign Policy* that "one-child" soldiers make for lousy troops in the People's Liberation Army (PLA). These soldiers comprised nearly half of the 2.3 million Chinese troops in the PLA in 2006. Though the one-child soldiers may have better computer skills and even communicate more effectively than comrades with siblings, "only-child recruits are not as tough; they don't like to go through the pain of intense training; they call in sick more frequently; and they struggle to perform some simple chores like doing their own laundry," Thompson writes.[17]

Demographics has been a key factor in China's economic rise in the past 30 years. Seventy percent of the population is of working age, a direct result of Mao's plan in the early 1960s to unleash a population explosion. Indeed, one of the employment challenges the national government faces is called the "20/30 Problem"—creating enough jobs for those in their 20s and early 30s.[18] However, it's not a problem China will have for too many more years.

China is aging fast. The number of young people entering the workforce between the ages of 20 and 24 will drop by half by 2020.[19] In other words, the majority of China's workers will be too old to keep the economy sizzling long enough for citizens' income on a per capita basis to catch up with America's or Europe's. China's "golden age" of productivity and wealth creation in China will only last until about 2030. The shift of the age-bulge also implies a change in the expectations of the testosterone-hazed "Little Emperors" who operate the machines in the "Workshop of the World"—they will not be so inclined temperamentally nor physically to stand day in and day out at factory machines; instead, they will make the effort to work smarter, not harder. They will reshape the country's service industry to increasingly cater to domestic middle-class demands and meet the requirements of a rapidly aging demographic.

GRAY TIGER POWER

In 2005, about 130 million people—roughly 10 percent of the population—were over the age of 60; by the year 2050, nearly half a billion Chinese—or one out of three people in the country at that time—will be more than 60 years old, with 100 million over the age of 80. China's population will peak at a little less than 1.5 billion in the year 2030, and then, through the medium of the one-child policy and the expenses incumbent in modernization, gradually decline. In 1975, before the population-reducing effects of the one-child policy, nearly eight workers supported the pension of every person aged 60 and older; in 2010, 13 workers paid a part of their salary into a retirement fund to support one elderly person. By 2050, China will only have two working-age people paying social security for each elderly individual.[20]

With fewer people in a Chinese household to support their relatives economically and physically, retirement homes are becoming a more socially acceptable alternative lifestyle for retirees. In 2010, five percent of elderly in the cities lived in retirement homes, while only two percent of the rural elderly live in such institutions.[21] A retirement home in Beijing such as the privately held Sunshine Care in Beijing can cost about 2,300 yuan (US$337) a month. Pensions can cover the costs; however, only about 200 million Chinese total are eligible for pension coverage. The national government plans to lift the number of Chinese covered by a pension scheme to nearly 225 million by the end of 2011. Large cities such as Beijing, Tianjin, and Chongqing are adding more retirement beds; Beijing intends to add as many as 15,000 new beds in 2010 alone—an increase of more than 40 percent from the previous year.[22] The private industry is getting in on the aging trend as well, with Singaporean investors establishing a "Scenic Health-Care Park" in Suzhou, near Shanghai. The park will be a retirement village with medical and food facilities on site, as well as rehabilitation and social programs for its residents—the first of its kind in China.[23]

China may well within the next decade see its one-child policy repealed.[24] Given Chinese xenophobia and its lack of enthusiasm for importing labor from other countries, government leaders will likely liberalize family-planning policies to bolster its labor force and try to shore up its national pension scheme. Meanwhile, a much more homogeneous China that is well-integrated through communication and transportation infrastructure might create the sort of network effects that work in lock-step to shake the leadership loose from its pedestal. Gray Tigers—that great bulge of half a billion Chinese over the age of 60—will be the first elderly generation in Chinese history who will be technology savvy, drawn closer together by the Internet, light rails, superhighways, and airport hubs. It's the Gray Tigers who may push China into its next political metamorphosis—with nary a shot fired.

HOT POT NATION

Modernization is exacting an unexpected toll on the Chinese population: homogenization. It's easy to perceive China as a mass of people and figure them all to be the same (to be fair, the Chinese have the same perception of Europeans and Americans). Nothing could be farther from the truth. Chinese are remarkably distinctive, even from town to town. China is made up of 31 provinces—including Tibet and the primarily Muslim Xinjiang, which modern China considers a *de facto* part of the country—656 cities, 48,000 districts, 235 distinct languages, and 8,000 dialects, not to ignore the 52 minority groups. Though much of the country understands and speaks Mandarin Chinese, which originally hailed from Northern China in a region near the Yellow River, many older locals can neither speak nor understand the country's *lingua franca*. Indeed, in the city in which I have my home—Suzhou, a half-hour bullet-train ride from Shanghai—many local residents over the age of 55 years simply cannot speak Mandarin. Nor can they have a conversation with someone who lives a 45-minute drive to the west of the city, in Wuxi; residents there have their own language. Suzhou locals can understand the language Shanghai locals speak, though Suzhou folk find it difficult to actually speak the Shanghai dialect: they must communicate in Mandarin (also known as *putonghua* 普通话, or common language). I recall one Chinese classmate from Guangdong telling me he could not understand our Chinese teacher when the teacher spoke the local dialect, though the two were from the same village. "Teacher is from the other side of the river," the student said. It took a year for the two to be able to communicate effectively in the local language.

Regional differences and habits can be even more revealing. Northern Chinese tend to be taller and stockier than their southern cousins, who share bloodlines with the indigenous populations of modern-day Vietnam, Thailand, and Burma, while northerners share more with Mongols. Northern Chinese tend to drink greater quantities of spirits than southerners, and prefer fighting to settle a dispute to simply arguing loudly, as most do in the south. Southerners tend to eat more rice than northerners, who favor an unleavened bread. Meanwhile, the Sichuanese, Hunanese, and residents of Guizhou love their spicy food; locals in Shanghai and westward in Jiangsu Province prefer their food sweetened with sugar.

Modernity is reducing the distinctiveness between regions. Exponential growth in road and rail links that increase travel between the countryside and cities—and between cities themselves—mass urbanization, a loosening of the *hukou* 户口 residence-permit system separating city dwellers and country folk, and cultural homogenization by consumer juggernauts such as McDonald's, KFC, and Starbucks are smoothing the differences in the vast population. China is becoming a great "hot pot" of homogeneity, much like the dish favored by almost every Chinese, no matter their hometown. Hot pot is a delicious chicken or pork broth brought to boil in a great stainless steel bowl over a gas flame or electric hot plate set in the middle of a dining table. Diners use their chopsticks to dip a variety of meats and vegetables in the broth until the morsels are well done, fishing the contents out to eat or to share with one another. After a while though, everything starts to taste the same—the mushrooms taste like the lamb chunks, the fish tastes like the egg dumplings, the beef meatballs taste the same as pig's brains—as the flavors intermingle and the broth becomes greasy from the meats that have been boiling away. The older generations who live in Shanghai see this happening all around them. They feel their local language and habits being replaced by the Mandarin Chinese dialect, as "outside people"—Chinese from other regions—have flooded into the city for educational and work opportunities. Young and hip locals in the metropolis also speak Mandarin with friends and classmates, conversing in the local Shanghai dialect only with their parents.

What modernization seems to be leaving in its wake in China is less differentiation between regions that were once uniquely colorful with their own foods, dialects, habits—and even their clothing. Only some of the most fundamental cultural values are remaining intact: an extreme dependence on close family relationships and associations with their hometowns, a reverence for history and ancestors, and an obsession with finding a mate and bearing children to satisfy parental pressure. Hard-core "traditional" values are noisily colliding with the values of a consumer-based modernity that accentuates individuality and individual expression.

Ironically, cultural homogenization is succeeding where socialism failed in the mobilization of thought and action in Chinese society. Nearly 100 years ago, the early Communists would send infiltrators ahead to villages, towns, and cities throughout China to turn the local population against the new Nationalist government and toward Communist ideology. In twenty-first century China, modern communications such as mobile phones, text messaging, Internet-enabled technologies (like Skype), blogs, and chat rooms have allowed ideas and opinions to spread, virus-like, more quickly throughout the country than ever before in its history. Fast trains operating at 340 kilometers an hour increasingly interconnect the smallest villages with the largest urban hubs, while subways knit together intracity districts for the first time ever. Airlines, highways, and bridges across rivers once considered impassable are also interweaving a society that historically relied on geography to maintain local customs and languages—at the same time providing local governments almost absolute control over districts. In essence, the Chinese are assimilating themselves.

Of course, though homogenization may work wonders for the reception of government precepts throughout the land, central and local governments by 2010 are already finding themselves increasingly under pressure for accountability from the farthest reaches of China. Regions once disparate are quickly coming to know about, understand, and even empathize with the plight of Chinese citizens thousands of kilometers away—and are able to do something about it. By the year 2020, they will be able to journey to these hotspots within half a day to "vote with their feet." By the year 2030, the one-child policy could be history. However, discontent born from the wedding of traditional values of family and the necessity of the one-child policy may provide a catalyst for challenging the Communist Party. The homegrown stresses of broken homes, underemployment, aging bachelors, childless men, overstretched health-care services and bankrupt social security tills may foment a riptide of change that trumps the one wild card the Party has been banking on since the Tiananmen Square protests to maintain its hold on power: Chinese nationalism.

END NOTES

1. Zhang Ming'ai, "Heavy Fine for Violators of One-Child Policy," China.org .cn, September 18, 2007, http://www.china.org.cn/english/government/ 224913.htm.

2. "Issues and Trends in China's Demographic History," Asia for Educators, Columbia University, http://afe.easia.columbia.edu/special/china_1950_ population.htm, accessed February 2, 2010.

3. "List of U.S. States and Territories by Population," Wikipedia, http://en .wikipedia.org/wiki/List_of_U.S._states_and_territories_by_population, accessed February 12, 2010.

4. http://agri-history.ihns.ac.cn/history/renkoubiao.htm; accessed March 30, 2010.

5. Lin Qi, "Young Couples Splitting from Tradition," *China Daily*, June 10, 2009.

6. "Issues and Trends in China's Demographic History," Asia for Educators, Columbia University, http://afe.easia.columbia.edu/special/china_1950_ population.htm, accessed February 2, 2010.

7. Gan Tian, "I'll Pay You to Be My Valentine," *China Daily*, February 13, 2009.

8. Dan Levin, "Wanted: Rental Boyfriend for Lunar New Year," *The New York Times*, February 11, 2010.

9. Tania Branigan, "Shanghai Encourages Second Child for Eligible Couples," *The Guardian*, July 24, 2009.

10. Gan Tian, "Embracing a 'Naked Marriage', *China Daily*, February 33, 2010.

11. Sharon LaFraniere,"Chinese Bias for Baby Boys Creates a Gap of 32 Million," *The New York Times*, April 10, 2009.

12. Christine Chan, Melissa D'Arcy, Shannon Hill, and Farouk Ophaso, "Demographic Consequences of China's One-Child Policy," International Economic Development Program, Ford School of Public Policy, University of Michigan, April 24, 2006.

13. "Chinese Man Spends 35K For 'Obedient' Vietnamese Wife," china SMACK, January 31, 2010, http://www.chinasmack.com/2010/ stories/chinese-man-spends-35k-for-obedient-vietnamese-wife.html, accessed February 26, 2010.

14. Ibid.

15. U.S. State Department Diplomacy in Action, China, March 11, 2008; http://www.state.gov/g/drl/rls/hrrpt/2007/100518.htm; accessed February 2, 2010.

16. "China Youth Crime in Rapid Rise,'" BBC, December 5, 2007, http://news.bbc.co.uk/2/hi/asia-pacific/7128213.stm, accessed September 15, 2010.

17. Drew Thompson, "Think Again: China's Military," *Foreign Policy*, March/April 2010.

18. William Dodson, "Out of Bangalore and into China," BusinessForum China, July/August 2009.

19. Simon Elegant, "Is China's One-Child Policy Heading for a Revision?," *Time*, July 27, 2009.

20. Dune Lawrence, "China Begins to Address a Coming Wave of Elderly," *The New York Times*, April 21, 2009.

21. Ibid.

22. Ibid.

23. "Golden Years," *China Economic Review*, October 2009.

24. Rachel Martin, "China May Relax One-Child Policy," National Public Radio, March 3, 2008, http://www.npr.org/templates/story/story.php?storyId=87851165, accessed September 12, 2010.

CHAPTER **10**

In the Shadow
of the Emperors

A CLASH OF CIVILIZATIONS

The American EP-3E ARIES II was flying a milk run, a routine mission along China's southeastern coastline that would likely see its crew back at Kadena Air Base in Okinawa by dinnertime. It was a bright Sunday morning, some 105 kilometers off the coast of Hainan Island, in the South China Sea. The crew would log the time at 08:30, April 2, 2001.The reconnaissance team was already familiar with the path that the spy plane would take as it scouted for the deployment of Chinese naval vessels staking their territory around rock outcroppings hotly contested by China and its neighbors for their mineral wealth and strategic importance; Chinese submarines based in Hainan Island that might come up for a breather; and missile batteries at the ready should Taiwan's rogue president Chen Shui-bian declare independence from the Motherland.

Two sleek Chinese J-8II interceptor fighter jets came up behind the lumbering propeller-driven craft. The fighters were like mosquitoes to the hippopotamus-like EP-3Es. The spy plane was awkward, slow-moving, pregnant with electronic-detection equipment, and bristling with antennae quivering with anticipation of discovery. The J-8IIs' job was to escort the U.S. surveillance craft from the border of international waters—a broad band of neutrality 200 nautical miles wide—away from the Chinese coast. It was normal operating procedure. The game had been played for decades by countries who wanted to get the drop on their neighbor's latest deployment of armaments. The neighbor, of course, always knew what was going on, and the tacit agreement was that when the neighbor felt enough, was enough it would lead its nosy counterpart away from its backyard.

The Chinese jets came up faster than usual, and closer. The EP-3E crew had already been briefed that for the past few months, Chinese fighter pilots were becoming more aggressive with their chases. This time, though, there was something more menacing in the way one of the jets crossed the nose of the EP-3E, in the devil-may-care acrobatics with which it tried to touch wingtip to wingtip. It was Leutinant Commander Wang Wei's fighter, the crew could see. He had already gained a reputation with American crews for showboating. The bearish U.S. craft could only continue on its path, however, locked on autopilot; gradually it would veer away from the supersonic wasps buzzing it.

At 09:15, Lieutenant Commander Wang Wei steered his craft to take another swipe at the EP-3E. It would be his last. The fighter bumped the EP-3E's left wing with its own wing. The fighter pilot could not control the slide, and watched as its own wing cut into the outside propeller of the American plane. The brief hold the outer propeller had on the sleek craft was enough to chuck the jet across the nose of the lumbering craft like a boomerang, sheering the tip of the black cone from the fuselage of the EP-3E. The pilot and co-pilot looked out the aft window to see smoke pouring from the stump of what had been the outer propeller; they still had three propellers, but with fuel leaking from the wing and the possibility of an explosion, they had no other option than to land the craft as soon as possible. That would mean taking the plane to the Chinese military base on Hainan Island itself.

As they radioed in their distress call, the crew watched the Chinese fighter that had collided with them spiral downward toward the blue floor of the ocean below. One of the crew spotted a parachute pop open near the fighter. It would be the last anyone would see of the pilot. The crew sent out numerous distress calls, all the while destroying the most sensitive equipment and records onboard. Requests to land at Lingshui airfield on Hainan Island went unanswered. The EP-3E, without recourse, made an unauthorized landing on the airfield. Armed Chinese soldiers surrounded the beached aircraft with orders to incarcerate the crew of 24.

The Chinese Foreign Ministry immediately demanded an apology from the United States as a victim of an incident clearly orchestrated to humiliate China. Without a detailed investigation into the causes behind the crash, the U.S. government was loathe to deliver any more than condolences over the loss of the pilot. Eventually, just to get the pilots back home, then-U.S. Secretary of State Colin Powell gave "face" to the Chinese government and its people by issuing a formal apology for causing the incident, though there still had been no objective investigation into circumstances. Eleven days after the incident, the entire crew returned to the United States, unharmed; five weeks later the plane followed, crated in pieces.

Emotions ran high in China as citizens protested American insouciance and performed the ritual stoning of the U.S. embassy in Beijing, which the central government permits from time to time to show the world its displeasure. The Chinese leadership had successfully shown its constituency it could keep its shores secure from unwanted and uninvited Western intrusion. Even further, it could make the mighty United States kowtow to its rising presence and importance in the world.

The Spy Plane Incident literally and metaphorically represented the first clash of civilizations between China and the United States since the Fall of the Berlin Wall in 1989. In 1998, Samuel P. Huntington wrote in his book, *The Clash of Civilizations*, that with political ideologies disintegrating after the fall of the Soviet Union, future conflicts would increasingly be divided along fault lines of civilization. The Spy Plane Incident provided China with its first opportunity of the new century to assert its evolving mythology of collective identity soaked in a blood-stained history of victimization and subsequent heroism. In other words, China has a chip on its shoulder. Its identity is still fragile, even embryonic, as it tries on modernization with Western characteristics, explores the boundaries of individual creative expression, arms itself against enemies of the past, and reluctantly assumes responsibilities as a heavyweight stakeholder in global institutions in which it had no part in developing.

If there is any single incident since the Tiananmen Square massacre in 1989 that exposes the collective insecurity underpinning China's massive drive to modernization, it is the Spy Plane Incident. It was much more than just a great deal of chest-beating or macho militarism on China's part; it showed up just how parochial Chinese society is, how clumsy its "coming out" onto the global stage has been, and the genuine confusion it is experiencing as it grafts Western technologies and world views onto its revisioned sense of history. The Spy Plane Incident revealed that much more is at play in the Chinese psyche during this time of great transition than mere flag-waving nationalism; instead, Chinese identity itself is at stake. A country that has heavily relied for thousands of years on historical precedent established by emperors is finding it must morph into a future leadership model without parallel in its own long history. China is simultaneously a developed country and a developing nation, and has no road map for the future—and no way to U-turn.

A CHIP ON ITS SHOULDER

In 1980, the Communist Party executed a huge about-face by refuting socialism and promoting capitalism. Nor could the Party claim the mantle of the Emperors, as they had just spent the previous 30 years refuting the imperial system (with Mao Zedong paradoxically playing the role of Emperor). That left the Party with only two tools with which to maintain its hold on power: the individual's quest for the good life (in some contexts interpreted as greed), and nationalism. The Chinese leadership has become expert in conducting the emotions of its citizens in an orchestra of "national outcry" against perceived foreign intransigence. The primary fuse the government can always ignite are China's grievances about foreign incursions into the country from the early 1800s until 1949. The grievances—many real, some imaginary, and all the fault of "the other guy"—have been whipped together to form a mythology that makes China the perpetual victim.

For instance, nearly a quarter of all national and local television programming in China is devoted to the wrongs perpetrated on the

Chinese people by any of the (fill in the blank): a) European and American colonizing powers; b) Japanese imperial army; c) Nationalist Army of Chiang Kai Shek (decamped to Taiwan after losing the Mainland to the Communists in 1949). On any given night on Chinese TV there will be at least one—perhaps even two—soap operas that involve the Japanese occupation of China and its brutality toward the Chinese. Most of the all-Japanese-are-dirty-bastards-that-rape-our-women-and-burn-our-villages soap operas begin with the fall of the Qing Dynasty in 1911, and trace the episodic tragedies of one or two families through the revolutions of the next two decades, tragically followed by the occupation of the Japanese from the early 1930s until their surrender in 1945. Inevitably, a lovely woman gets raped by a Japanese officer with a Hitler mustache, while her husband/son/father (fill in the blank), forced to watch the violation, is eventually bayoneted by lascivious Japanese foot soldiers. All the miniseries (which run to 30 or 40 episodes) end with the sheer joy citizens express when Communist Party soldiers march through their town's gates at the end of the war. It would be the equivalent in the United States to a quarter of all network television channels devoting prime-time viewing hours to documentaries, movies, and soap operas about the Civil War and slavery (with Union soldiers triumphantly marching through the streets of Richmond, Virginia). The shows are hugely popular with Chinese of all ages. In other words, the central government does not have to work very hard to shore up Chinese outrage at "The Others".

The effect, of course, is reinforcement of a xenophobia that China has suffered since antiquity, and a consolidation and homogenization of modern Chinese thinking about the world outside its borders. "The Great Media Wall of China" effectively builds walls to resist incursion of the idea that foreigners are human beings too. Indeed, not until the end of the Qing Dynasty in 1911 were foreigners able to travel beyond the designated port areas Western colonial powers had wrested from the insular government of the time. Throughout most of China's history, the only contact Chinese had with foreigners was through the Silk Road. *Entrepôts* such as Xi'an and, to the south, Dali, were some of the few places where foreign traders could kick back after years on the road. One of the reasons the stories of Marco Polo are so significant is that the volumes are the first recorded observations of China beyond the Silk Road. As Rob Gifford points out in his book, *China Road*, it wasn't until the eighteenth century that the Emperor commanded that the written character for foreigner have stripped from it the radical for dog, indicating an outsider's status in Chinese society. Chinese—despite their regional tastes in food and local dialects—are remarkably lockstep in their response to foreigners as not being quite as clever as they are, or as civilized. I recall during one language exchange session with a Beijing manager (one hour of English conversation/one hour of Chinese language conversation) in the late 1990s her remarking how "primitive" it felt for her to speak English. Chinese believe themselves the most culturally advanced civilization in the world, their language—because it's devilishly difficult to learn—the most cultivated.

PLASTIC MYTHOLOGIES

The flip side of mythologizing Chinese victimization is an adoration of imperial rule. Most Chinese, no matter their socioeconomic status, love the imperial line and accept everything about it. It rather seems to me the more highly educated the Chinese, the more they relish and try to emulate the imperial way, in business and in government. While upward of a quarter of television dramas beat the drum of foreign incursion that must be despised in every way, another quarter of prime-time television viewing is made up of soap operas typically set in one dynasty or another; the last imperial dynasty, the Qing, is a favorite historical setting. Despite the Qing having been foreigners themselves (northern "barbarians" from Manchuria), 40 or even 50 hours of drama is devoted to pulling heartstrings that have viewers empathizing and commiserating with emperors, courtesans, and eunuchs. At the beginning of 2010, a popular historical epic centered around the young and willowy Cixi, who would one day become the Empress Dowager—the original Dragon Queen. The young Cixi, how-ever, had been bullied and herself intrigued against, providing all the justification producers of the show and government censors needed to frame her later imperial missteps in a sympathetic light. It was the Empress through her scheming, her insularity, her arrogance, and her lifestyle that would put any oil sheik to shame who ushered in the downfall of the Qing dynasty in 1911.

Chinese cinema reflects the same sort of dichotomy. The vast majority of films coming out of Chinese movie studios are historical dramas with lots of armor and high body counts, or those "dirty-Japanese" World War II films, or films that glorify the heroism of Communist Party personalities. As the award-winning film director Zhang Yimou said in an interview: "Only if we situate the stories in ancient China can we express ourselves more freely."[1] Zhang is maker of the lush historical dramas *Raise the Red Lantern* and *Red Sorghum*. He was also creative director for the visually stunning Beijing Olympics opening performances in 2008, during which thousands of coordinated performers laid out the high points of Chinese history for the world to see.

Communist Party *apparatchiks* from a half-dozen media-industry-related ministries believed in the winter of 2010 that they could clobber audiences over the head with Party-think by releasing a historic blockbuster with internationally renowned Hong Kong actor Chow Yun Fat as the sage Confucius, set in fifth-century BC China. Censors looked forward to usurping two-thirds of China's big screens from the Western blockbuster *Avatar* in the runup to Spring Festival, which started in mid-February of that year. Chinese who had not yet seen *Avatar* on the big screen were not amused by the announcement that *Avatar* would be pulled from most cinemas in China. Internet users flamed government censors and let it be known citizens would become unruly if they could not get their *Avatar* fix. Film censors backed down, allowing *Avatar* to continue running on most screens, while ensuring *Confucius* still had a fair run. Viewers, though—especially those in their 20s and early 30s—universally panned the film *Confucius* as lumbering and forced. Social tectonic fault lines running along the length of what differentiates authoritarianism from totalitarianism in modernizing China had once again shifted in favor of popular sentiment, similar to the way in which the government fell back from its proclamation in 2009 to put censorship software on every computer sold in China.

Online, Chinese audience responses to *Avatar* revealed unexpected social associations between changes in their own society and the upheaval of the indigenous characters in the film. Chinese used the

Internet to decry the forced evictions and subsequent destruction of so many Chinese homes and entire towns to make way for commercial and infrastructure construction interests throughout the country. (The Chinese government subsequently publicized a regulation forbidding such forced evictions by local governments, just weeks after *Avatar's* opening; a policy that had likely been in review for months if not years before the movie's release to the public). However, never did Chinese viewers draw the parallel between the wholesale destruction of an indigenous people and their way of life in the film *Avatar* with the recent history of China's colonization of Tibet and Xinjiang. That is because it is an axiom of the modern Mainland Chinese psyche that Tibet and Xinjiang as well as Taiwan fall within the borders of China's national sovereignty. If there is any single ideology that binds Mainland Chinese to one another and the people to its government, it's the concept of national sovereignty—supreme authority over a region and its people—and the legitimacy of the imperial line that has maintained the integrity of the region. For Chinese, the eastern Asiatic continent is for the Han people to control. ("Han 汉" is the name Chinese people give their ethnic group.) End of discussion (as far as Chinese are concerned).

Chinese nationalism knows no borders except its own, and it flares up in the most unexpected ways and places. One nationalistic con-flagration that ignited during the 2008 protests of Tibetan citizens against Chinese occupation of the country engulfed a Chinese citizen on the other side of the world. Chinese netizens branded Grace Wang a traitor to China. Grace was a freshman student from Qingdao attending Duke University in the United States that year. Politically aware, Grace always tried to see both sides of an argument and worked to mediate a workable understanding between the two sides. Chinese in Mainland China took direct affront to her efforts at public mediation during the Tibetan protests of 2008, when Beijing squashed dissent in Tibet with riot police and used its army to keep a lid on further protests and contact with the outside world. Grace was photographed shuttling between two Chinese pickets on campus, placing herself between students who were hurling epithets and brandishing placards at each other. All the students on the Repress-Tibet side of the protest were Chinese; all on the Free-Tibet side of the protest were from other countries. To be Chinese was to be pro-Chinese government in this instance. Any other stance was unpardonable.

A Chinese who personally considered Grace's actions treasonable posted the photo on the Internet, whereupon netizens in Mainland China took it upon themselves to perform a Human Flesh Search. They unearthed her name, her address in the U.S., her parents' address in Qingdao, and labeled her a traitor to her country for not supporting the Chinese presumption that Tibet is a historical subject of China, to be done with as China chooses. Her parents in China went into hiding to escape retribution for their daughter's actions; a photo was posted exhibiting feces that had been dumped at her family's doorstep. Many of the thousands of blog posts and e-mails vilifying her took a tone similar to an e-mail message anonymously posted on a Chinese bulletin board system: "If you return to China, your dead corpse will be chopped into 10,000 pieces." Even Chinese who disagreed with her stance as a mediator in such a politically charged matter considered the backlash against her as over the top.[2]

The American history equivalent of such an aggressive form of national sovereignty is Manifest Destiny: the precept that it was the white man's preserve as declared by God to civilize the entirety of the North American continent. Indeed, Chinese are well-aware of American colonial history and the spread of European civilization westward across the continent. Chinese believe themselves to be bringing the same sort of civilizing influence to a Western frontier with lots of space and natural resources but bereft of infrastructure and wealth-creating enterprises. Chinese, though, don't see themselves as neocolonialists. They are not willing to lump their activities in Tibet and Xinjiang with the same historical injustices against which they still rail today. They instead believe in the fundamental economic good of their patronage to what their government-controlled media services call "backward" societies. The cognitive dissonance between reality and revisioned history creates a stridency that will lead the country to continued blunders in foreign affairs and a furthering refraction of social perceptions of what is real and what is mythology.

Any conception of a God or gods in the Chinese world view has never served as a centerpiece of domestic or foreign policy. "Chinese-ness" has. As Fareed Zakaria writes in *The Post-American*

World: "In the case of Britain and the United States, perhaps because they have been so powerful, the Protestant sense of purpose at the core of their foreign policies has made a deep mark on global affairs. China, in contrast, may never acquire a similar sense of destiny. *Simply being China* [his italics] and becoming a world power, in a sense, fulfills its historical purpose. It doesn't need to spread anything to anyone to vindicate itself."

G.I. ZHOU GETS A NEW UNIFORM

The Chinese leadership and Chinese people have no doubt they must be strong militarily and use "every trick in the book" to keep from repeating the bit of history that saw foreigners running the affairs of nation for nearly 300 years until the Communist Party declared a new country in 1949. Though the country's military defense spending may have been rising in double digits from 1989 to 2009, making China the second-largest spender on defense-related outlays in the world, China runs a distant second behind the United States with an estimated US$100 billion to US$150 billion in 2010—only about 1.4 percent of its GDP. Meanwhile, the U.S. uses about four percent of its GDP to make up nearly half the world's expenditure on the military with a budget of more than US$700 billion in 2010—more than the next 15 big spenders combined, including China, Russia, France, and Japan.[3]

Still, being a distant number two in military spending has not deterred the Chinese from aiming to complete construction of two aircraft carriers by 2020, nor of developing the largest missile program in the world, according to the Pentagon, many of which are aimed at U.S. bases in Guam and Japan. China has several dozens of land-based nuclear missiles capable of hitting some parts of North America, with longer-range missiles under development. The leadership plans to mount nuclear ballistic missiles inside some of its submarines, which have become increasingly sophisticated. However, the United States Navy's "Sputnik" moment came in November 2007 when a Chinese Song-class nuclear attack submarine surfaced 49 meters from the U.S. aircraft carrier U.S.S. Kittyhawk. Sputnik was the Soviet Union's satellite program in the late 1950s that crystallized American fears of losing the race for outer space. The 1,000-foot-long Kittyhawk, with 4,500 personnel onboard, was being escorted by at least a dozen other naval vessels and two submarines at the time. The sub had been running on super-quiet electric motors, a technology of which the West did not know China was capable. The Chinese crew revealed its presence to the Americans in waterways near Okinawa. U.S. naval leaders were apoplectic at the Cold War tactic, while the diplomatic corp lodged angry complaints with the Chinese government. Beijing offered it had been ignorant of the submarine maneuvers and suggested the encounter was a coincidence.[4] The surprise served as a rude awakening to U.S. policy makers that the Pacific Ocean was no longer the preeminent domain of its navy.

The U.S. National Security Agency (NSA) had its "Sputnik" moment in January 2007 when China launched a mid-range ballistic missile from Sichuan Province to successfully shoot down one of its own weather satellites. Though the target was a missile in low-orbit around the Earth, the Taiwanese felt immediately threatened they would lose the American "eyes in the sky" that help monitor Chinese military activity around the island. Three years later to the month, in 2010, China succeeded as the only country after the United States to successfully destroy a missile traveling outside the Earth's atmosphere with another missile.

China has heavily invested in Russian-made Su-27 and Su-30 fighters—which experts say are high-maintenance and require parts from Russia—and in its own fighter, the J-10. One of the most expensive aspects of its military, though, is the People's Liberation Army, made up of nearly 2.5 million individuals who require pay grades and housing at least on par with the civilian world. Military retirees and their pensions are also a major drain on the military's budget.

Chinese policy makers are well aware of the asymmetric nature of their relationship with the West, America, in particular. They know they will never be able to spend as much as the U.S. on men, material, research and development, and offensive and defensive technologies. They know that if they ever had to confront the United States in conventional warfare on land, sea, or air, they would at best give America a bloody nose; however, in the minds of the Chinese leadership and people, that would be a victory in and of itself. The two greatest weapons the Chinese have always wielded effectively in their encounters with foreign incursion are time and population. This was especially true during the Japanese War of Aggression, which started with gusto in 1937 and which the U.S. did not formally enter until the bombing of Pearl Harbor in 1941. Generalisimo Chiang Kai Shek, fully well knowing his Nationalist forces were outed in every way, fell back from the east coast of China to Chongqing, in the rough mountains of China's interior. To buy his forces time for a counteroffensive from the city of Wuhan, in south China, Chiang directed the levies of the Yellow River in the north be opened to flood the plains. The Nationalist government did not warn the civilians of the impending flood, which inundated millions of dwellings and killed hundreds of thousands. The flood helped stagnate the advance of the Japanese forces until the end of the War. Once in Chongqing, he effectively waited out the invasion until the Japanese overextended themselves in other theaters of the War, while spoiling as much of the advance of the Japanese as possible with the sacrifice of millions of ill-equipped and malnourished soldiers. Civilians in their numbers, too, played their part by tying Japanese lines down to the mundane job of managing the daily affairs of millions of war refugees.

China has also been upgrading its ability to wage battles through the development of its ability to control and defend its Internet space in the same way it would any part of its natural geography. The Golden Shield project, begun in 1998, is the equivalent of America's space program in the 1960s to scratch out the boundaries of Chinese cyberspace. The Golden Shield initiative was meant to create an information and civil service infrastructure that would systematically filter any content that authorities considered socially or politically unacceptable. A significant part of the Golden Shield is "The Great Firewall of China," a moniker coined by Westerners to compare the system with the expansive and ineffective effort of ancient Chinese emperors to keep marauding hordes from the north from sweeping southward into the homeland. At a cost of about US$800 million, the first phase of Golden Shield technologies sniffed out key words on Websites, blogs, and electronic bulletin board systems based on a list of tens of thousands of Internet addresses that the Communist Party considers politically incorrect. Phase two of the project started in 2006 and finished in 2008 with an army of some 30,000 staff at national and local levels following up on suspect searches and posts.

Since stabilizing and strengthening the Great Firewall, the Chinese leadership has been bolstering its offensive capabilities by hiring and training computer programmers to "hack" foreign Web sites, databases, and other online resources. Western governments now believe not only their companies, but their state utilities—water, electricity, transportation, and the like—are vulnerable to enemy incursion through the Internet. China was caught in the spotlight in early 2010 when Google accused the country's leadership of sponsoring Chinese hackers who broke through Google's e-mail security to re-route the mail of Chinese dissidents to Party inspectors, and of Beijing-based Western journalists to an e-mail account controlled by the hackers. A dozen other high-profile technology companies also announced their e-mail servers had been attacked as well, including Oracle, Cisco, and Microsoft. In mid-2009, University of Toronto researchers published a comprehensive study that discovered that servers in China had been the launch pad for hackers that had invaded 1,300 computers in more than 100 countries. Favorite targets were government institutions and media enterprises that held information about China's national security issues, including Tibet and Taiwan.[5] The Chinese leadership describes the interconnectivity of networks of commercial and government computers as the "soft ribs" of American dominance in business and military affairs.

Diplomatically, China consistently plays the role of spoiler to stagnate international initiatives with which it disagrees, especially if China feels the international community is attempting what it deems "interference in its internal matters". United Nations resolutions that the Security Council votes on to censure recalcitrant nations—for instance, the government of Sudan in its genocide in Darfur, or Iran's development of a nuclear bomb program, or even North Korea's own belligerent activities—receive abstention votes as other UN members attempt to end or preempt events that will clearly have dangerous results for citizens or a region. The Chinese official media was vocally proud of the Chinese delegation's spoiling tactics at the Copenhagen Climate Change Conference in December 2009. He Yafei's sound bites went over particularly well for Chinese consumption. He Yafei was

China's vice-foreign minister and lead negotiator at the climate change conference. He made such pithy statements as: "China will not be an obstacle [to a deal]. The obstacle now is from developed countries," and "I know people will say if there is no deal that China is to blame. This is a trick played by the developed countries. They have to look at their own position and can't use China as an excuse. That is not fair."[6] China's delegation preferred to leave emissions-reduction goals and regulatory mechanisms vague at best, while assembling a coalition of smaller countries less wealthy than American and European counterparts to obscure proceedings with arguments about the unfairness of requirements for developing countries to bow to Western arrogance. Chinese leadership was triumphalist upon return to its home audience, which saw negating the debate with "patronizing" Western economies as the highest form of well-executed, political brinkmanship.

Asymmetry in China's relationship with the world works the other way, too, with the country's neighbors increasingly seeing China as a brutish bully. China's increased wealth—cultivated in an incubator of nationalist gases and instinctively driven to move beyond its borders to secure the natural resources it needs to flourish—have driven it to more frequently clash with countries in the near beyond. In the autumn of 2009, Indian newspaper columnists and bloggers flamed China for its belligerence in territories that India considers its own. Most contentious is a slice of land through the Indian state of Arunachal Pradesh, which the Chinese call South Tibet. The protests in Tibet in 2008 brought the region back onto the radar of Chinese officialdom. The colorful and insightful language of the Indian press—with official Chinese articles and unofficial Chinese blogs lobbing insults back—made negotiations over the disputed territory as emotionally charged as any since the countries went to war over the mountain range in 1962. The Chinese government early in 2009 sent soldiers into the territory to stake China's claim, evicting a family of herders from the region. The importance of the rough terrain is magnified for the Chinese leadership insofar as the region served as the Dalai Lama's escape route to India when the Chinese army invaded Tibet in 1950. Further, the melting glaciers in the Himalayas as the source of the greatest rivers in India and China have only served to ratchet tensions more tightly. Some experts predict the glaciers will disappear completely by 2035 due to global climate change, leaving both countries without water for their farms, their factories, and their cities. Hydroelectric projects near the glaciers from both countries also may prove flashpoints as the countries argue about which countries "own" the diminishing glaciers and their life-giving runoff.

India also claims China is building a commercial "string of pearls" that cordons India from its own neighbors. China has been offering loans to build port facilities in Sri Lanka, Pakistan, Bangladesh, and Burma, as well as to Nepal to build rail lines. China is investing in these countries to build new markets for its goods, with improved infrastructure aiding distribution of Chinese products throughout the region. In Sri Lanka alone, China has invested upward of US$6 billion for a huge port, an international airport, and to redevelop Hambantota, which had been destroyed during the tsunami of 2004, into the second-largest city after the capital, Colombo.[7]

Countries nearer China, though, see Chinese commercial might as much a threat as an opportunity to bolster their own fortunes. Islands off the coast of China, Japan, South Korea, Vietnam, the Philipines, Malaysia, and Brunei—such as the Paracel and Spratly Islands have long been flashpoints for the dissatisfaction of the smaller countries. International research teams have found the waters surrounding the islands to be rich in oil and metals. China is increasingly asserting its claim that the island chains have always been its own to do with as it pleases. At the start of its "Year of Friendship" with Vietnam in 2008, China announced it was turning the Paracel Islands into a tourist resort. China has controlled the Paracels militarily since 1974, with the People's Liberation Army inhabiting the sandy outcroppings—a contentious position since Vietnam also considers the islands its own. Meanwhile, the Japanese agonize at Chinese designs over the Chunxiao gas field in the East China Sea, which lies underwater halfway between both countries. Despite an agreement to exploit the field jointly, the Japanese observed the Chinese in 2008 unilaterally moving engineering equipment into the waterway.

Vietnam's approach to "disarm" China in the South China Sea is to work with other countries in the dispute to create a multinational representative body with which China has to deal, much as China had created a consortium of developing countries during the Copenhagen talks to foil European and American attempts at accountability for meeting emissions targets. Vietnam hopes the Lilliputian Net it throws over China will force international attention on the dispute and perhaps draw the attention of other countries with which China is coming into contention.

Jeffrey Garten, a professor of International Trade, Finance, and Business at Yale, proposed in 2010 that America in its weakened financial condition after the Great Recession of 2008–2009 should also adopt a strategy of multilateral engagement with China. With the U.S. banking system fragile and commitments in the Middle East continuing to stretch its military and its finances, America is at a disadvantage in trying to balance out Chinese assertiveness. Instead, Garten suggests the United States should lead the way toward working with other nations to support international institutions, such as the World Trade Organization, "where China is obliged to play by the rules that a number of leading countries have subscribed to, and which has an orderly process of adjudication. While it still has leadership clout, the centerpiece of U.S. efforts ought to be marshaling multilateral support for other such arrangements." Examples of such multilateral efforts include an enforceable international climate change treaty, multilateral Internet standards, and a strengthened global monetary system.[8]

Further afield, African countries and Central Asian countries have since 2005 been bathing in the infrastructure largesse that Chinese financing is lavishing on their poor societies, without the sort of macroeconomic and political strings attached by Western nations and the International Monetary Fund. Perhaps no other non-African country has been held in as high esteem by Africans as China, which has gone to considerable lengths to improve the infrastructure of the resource-rich regions.

While the U.S. and Russia were stricken with economic problems at home during the recent recession, the Chinese saw opportunities to pedal more than just influence in its own backyard—Central Asia. One high-profile energy project had leaders of China and Kazakhstan opening the Kazakhstan portion of a 7,000-kilometer pipeline in late 2009, which starts at a gas field in Turkmenistan and will end in

Xinjiang when completed in 2013. Russia, of course, still considers the Central Asian countries as part of its own sphere of influence, and looks on at Chinese movements in the region in much the same way as the Indians view Chinese activities along its borders; that is, as suspect, if not outright provocative. Central Asian citizens, meanwhile—all part of the same Turkic Muslim civilization as Xinjiang—watch with horror as China muzzles Xinjiang and continues to import Chinese immigrants into the territory. They wonder if and when they will be next.

If Chinese commercial interests with strategic intent come under threat in Africa—for instance, if Congolese rebels take over oil installations into which China has plowed billions of dollars—China will resort to the same tactics it already has with the government of Sudan, which has been intent on making a clean sweep of the Muslim population of Darfur. China provides the armament and the encouragement implicit in the sale, and the local army does the rest. China has neither the military technology, logistics support, political leverage, nor warfare experience to launch a full-scale assault in a land as distant and alien to China as the Middle East is to America.

However, in the case of a threat to energy supplies in Central Asia, Chinese leadership bolstered by historical precedent might see that protecting its commercial interests through military force is preferable to losing the investments and the flows of oil and natural gas into its borders. By 2025, one billion people in China will be counting themselves among the middle class. With all the greater requirements for consumption incumbent on any material class, the Chinese leadership could promote the country's historical "imperative" to take back Kazakhstan, Krygyzstan, and southeastern Uzbekistan for defeats that Tang Dynasty generals suffered at the hands of Arab armies in the Battle of Talas in 751 AD. Twentieth-century modern history has already shown repeatedly that Great and Small Powers will go to any length to justify claims on energy supplies and trade routes, contorting cultural mythologies for motive; China, with its rich history of successive expansion and contraction of its borders, has more than enough mythology that can be reshaped to justify usurpation of geographies that support its resource requirements. China's military also has experience fighting just beyond its borders, and will have the armament, logistics, and manpower to mount an assault that would overwhelm any of its neighbors.

TOWARD A CHINA WITH DEMOCRATIC CHARACTERISTICS

All of this supposition presumes that China is led by a Chinese Communist Party (CCP) boss—a modern-day emperor—who impresses his will on his government minions and can unilaterally deploy the military at his bidding. Instead, the Communist Party leaders who the West sees hobnobbing with Western dignitaries and announcing their "anger" at this or that perceived provocation are beholden to what Susan Shirk, author of *China: Fragile Superpower*, calls "the control cartel," made up of the CCP Organization Department, which controls personnel appointments; the CCP Propaganda Department, which controls content of the media and culture; and the Ministries of State Security and Public Security (the internal police). The People's Liberation Army and the People's Armed Police—the paramilitary internal security force spun off from the PLA—round out the cartel that hold "exceptional political independence and leverage over the top leaders". In other words, the Communist Party is an oligarchy—a political system run by an elite—made up of deeply entrenched, extra-ordinarily forceful interests that sometimes operate counter to the interests of others in the group; including the two most visible posts: the president and the premier, held by Hu Jintao and Wen Jiabao in 2010, respectively. The apparatus is actually the most liberal in Chinese history, though, underscored by Jiang Zemin voluntarily stepping down as CCP general secretary and president in 2002-03, the first time a leader in China and in any large communist country gave up power without fighting to remain or without dying. In 60 years of rule, the CCP is the least totalitarian it has ever been, with the exception of its rule of Xinjiang and Tibet.

The great lesson the Chinese Communist Party (CCP) took away from the Tiananmen Square massacre of 1989 was to always present the people a united front, however divided the Party might be internally. The incident sparked a hundred other mass protests throughout the country. Ostensibly started as a small student move-ment against government corruption, the movement got out of hand when students perceived mixed messages coming from the central government: on the one hand Zhao Ziyang, then general secretary of the Communist Party, sending signals of appeasement to students; while Deng Xiaoping, *de facto* leader of the Party, publicly denounced the mass protest as "a well-planned plot". Since that time, as Shirk writes, the CCP learned that "if they don't hang together, they could hang separately". Ultimately, all agendas in the CCP coincide: self-preservation. Internal threats are a greater danger to the Party's hold on power than international imperatives.

Chinese citizens, by and large, maintain the tacit agreement with the CCP that the integrity of the country and economic development trump the Party's autocratic ways. When citizens are convinced the institution of democracy will do a better job of perpetuating the wealth and well being of themselves and family members, and protect against foreign encroachment in their historical domain, then they will push for it *en masse*. So far, the Communist Party has delivered on those values on a macro level as every economic sign—and many social—would indicate. Especially after the meltdown of the West's financial system in 2008 and the subsequent deadlock in which many Western democracies found themselves in healing their economies, the majority of Chinese have formed a "Beijing Consensus" that authoritarian leadership and management of an economy by fiat is preferable to the dillydallying that they see has cost jobs and social unrest in the West. As such, the Party looks set to remain at China's helm until much of the country's urbanization and infrastructure development is complete, sometime around 2025.

The Achilles' heel of the government apparatus, though, is the lack of an independent, well-trained judiciary to impartially hear grievances of even the most petty sort. The lack of this democratic institution—an impartial judiciary is unknown in Chinese history—particularly grates on modern-day Chinese sensibilities, especially as they acquire property and find their ownership rights infringed upon; or, as they seek to acquire wealth or ensure well being, they find their efforts obfuscated by individuals, corporations, or even the government.

An impartial judiciary will diffuse the kinds of grievances that can aggregate to create just the sort of social instability that the leadership is so anxious will topple its regime. Though China's statistics are often questionable, anecdotal evidence seems to support a rise in what the

Chinese government calls "anger-venting" mass incidents in the runup to 2010. In the mid-2000s, foreign journalists often cited that China had annually seen some 80,000 to 100,000 mass disturbances. But the source of the statistics, a government website, lumped in any disturbance from assemblies of disgruntled property owners to mafia-gang fights, orgies, and insulting the flag. "Anger-venting," though, does seem on the rise in smaller towns and cities. It typically starts through a small, arbitrary dispute and then grows out of control into a hodgepodge of grievances that citizens have with local authorities. Ten thousand people setting light to a police station in Guizhou in 2009— upset over the news that relatives of local government officials had possibly committed, and then tried to cover up, a murder—would qualify as venting anger.[9]

Mass protests in China are like forest fires in which the forest has not been cleared of underbrush in years. A random spark from a lightning storm, or a single lit match, scorches thousands of hectares. The potential for mass demonstrations that "rage out of control" actually increases—not lessens—as the country's information and transportation infrastructure ties citizens more closely together and the overwhelming majority of citizens move to homogenized urban centers from rugged, sometimes inaccessible, rural patches that would otherwise create "firewalls" between banded dissent.

Independent judiciaries offer a channel through which local governments can "clear the brush" and the central government can more proactively mitigate the risks of explosive situations getting out of hand. Illegal land seizures or inappropriate compensation for property have proven to be incendiary, sending thousands of protesters at a time to battle with police. Local government malfeasance, collusion, and corruption—especially in real estate and deals involving highly polluting industries—also send citizens baying for the blood of officials. The CCP, though, in order to present a united front that the public is unable to pry open, is loathe to institutionalize a "separation of powers", especially with a judiciary that could upset the delicate internal balance the CCP has worked decades to build. Voting, a further step toward democratization, is even more anathema to an oligarchy that prefers to stay where it is — in control of the most populous nation in the world. It is no coincidence, then, that cadres study the implementation of models of democracy that sees a single party in power for generations at a stretch with a seemingly immortal bureaucracy and its own authoritarian streaks; as in Singapore, Taiwan, and Japan.

International interests in China will remain viable as long as national, industrial, and technological "branding" align with China's self-image. Unfortunately, that self-image can take sudden shifts, depending on the society's and leadership's domestic or international imperatives. For instance, despite Chinese aversion to engaging Japanese on a personal level for historic reasons, Chinese are typically happy to buy Japanese brands of cosmetics, electronic appliances, and cars, believing in the cachet of the brands and the high-quality content of the products. However, when the Japanese government pushed for a permanent seat on the United Nations Security Council in the spring of 2005 and at the same time released a revised version of its history books for schools all but expunging its war crimes in Japan, Chinese protested in the millions throughout the Mainland. Japan's revision of its own history and attempt at upgrading its status in the world ran against the grain of China's own self-image as a continued victim of Japanese aggression: foreign "investment" in factories and retail outlets became foreign "invasion." In Shanghai and other cities throughout China, protestors smashed the storefronts of Japanese department stores, destroyed Japanese products, and boycotted purchase of Japanese brands. Sentiments the government itself stoked became increasingly difficult for the central authority to control, as protest gatherings grew larger and more vocal and undisciplined. Eventually, the central government signaled it was time for protest organizers to end the demonstrations. Censors used the Internet and phone-messaging systems to filter out references to the protests, while the central authority announced an official end to the mass action.

During the demonstrations, I was acquainted with a Japanese businessman whose family owned several factories in China that made *tabi* socks—split-toe socks used with sandals—for export to Japanese consumers. He had barricaded the front door of his downtown Shanghai apartment during the protests, afraid for his life, watching protestors parade on his TV and out his window. Afterward, he told me that he and other Japanese investors were diversifying investments out of China, considering the environment too volatile in which to place all their operations. The French also suffered a commercial setback in the runup to the Beijing Olympics in 2008 because of Chinese consumer anger at French behavior during the Olympic torch relay.

In China, sentiment is fluid, shunted through the vanes of Communist Party interests. Most, if not all, of those interests are based on an asymmetrical relationship with the world, in which China sees itself as the perpetual underdog, occasionally bullied by other, richer countries who gained their wealth and technology at the expense of China. Asymmetry informs its military policy; its approach to Internet censorship and cyber-warfare tactics; its diplomatic policy; the social controls it places on its population; and its foreign investment priorities. The sense of "us against the world" is one of the reasons the Chinese leadership is slow to reign in Intellectual Property Rights (IPR) violations. The country sees IPR as another expression of the unfair advantage other countries have gained at the expense of China, keeping her masses downtrodden and her place as a developing country immutable. Companies whose wealth derives from proprietary technologies and processes will continue to need to guard their secrets zealously if they should introduce those jewels into the Chinese marketplace as producers. Only when the sentiments of the man on the street shift about perceived Chinese asymmetrical relationships with foreigners can IPR policies already in place in China be adequately enforced.

China's sense of asymmetry with the rest of the world has as much to do with the lack of avenues available to its citizens to reflect on and debate its recent tumultuous modern history as with the very real crimes some foreign powers did commit against the nation and its people. However, as long as its citizens have neither the desire nor the opportunity to candidly revisit its various governments' roles and decisions during tragic events such as the Opium Wars, the Japanese War of Aggression, the Great Leap Forward, and the Cultural Revolution, society will always reach outside its borders for the nearest and most simplistically delineated Bogey Man at hand to narcotize its seemingly endless pain and anger. Modernization and the closer relationship with the rest of the world that technological innovation implies may prove to be a catalyst that forces normalization of Chinese self-image and its place in the world. The advantage democracy brings to society is in providing those avenues of social reflection and discussion that allow a nation to agonize over the less savory parts of its history without tearing itself apart in revolution.

Democracy in China, then, is not just a matter of the powers-that-be developing institutions that normalize, share, and balance power throughout the society; the society itself has to be ready to accept and adapt to a model of relationship between the government and its people that flies in the face of a national identity steeped in 2,000 years of imperial mythology and foreign encroachment in its domain. The continuity of absolute hierarchy and victimization permeates nearly every facet of life in the country, though. The shadow of the Emperors' past is long, and the Chinese people's attachment to their revered history deep. Democratic change—if and when it happens, however necessary leaders and citizens believe it to be to preserve the wealth of individuals and the hegemony of the country—will have characteristics perhaps unrecognizable in the West—in a world with challenges we can scarcely imagine.

END NOTES

1. Geoff Dyer, "Zhang Yimou on His Creative Independence," *Financial Times*, December 11, 2009.
2. Shaila Dewan, "Chinese Student in U.S. Is Caught in Confrontation," *The New York Times*, April 17, 2008.
3. Micheal Wines and Jonathon Ansfield, "China Says It Is Slowing Down Military Spending," *The New York Times*, March 4, 2010.
4. Matthew Hickley, "The Uninvited Guest: Chinese Sub Pops Up in Middle of U.S. Navy Exercise, Leaving Military Chiefs Red-Faced," *The Daily Mail*, November 7, 2007.
5. Katherin Hille and Joseph Menn, "Hackers in Front Line of China's Cyberwar," *Financial Times*, January 13, 2010.
6. Fiona Harvey, "China Signals Climate Funds Shift," *Financial Times*, December 13, 2009.
7. Vikas Bajaj, "India Worries as China Builds Ports in South Asia," *The New York Times*, February 15, 2010.
8. Jeffrey Garten, "The U.S. Can No Longer Go It Alone with China," *Financial Times*, February 8, 2010.
9. Will Freeman, "The Accuracy of China's 'Mass Incidents,'" *Financial Times*, March 2, 2010.

Afterword

The modernization of China and its changing relationship with the world outside its borders is very much a story about asymmetries that teeter across fulcrums constructed of international standards and, for the most part, Western norms. Its self-image is reflected and refracted through a prism of historical mythologies it plies and applies as circumstances see fit. Its economic development strategy, its foreign policy, its militarization, its control of Chinese-language cyberspace, its consumption patterns, and its quest for natural resources are all based on the premise that it is and will always be at a disadvantage relative to others. The Chinese believe they have the short end of every engagement; there's always more to be gained, to be won, to be shown off, they fret. Chinese feel they can seldom arrange an equitable deal between themselves or especially with foreigners in most transactions, and they have even less faith in their own government to do right by them. Meanwhile, their own government believes it will never be treated fairly by the West—hence, China's mercantilist approaches to international trade and finance, and the guerrilla tactics of Mainland Chinese business and government representatives in dealing with outsiders. Chinese do not believe in "safe zones", where win-win is the standard operating procedure.

However, there are asymmetries China has that work to the country's advantage: for instance, the ability of its people to mobilize with great energy and speed to achieve monumental tasks. A prime example is that while New Orleans remains shattered some five years after the awful destruction wrought by Hurricane Katrina in 2005, China has built scores of new cities and torn down and rebuilt dozens of others. Another advantageous asymmetry is that its population is and will be for decades to come the largest in the world, implying the potential for the development of great and unique works of art and science in the future, and the largest educated consumer base in the largest rationalized marketplace on the planet. Population pressures on the environment and natural resource consumption combined with the kinetic pace at which its citizens take on new challenges is already resulting in alternative microeconomic models. Urban and transportation schemes currently under development in China may one day point the way to approaches to energy conservation and even alternative energy generation on an evermore crowded Earth.

The advantages of China's asymmetries with the world are quickly canceled out, however, when one examines its "balance sheet" for its ecology and its natural resources: both show tremendous debits that will take generations to pay off. However, the Chinese argue, China is only pursuing a model that dozens of other countries the past 200 years have followed to provide greater economic opportunity to their citizenry and a greater level of security to their societies. The benefits that modernization has provided China are there for all to see: longer life spans for its citizens, higher education levels, greater degrees of freedom of creativity and expression, more opportunities to lead fulfilling lives. The downside is also in plain view: pollution on an unprecedented scale, human-rights violations, untold stress on natural resources and strained relationships with neighbors. However, many of the Western countries that consolidated the gains of modernity after World War II also at one time or another denied rights to their own citizens, fouled their land and waterways, and even tested the limits of democracy. It is the West at this writing that has perpetrated one of the greatest ecological disasters in human history with the explosion of an oil rig leased by British Petroleum off the U.S. Gulf Coast. Had such an event occurred in the South China Sea off the coast of Guangdong Province on a rig run by the Chinese state-owned enterprise Sinopec, for instance, it would likely have been framed as a Chinese quality issue caused by the precipitous growth of the economy and an utter lack of concern for the environment and worker safety. The American and British spin on the spill in the Gulf of Mexico is that it was a matter of corporate negligence exacerbated by shareholder greed for quick and fat returns; little or no mention has been made about American society's own addiction to the slick stuff, the Congress's loosening to extraordinary lengths of the regulatory framework around offshore oil drilling, and the stunning degree to which the U.S. administration put its trust in multinational corporations to do the right thing in preventing such disasters from ever happening. Of course, China has thrills and spills aplenty in the exploitation of its own environment, but has yet to reach the level of sophistication as British Petroleum in destroying such a large swathe of ecosystem. However, if the spoiled wilds of modernized societies are at all sign posts, China too will one day have its chance at despoiling an environment wholesale, overnight.

China's contribution to the discussion about the earth's environment comes framed in the geographic extent, continuity, variety, and sustainability of its pollution. Therein China is a record holder. No other country in history has created so much pollution for so many to bear in such a short period. Further, China's pollution is slopping over into the ecosystems of other countries in ways that should force us to remember we all live on the same planet. The ocean patterns, wind currents, and storm fronts of the world have no firewalls that separate the filth of one country from the muck of another.

Perhaps one of China's greatest contributions to the world, then, is as the proverbial "canary in the coal mine"—the bird caged in coal mines in historic times that would indicate when gas and noxious fumes emitted underground were dangerous. When the bird died, it was time for miners to get out of the shaft and "run to the hills" for safety. China has compressed 200 years of industrialization into 30, stressing not only its environment and resources beyond reckoning but that of other nations as well. The world is waiting and watching, collective breath held, to see how China will manage any ecological catastrophes that lie in waiting.

Yet, what is the alternative model for a country that wants to live the same way it sees Westerners living on TV and in Hollywood movies? The United States is certainly not leading the world from a policy vantage in developing clean and renewable energy sources. The European Union has not legislated its companies to move to sustainable models of doing business or bear penalty. Japan is, as ever, mute on the subject, its moribund government forcing its society to live off the savings of its rapidly aging and decreasing population. So, China rightfully believes it can press on without shame in the development of a middle class that—until they open their mouths to speak or sit at a round table of hot pot—increasingly looks and acts for all the world like Americans, albeit with Chinese characteristics. If imitation is the best form of flattery, the United States, the National Basketball Association, the New Kids on the Block, McDonald's, and Barbie should all take a bow. The stress of obtaining a home of one's own—and of keeping it in the face of arbitrary government policy and development interests— educating one's children; finding and keeping a job when hundreds if not thousands are equally qualified; and of being properly cared for in times of ill health or disaster, weigh mightily on the new middle class. Still, citizens know there is no turning back to socialism. They can only soldier on in hopes of opportunities to change a system that in many ways is stacked against them. Knee-jerk protectionist policies by the United States and the European Union only put more strains on and further insulate a system that can explode if sealed too tightly and pressurized beyond reason.

China is building cities like there is no tomorrow for its villagers and peasants, to get them running water, hot showers, and electricity for their washing machines and televisions. The leadership is doing it as quickly as it can with its own underclass, who are defined by residence permit policies. Why import workers from another country when *hukou* 户口 policies maintain a divide between country folk and urbanites that forces more than half the country into servitude, the least anchored of which float between construction work sites around the nation. Transportation-infrastructure and urbanization-construction projects delivered an adrenaline boost from the government's US$2.4 trillion fiscal stimulus during the global economic downturn, keeping workers busy seven days a week, 24 hours a day. They are helping China remake its countryside in dramatic ways, and lifting the expectations of millions of citizens in some of the most disenfranchised regions of the nation. So while economic inequalities in China may rival those in the United States, the majority of Chinese have American-style Hope (with a capital "H") that with enough hard work and a few breaks they too will live a prosperous life. Americans need to understand and appreciate how special "the old world" considers America's world view that through individual grit, life can indeed be better one day. American optimism has suffused the last 50 years of the past century with a sense of endless possibilities that operates to this day, especially in China. Americans, through trade and cultural exchange, need to continue to share the unique quality of its energy with China (and other developing countries) to encourage further equality and creativity in Chinese society and in its relations with the international community of nations. As Americans themselves discovered with the terrible destruction of the Twin Towers in Manhattan on September 11, 2001, a country that tosses hope aside to play the role of victim can itself become a marauder of others. China has more than enough reasons and resentments from its recent historic encounters with foreign countries to forgo hope in favor of pursuing less constructive paths of engaging the world; the United States should not allow China through laziness or lack of imagination or expediency to traverse any such dead ends.

Though many of China's Communist Party at national and local levels are helping themselves to the wealth that the country has accumulated through its privatization policies and export-driven largesse (courtesy of United States and European Union consumers), the "proletariat" have twigged onto them through Human Flesh Searches that investigate, confer, levy judgment, and mete out justice as quickly as it takes to google details of the Tiananmen Square demonstrations in 1989—faster, actually, since references to the protests of that dreadful summer are blocked in China and require additional software to get round. Still, likely the most thrilling aspect of China's modernization is that the social hierarchy separating "the Emperor" above from his minions below is the flattest it's been in the past 2,000 years of China's imperial history. The Internet and telecommunications technology has succeeded in infusing social equality into the society in a way that Marxist-Leninist Mao Zedong Theory never could. As quickly as it takes the Chinese leadership to roll out commandments intent on boxing individual expression and group discourse in cyberspace, the *cognoscenti* regroup with new technologies or code words or entire imaginary beings instilled with wonderful, contrary meaning for the more than 400 million Internet users (by the summer of 2010, and counting) who want to know about the country in which they live and the world in which it is couched. Government officials that the people are able to catch red-handed wantonly abusing the system are being exposed at a rate never before seen, resulting in new measures by the national government that increase the transparency of the offices

administrators keep. Still, Human Flesh Searches and official pro-
nouncements of clean government are no substitute for a proper judiciary with trained judges and lawyers who do not fear for their careers
or their lives when they represent client grievances that clash with
Party interests.

Most of China's cybernauts are on average a decade or more younger than those in America. Today's young Chinese, though, are not
wealthy, whether they live in the cities or in the countryside, and they
know it. However, having been the center of attention as the single
child in most families, they are impatient for gratification through
acquisition of the trappings of modernization. Since the late 1990s,
wages as a percent of the country's GDP have remained stagnant; in
other words, while the country's wealth inflated beyond all expectations, the average Chinese income did not change. However, the state-
owned enterprises and the infrastructure projects of local governments
benefited handsomely, with the bosses of private export-led factories
huffing and puffing to keep up. It is no longer enough for young
Chinese to simply have a factory job, as their parents had. They want to
do more than work, sleep, and eat; they want to have mobility, they
want playthings, and many of them want the wherewithal to have
husbands and wives one day, and to settle down with property in
middle-classdom. The run of suicides in the spring of 2010 at the enor-
mous factory campus of Foxconn, the Taiwanese contract manufacturer
in Shenzhen, as well as the protests at the Honda automotive components plants in Guangdong Province both presage the degree of
dissatisfaction youth are having with the role of self-sacrificing worker
bee. The Internet generation of China has discovered it's glorious to
have a life beyond work; the worldwide consumers of goods made in
China will find out the prices of their toys, sneakers, and electronics
will begin to rise as employers in China have no choice but to raise the
standards of employment for their workers.

The development of a healthy and robust service sector is of
paramount importance in creating opportunities for the youth who
cannot find factory jobs or who have graduated from university with
expectations and learnings inappropriate to a shop floor. However,
social taboos and a lack of a civil society make development of a service
sector particularly challenging, as service staff must learn entirely new

ways of interacting with others, and organizations must reach for and grasp increasingly higher service levels to remain competitive. Service industries such as research and development and information technology will continue to suffer from policy suffocation as the central government pursues investment in huge infrastructure projects, export-led growth in the economy, and the maintenance of state-owned enterprises too big to fail. Western companies will for the foreseeable future continue to feel they are being forced out of entire industries in China, as policy makers hypnotize themselves into believing mountains of cash are enough to learn how to innovate and compete on the world stage. The Party is loathe to accept a true innovation culture that leads to major disruptions of industries, and, sometimes, to societies, as well. As a result, much of China's creative and pure research industries will be mired in revisions of Chinese history and *ad hoc* propaganda that are irrelevant to the needs of a high-tech society that must remain integrated with the rest of the world to meet its citizens' desires for gratification.

While Party leaders are mostly concerned with curbing the enthusiasm of a youth that knows little if anything about the Tiananmen Square massacre, preferring instead to bring that slice of demography to heel to sustain its power base, the Party should instead concern itself with a demographic that is shifting as quickly as the dunes of the Gobi desert are encroaching on Beijing. Chinese who are now in their 40s are wealthier per capita than at any time in the country's history. Chinese in their 20s and 30s are working harder than ever to get their slice of economic reward. Now, society is beginning to reframe its concerns around a middle-aged bulge instead. An older and more cynical and anxious group that is flabbier and less fit than previous generations is increasingly commanding the scenery. As the forty- and fifty-somethings become lifetime members of the Gray Tigers, they will be ever more demanding and far more sophisticated than previous generations in getting and holding onto what they want and what they need. Social services, certainly, will be near the top of their list of demands; keeping the wealth they have acquired and passing their gains onto future generations will take first place in their agenda, however. Property rights will be at the center of their concerns as the average property built in China is constructed to last a mere 30 years or less[1], implying property devaluations in the retirement years of millions of citizens, and perhaps even wholesale reclamation of property by the state or by savvy property developers. The Gray Tigers risk losing a great deal of their wealth within the next 10 to 15 years. Their dissatisfaction may be heard around the world as the Communist Party attempts to suppress the sophisticated and coordinated protestations of an ornery generation that wants a refund and refuses to back down.

The outward-bound investment trend will continue apace as Chinese business and government leaders and the *nouveau riche* place assets offshore to protect against an inevitable downturn in the business climate (remember, what goes up and up and up. . . .), or to sidestep capricious policy decisions passed down by the central authority to cool an overheated economy. State-owned enterprises in the natural resources business will continue to make forays into foreign markets to stake their claims, as money is still to be made from the energy needs of a growing middle class, and as urbanization and transportation infrastructure projects continue into 2020. Interestingly, Western fears of China conquering the world will come to naught as international institutions such as the International Monetary Fund, the World Bank, and the World Trade Organization increasingly educate and exert influence on a China that—despite its thousands of years of history—is a novice in globalization circles. The rule of law and even norms of fair play in Anglo-American countries and in the European Union will sap the cavalier approach that China has been taking to investing abroad. Its domestic imperatives—natural resource depletion, pollution, and population pressure—will narrow its attention even further. Already, some African countries have complained that China has imported environmental and human-resource violations that Chinese bosses consider *de rigueur* back home. Still, it cannot be denied that Chinese investment in many developing countries—from Bangladesh to Sri Lanka to Nigeria—has done more to bring economic opportunity and raise living standards in the past five years than the last 50 years of the West's donor philosophy or the macroeconomic policies of the International Monetary Fund. Though China's approach is mercantilist to the core, the U.S. and the European Union have much to learn in uplifting developing nations, instead of merely hectoring them to follow the same Western economic growth models that kicked off the global economic downturn in 2008. One day, America itself may need these far-flung neighbors to balance the influence of a sprawling China.

Chinese society has major challenges ahead as it navigates the defining trends discussed in *China Inside Out*. Sometimes these trends intersect, creating serious disruption to the society and causing collective reflection on the momentum of the country's development and the country's national identity. For instance, the stress between urbanization and the migration of the population from the countryside to the cities has already created social dislocation for millions of families trying to bridge the culture gap between the two worlds. Or when pollution issues come to roost in urban centers where the affluent are able to organize and articulate their dissatisfaction with local authorities more effectively than their cousins in the countryside. China's urbanization, infrastructure development, and absorption of the western regions Tibet and Xinjiang—resulting in mass protests by the indigenous populations—come into direct conflict with the trend toward increasing definition and assertion of a national identity that prides itself on "non-interference". The tremors from the intersection of the trends and the collisions between the social plates resulted in military action on an unprecedented scale that saw a complete communications blackout of the territories, including all Internet access in Xinjiang for nearly a year. The colonial exercise presages another, possibly more dramatic disruption when China's quest for natural resources crosses vested interests in contested or controversial regions around the world, igniting uncontrollable nationalist indignation that forces the central government to black out the communications of the entire country to maintain law and order. Even more dramatically, the central authority may order a complete blackout of the country's information highways and by-ways in the event of a major perceived threat to the country's (or the Party's) sovereignty. Low probability, high-impact events such as these imply companies need to have airtight contingency plans and possibly even exit strategies for their operations. Of course, the last scenario would see foreign direct investment into China dry up, and current foreign operations to halt completely, possibly for several years, as had been the case after the Tiananmen Square massacre. But by that time, the Chinese government might believe it can "go it alone," and damn what the West might think. Meanwhile, China's leadership, its international power heavily moderated by a welter of global institutions and multilateral agreements, will be forced to find a way to reconcile its population's self-image with how the rest of the world sees it.

The greatest challenges to Chinese society and to *the raison d'etre* of the Communist Party will come as defining trends wind down to a natural conclusion: all the cities the land can support are built; all the people the cities can house have moved from the countryside to the urban centers; the great bulge of twenty-somethings whose vitality manned the factories in the early 2000s will move into the demanding middle age; the Cultural Revolution generation of Red Guards that kicked off economic liberalization will become Gray Tigers, straining family ties and social welfare systems; and China will run out of water—climate change, overpopulation, waste and mismanagement of an irreplaceable resource having caught up with it with unimaginable finality.

Ultimately, what America and the rest of the world have most to be concerned about are the network effects of a society homogenizing in temperament, in language, and in culture. The insurmountable topography within the borders of China is disappearing as light rail replaces Stalinist-era locomotives and flights tie together even the most remote yurts in Mongolia with the high-rises of Guangdong. Telecommunications technologies and the Internet allow news, information, and gossip to travel near the speed of light. At the start of the twenty-first century, central authority and local governments could squelch protests and dissent over institutional gangersterism and resentment about economic inequality with impunity. Then, all the cities and towns in China—especially in the countryside—were relatively isolated from one another. Geography created natural firebreaks that cordoned the communicable, destructive sentiment of local citizenry. However, as China and Chinese people truly become unified, dissent will resonate more easily and freely than ever before in the country's history. As the power trends discussed in *China Inside Out* devolve while the population's expectations for modernity amp up, discontent will spread virally in a way that will truly shake the Communist Party's foundations.

Chinese leadership will have to evolve even more radically than it has since the death of Mao Zedong. The Party leadership has seen itself go from totalitarian, despotic rule in the mold of the emperors to a more porous and insecure oligarchy that backs down when popular sentiment runs against its sometimes arbitrary dictates. Though the Party at times falls back to the Soviet-era ways of the bad old days, self-preservation is motivating it to evolve into something approximating its nemesis, the Nationalist Party of Taiwan, which has managed within a nominally democratic framework to stay in power nearly 60 years, with the island-state's brief excursion into leadership by an opposition party. Or, China could become a Singapore-on-steroids, guided by the iron hand of a single party supported by a well-educated, elite bureaucracy with enough of the trappings of democracy to be beyond reproach internationally, yet still deliver the economic benefits it promises its constituency anew.

We assume in the West that China will have a *"Magna Carta Moment"* in which competing factions or the people will serve the Communist Party a warrant, whereupon the country will become enlightened and then embrace democracy. The Internet would seem an appropriate platform upon which such a revolution could occur. However, the level of reverence that Chinese people have for their imperial history as well as the entrenched factions within the oligarchy preclude such a moment of truth, even in cyberspace. Instead, the country generates "micro-truths" with each clash of interests. The friction between social plates—public, commercial, criminal, generational, and governmental (with even local governments sometimes rubbing the central government up the wrong way)—releases small amounts of a transformational energy that is working its way through the deeply insular society. The sparks of micro-truths shoot into increasingly porous media channels that give stakeholders the opportunity to chatter about their value system in ways that are very Chinese: noisy, raucous, and full of verve. Sometimes the chaos results in a momentary state of relaxation; sometimes in a wholesale reversal of direction, with the government and the people in lockstep; while at other times, the people acquiesce while the government leads the way.

Chinese political and industrial factions are hardly sitting on their hands, to be fair. They are attacking the country's multitude of domestic issues to move China up the industrial value chain, away from low-end manufacturing, and into research and development projects, services outsourcing, renewable and clean energy generation, sustainable business models, and aggressive resource conservation projects. China now is only second to the United States in the number of patents registered every year and in the number of scholarly research papers published; by 2020, it will be the third-largest investor in research and development as a percent of GDP, just behind the United States and the European Union. China has already shown its commitment to being the world leader in renewable energy generation, with investments in alternative energy projects of nearly US$35 billion in 2009 alone, twice the amount the United States invested during the same period. Environmental degradation, energy consumption imperatives, natural resource constraints, social welfare issues, and international commitments may force China to become the most progressive country in the world.

But that's a whole other story completely.

END NOTE

1. "Feeding the Beast," *China Economic Review*, May 2010.

Bibliography

Buchanan, Mark Nexus. *Small Worlds and the Groundbreaking Science of Networks*. New York: W.W. Norton & Company, 2002.

———. *Ubiquity: Why Catastrophes Happen*. New York: Three Rivers Press, 2000.

Carr, Edward Hallet. *What Is History?* New York: Vintage Books, 1967.

Clissold, Tim. *Mr. China: A Memoir*. New York: Harper Collins, 2004.

Crow, Carl. *400 Million Customers*. Hong Kong: China Economic Review Publishing, 2008.

Diamond, Jared. *Collapse: How Societies Choose to Fail or Suceed*. New York: Viking, 2005.

———. *Guns, Germs, and Steel: The Fates of Human Societies*. New York: W. W. Norton & Company, 2005.

Fallows, James. *Postcards from Tomorrow Square: Reports from China*. New York: Vintage Books, 2009.

Fenby, Jonathan. *The Penguin History of Modern History: The Fall and Rise of a Great Power, 1850 – 2009*. London: Penguin Books, 2009.

Fishman, Ted C. *China, Inc.: How the Rise of the Next Superpower Challenges America and the World*. New York: Scribner, 2005.

French, Paul. *Carl Crow: A Tough Old China Hand—The Life, Times, and Adventures of an American in Shanghai*. Hong Kong: Hong Kong University Press, 2006.

French, Paul. *Through the Looking Glass: China's Foreign Journalists from Opium Wars to Mao*. Hong Kong: Hong Kong University Press, 2009.

Friedman, Thomas L. *Hot, Flat, and Crowded: Why the World Needs a Green Revolution—and How We Can Renew Our Global Future*. London: Allen Lane, 2008.

———. *The World is Flat: the Globalized World in the Twenty-First Century*. London: Penguin Books, 2006.

Gifford, Rob. *China Road: A Journey into the Future of a Rising Power*. New York: Random House, 2007.

Gladwell, Malcolm. *The Tipping Point: How Little Things Can Make a Big Difference*. New York: Little, Brown and Company, 2000.

Harney, Alexandra. *The China Price: The True Cost of Chinese Competitive Advantage.* New York: The Penguin Press, 2008.

Hewitt, Duncan. *Getting Rich First: Life in a Changing China.* London, Vintage Books, 2007.

Huntington, Samuel P. *The Clash of Civilizations and the Remaking of World Order.* London: Simon and Schuster, 1996.

Jocelyn, Ed and Andrew McEwan. *The Long March: The True Story Behind the Legendary Journey the Made Mao's China.* London: Constable, 2006.

Kynge, James. *China Shakes the World: A Titan's Rise and Troubled Future—and the Challenge for America.* New York: Mariner Books, 2007.

Leeb, Stephen. *The Coming Economic Collapse: How You Can Thrive When Oil Costs $200 a Barrel.* New York: Warner Books, 2006.

McGregor, James. *One Billion Customers: Lessons from the Front Lines of Doing Business in China.* New York: Wall Street Journal Books, 2005.

Prestowitz, Clyde. *Three Billion New Capitalists: the Great Shift of Wealth and Power to the East.* New York: Basic Books, 2005.

Rose, Sarah. *For All the Tea in China.* London: Hutchinson, 2009.

Ross, Andrew. *Fast Boat to China: High-Tech Outsourcing and the Consequences of Free Trade—Lessons from Shanghai.* New York: Vintage Books, 2007.

Shenkar, Oded. *The Chinese Century: The Rising Chinese Economy and Its Impact of the Global Economy, the Balance of Power, and Your Job.* Upper Saddle River, New Jersey: Wharton School Publishing, 2005.

Shirk, Susan L. *China: Fragile Superpower.* New York: Oxford University Press, 2007.

Spence, Jonathon D. *God's Chinese Son: The Taiping Heavenly Kingdom of Hong Xiuquan.* New York: W.W. Norton & Company, 1996.

———. *The Gate of Heavenly Peace: The Chinese and Their Revolution.* New York: Penguin Books, 1981.

Strahan, David. *The Last Oil Shock: A Survival Guide to the Imminent Extinction of Petroleum Man.* London: John Murray, 2007.

Tainter, Joseph A. *The Collapse of Complex Societies: New Studies in Archaeology.* Cambridge, U.K.: Cambridge University Press, 1988.

Taleb, Nassim Nicholas. *The Black Swan.* London: Penguin Books, 2007.

———. *Fooled by Randomness: The Hidden Role of Chance in Life and in the Markets.* London: Penguin Books, 2007.

White, Theodore H. and Annalee Jacoby. *Thunder Out of China.* New York: Da Capo Press, 1980.

Zakaria, Fareed. *The Post-American World.* New York: Norton, 2008.

Index